Andrew
unsuccess
school at ... ssex, he became a shipping clerk in London, where he joined the punk rock explosion of 1976 and formed his own, now legendary group.

Giving up his punk ideals in favour of his life-long interest in paranormal mysteries in 1979, Andrew became a journalist on the magazine *Strange Phenomena*. Here he teamed up with fellow researcher and psychic, Graham Phillips. Working together, they played out what has become one of the century's most sensational supernatural adventures—the dramatic hunt for a green talismanic jewel, known as *Meonia*, and a sword bearing Mary Queen of Scots' personal monogram. The discovery of these historic artefacts is told in his own book *The Sword and the Stone* and in *The Green Stone* by Graham Phillips and Martin Keatman.

Andrew coined the term psychic questing to describe his and Graham's own unique brand of discovering hidden artefacts and lost secrets of the past using psychic and mystical processes. Its mixture of modern-day magic, sorcery and supernatural drama has made questing the most exciting, and yet controversial form of psychical research currently taking place in this country.

Since 1984, Andrew has been working with a talented psychic named Bernard. Their working partnership has taken them on mystical quests across the British landscape.

Andrew is a full-time author and publisher of his own books.

By the same author

THE SEVENTH SWORD

Andrew Collins

THE BLACK ALCHEMIST

ARROW BOOKS

Published by Arrow Books Limited
20 Vauxhall Bridge Road, London SW1V 2SA
An imprint of Random House UK Limited
London Melbourne Sydney Auckland Johannesburg
and agencies throughout the world
First published in 1988 by ABC Books
Arrow edition 1992
1 3 5 7 9 10 8 6 4 2

Printed and bound in Great Britain by
Cox & Wyman Ltd, Reading
ISBN 0 09 916551 1

DEDICATION

To Bernard and Graham, without whom this book would not have been possible.

ACKNOWLEDGMENTS

Thanks to, in alphabetical order: Christine Baxter, Bernard, Gerry Beskin, Eric Briggs, Ann Chadwick, Alan Cleaver, Brian Fenning, Bob Gilbert, Rita Goold, Clive Harper, Fiona Kaye, Johnny Merron, Debbie Newman, Joan Newton, Toyne Newton, David and Marilyn Overton, Colin and Gelly Paddon, Graham Phillips, Hugh Pincott, Chesca Potter, Terry DuQuesne, Carole Smith, Ken Smith, Gilly Street, Gaynor Sunderland, Marion Sunderland, Cara Trimarco, Charles Walker and last, but not least, Caroline Wise.
Cheers, and happy reading.

Contents

Preface

This book is not just based on fact — it is a very real account of very real events. Every measure has been taken to ensure that its contents are accurate in every respect. Where certain conversations, meetings or situations have been condensed together, it has been clearly marked and explained in the extensive notes at the end of this book.

Nothing has been exaggerated. Everything in *The Black Alchemist* is exactly as it happened, as taken from the author's comprehensive collection of papers, diaries and original notes recorded at the time.

The different people who play a role in the account have each checked and verified the accuracy of their portrayed participation in the book, having been shown the unpublished manuscript to correct and comment upon the sections in which they appear.

The Black Alchemist features the close working partnership between the author, who is an experienced psychic researcher, and a talented psychic presently living in Essex, who wishes only to be known by his Christian name of Bernard. This decision I have respected, as his position as a company director, as well as his cherished privacy, would no doubt be at risk should knowledge of his psychic activities become publicly known.

Many readers of this book will possibly question the authenticity of its extraordinary contents; some of which calls to question our very understanding of human capability. This attitude I can only understand and respect, although I would ask them to fully absorb the entire story before drawing their own conclusions.

Andrew Collins, September 1988.

What is Psychic Questing?

The Black Alchemist is a book about psychic questing, the most exciting, and yet controversial aspect of psychical research in this country today. In simple terms, it takes the psychic out of the seance room and into the landscape. Visionary experiences, powerful dreams, supernatural encounters, the retrieval of concealed relics and other, more clandestine activities all blend together to form the basis of this fast-growing occupation which, to some, may sound as if it has come straight out of the pages of a Dennis Wheatley or J. R. R. Tolkien novel.

The modern revival in psychic questing, or just 'questing,' as it's now known, began in 1979 when the author and a parapsychologist named Graham Phillips were led by an extraordinary series of psychic events to a secluded pool in the Worcestershire countryside. Here, under the cover of darkness and a race against time, they unearthed a sword bearing Mary Queen of Scots' personal monogram, before going on to discover further hidden treasures, including a green talismanic jewel found in an ancient brass casket.

Since that time both Graham Phillips and the author have worked independently with different psychics uncovering the mysteries of the landscape and many more age-old artefacts. Their exploits form the backdrop of questing as it stands today.

The Black Alchemist is the first in a series of books by the author on psychic questing. Details of future titles are available from the publisher.

A list of questing slang is included at the end of this book.

Portent

Spring Equinox 1985. The thud of a car door closing broke the silence of the cold, pre-dawn air. Moments later a silhouetted human form emerged from the vehicle's shadow and began a slow ascent along the narrow, brick-lined path towards the darkened churchyard.

The figure was worried; even a little scared. He knew only too well that the owner of the little cottage to the left of the track possessed an accursed dog which barked wildly whenever visitors passed by. If he awoke this animal then his clandestine presence would be discovered; and he would fail. The churchyard had to be reached before sunrise, or the ritual could not be completed and *he* would not come. A lifetime of dedication to the Great Work would all have been in vain.

The thought agitated him. But the dog was nowhere to be seen, so he moved swiftly on towards his destination.

With fear still mounting, the hooded black form passed through the gate into the tree-lined churchyard and walked among the few remaining gravestones scattered about here and there. His bitter scrutiny of the sentinel-like church betrayed his hatred and revulsion of this house of God; their god. Yet its stillness reassured him; Christianity slept at this strange hour of the day.

The first light of the approaching dawn picked out a low rectangular block of stone and mortar, all that now remained of the church's old nave which had been pulled down long ago. This would be his altar.

In readiness, he set out his occult instruments of ritual upon the uneven foundations. A yellow cord was untied from around his waist, which allowed his black cowled robe to hang loosely. To one end he attached a short dagger, and to the other he tied a crude wooden stake, which was then thrust into the soft, matted grass a few feet in front of the stone altar.

Using the long cord as the radius of a wide circle, the hooded man cut a ring into the ground with the dagger's sharp blade, before shortening its length and carving a second circle several inches inside the first. This would represent his magic ring of protection against any outside psychic interference.

Slow, chilling minutes passed as the figure waited for the sun's glowing red orb to show its face above the eastern horizon and touch the ageing gravestones with its first, finger-like rays of solar light.

The black-robed man stared into the sun's eye and watched for the precise moment before hesitantly raising his arms above his head.

Now was the time.

Strange sounds in a gutteral, hissing-like voice issued forth from his mouth, and then silence. More words followed; slow, decisive and this time in English. 'The First Matter has been achieved; the work is complete. By the power of Zosimos, teacher and guide, release the divine essence. Free the spirit. Cut loose the head from its body, sacrifice the soul and carry it through space to the centre of centres. Then let *him* return to raise the head.'

At this, he reached down to the stone foundations and picked up a slim length of grey stone fashioned into the shape of a spearhead and inscribed with magical characters. As if to show some kind of allegiance to this apparently lifeless artefact, he stared at it with an unsure smile before gripping it hard and plunging it into the ground by his feet.

'I seal the purpose. Now let *him* come.'

The ritual was complete. The Black Alchemist had set his stage.[1]

One
The Stave of Nizar

Tuesday, 7th May, 1985. It was late afternoon when Bernard's car pulled into the car park adjoining Tewkesbury Abbey; Gloucestershire's finest remaining example of Norman architecture. As he locked the vehicle and ambled his way along the flagstone path through the grounds to the entrance doorway, a sudden chill ran through his body. Perhaps it was just the cold air, he considered, or maybe there was another, more curious explanation.

He had been called to the area that day on business, strange in itself, since his line of work did not usually take him outside his home county of Essex. However, the coincidence lay, not in this, but in the very fact that he had wanted to visit the abbey for some months to inspect the tomb of its founder, one Robert Fitzhamon, a man who, in his day, had been one of the most powerful Norman barons in England and a right-hand man to King William Rufus. He had also been a member of the notorious St Clere family, whose very name had been synonymous with mystical intrigue and religious heresies in both France and Britain. Bernard was tracing the genealogy and history of Robert Fitzhamon and felt the need to inspect his tomb at close quarters, for some unapparent reason.

Yet with thoughts of Fitzhamon's tomb put aside for a moment, Bernard stopped to gaze up at the radiant splendour of the twelfth century building's perfect state of preservation. Apparently, when King Henry VIII had dissolved the monasteries of England at the time of the Reformation, the people of Tewkesbury had got together and purchased the abbey building so that it could continue on as their own parish church. In this way they guaranteed its future preservation against the destructive might of the king's men; *and* the local stonemasons. And so, to that day, it remained the most outstanding and complete example of a Norman abbey in the country.

Inside Tewkesbury Abbey Bernard gained psychic communication with its founder, Robert Fitzhamon (Photograph: Bernard).

Inside, Bernard walked slowly down the central aisle towards the high altar at the eastern end. Snippets of the abbey's long history of monastic and parochial devotion were caught by his psychic ears in the form of audible voices; clairaudience, as it was referred to by the psychic researchers.

'They come at the sun's height,' someone proclaimed from behind him. Yet, upon turning around, he saw that he was alone.

'It is the sign of the Lord,' another voice shouted from somewhere out of the stillness of a side aisle. He looked, just in case, but, once again, no one was there.

He was on guard, but still quite settled in mind. The atmosphere was one of anticipation and expectancy; and a shiver ran down his spine. He knew this would be no ordinary visit. Something was going to happen. Something of importance.

Robert Fitzhamon's Gothic-styled box tomb, Bernard found, was situated in a small chantry on the left-hand side of the high altar. However, he had not anticipated that access to it would be barred by a locked wrought iron gate and a low altar rail separating the chancel from the nave. He stood, frustrated, staring helplessly in the direction of the chantry. Had it been a wasted journey after all?

'Is this your first visit to the abbey?' an attentive voice asked from somewhere behind him.

Bernard turned around to see a tall gentleman in a red robe, a verger he decided, waiting for a reply.

He said it was and then voiced his wish to study the tomb of Robert Fitzhamon. Could this be done?

The verger lowered his head with regret. 'I'm sorry sir, but no one is allowed beyond the altar rail or into the chantry unless prior arrangements have been made.'

Undeterred, Bernard pointed out that he had travelled a long way to see this tomb and had been studying Robert Fitzhamon's family for some time. Couldn't he just 'nip in' for a minute or two?

The robed man shook his head, but then relented. 'I will see what the rector has to say on the matter,' he said, turning to walk away.

Minutes later he returned and, with a reserved smile, said: 'Yes, the rector says you can view the tomb, but only for a few minutes. Come on, you'll have to follow me.'

Without further word, the verger led Bernard into the chancel, unlocked the wrought iron gate into the chantry, and disappeared to leave him on his own.

Inside the tiny stone room, he studied the badly worn tomb. It was a disappointment, he decided. Robert Fitzhamon's brass effigy and inscription had long since vanished, leaving only the outline of his body carved into the top of the huge stone matrix slab. Still, it did not really matter. He had now seen it if nothing else.

So what could the tomb tell him about the life and times of this powerful Norman baron? To answer this, Bernard decided to psychometrise or psychically attune to the memorial by reaching out with his right hand until it made contact with the cold stone. Closing his eyes, he let his mind relax and waited patiently for some sort of response. Moments later a stern and authoritative male voice entered his mind and addressed him.

'Who are you with knowledge of me that stands so quiet at my resting?' it indignantly enquired, as if the inquisitive visitor was intruding upon his eternal slumber.

It was the discarnate voice of Robert Fitzhamon. It had to be. 'I know of your family,' he responded, hoping to gain the voice's confidence.

'Do you know of the finding of the Stave of Nizar?' Fitzhamon asked. 'It was mine.'

'No, what is it?' Bernard queried, in complete puzzlement.

'Handed to me by a companion in France; from a Crusade, and belonged to Nizar. Before my friend died on the battlefield he requested that I have it. My request was that it be laid with me (upon my death). But it was taken.'

Intrigued, Bernard asked who took it, and to where.

'The bastard sons of the half-wit Robert of Montaigne,' came the angry reply. 'Where, I know not.'

With his curiosity now well and truly aroused, he began to ask Fitzhamon further questions about this 'Stave of Nizar,' yet none were answered. No more came from the Norman baron who had been dead for nearly 880 years. Yet the psychic communication was by no means over as new images and impressions began to fill his mind.

Bernard could psychically, or clairvoyantly, see a magnificent vision — a solid gold rod, some three to four feet tall, fashioned to look like the branch of a tree. Spiralling its way around the entire length was a golden snake or serpent, its head resting on the top of the rod, its mouth agape and two red rubies for eyes. This, it seemed, was the Stave of Nizar.

Accompanying this vivid clairvoyant image were a series of rapid impressions concerning the rod's long history. It had apparently been fashioned in Ancient Egypt thousands of years ago and had passed through many hands since that age. What was more, he felt its past had involved the spilling of blood, almost as if, at times of desperation, it had been used as a bludgeon to ward off would-be attackers and thieves.

No more came to him inside the small chantry. So, with thoughts of this desirable artefact still firmly fixed in his mind, Bernard walked out into the nave and stood in front of the high altar. Did such a thing really exist? If so, then where was it today? Was it hidden? More importantly, was he meant to find it?

The mere idea of a quest to find the Stave of Nizar appealed to his normally restrained sense of adventure. Mentally, Bernard asked where the 'sons of Robert of Montaigne,' whoever they were, could have taken this rod. Contemplating an answer, his eyes glanced up and became transfixed by the majestic beauty of the stained glass that made up the eastern window.

'WILMINGTON,' a voice bellowed into his ears from over his shoulder.

Startled, Bernard twisted around quite expecting to find someone, the verger most probably, standing right behind him. But no one was there. It had been a clairaudient voice.

Wilmington. He repeated the word over and over in his mind as he moved to a convenient pew and sat down. What did it mean? More names began to pass through his mind in quick succession: 'Samson . . . John . . . William de Jumieges.'

'Who?' he asked himself. Only further words came in response: 'Priors . . . Wilmington . . . Honfleur . . . Gristaine . . . mother . . . France . . . Contaville.'

'Explain,' he requested. For a moment, there was no reply, but then additional words flowed through his mind: 'William . . . Paganus . . . church . . . woods . . . mound.'

'Explain,' he insisted once more. Nothing happened. 'Who is speaking?' He waited, but no answers came. Yet then, as he was about to get up and walk away, another clairvoyant image stabbed at his mind. It was of a dark, damp stone room, without any feeling or presence of modern-day life. This place, he sensed, was an underground crypt of some sort, associated with a medieval priory. It was inside this room that an important clue as to the eventual destiny of the fabulous Stave of Nizar would be found. But where was it?

Mentally, Bernard asked for the precise location of this priory crypt.

'Wilmington,' came the reply.

By the time he sat down in the comfort of his dining room that evening, Bernard had been given enough time to fully digest the incredible events which had befallen him inside Tewkesbury Abbey that afternoon. Along with a few further explanatory images and impressions he had received on the long journey back from Gloucestershire, he now felt able to put the whole story into some sort of perspective. So, picking up a pen, he began to scribble down his feelings on a large notepad.

It was a tale which appeared to have begun in Ancient Egypt, during the time of the pharoahs, when a gold serpent rod of some magnificence had been fashioned as an instrument of religious ritual. It had been passed on from one high priest to the next until the eventual collapse of this great Middle Eastern empire just before the birth of Christ. After this time, the ceremonial stave had no longer been seen as a treasure of religious significance. Instead, it became an object of curiosity and greed, to be stolen or sold from one person to the next; and even used as a murder weapon when necessary. Eventually, this golden rod became known as the Stave of Nizar, seemingly after a person of this name, before falling into the hands of a French nobleman taking part in a religious Crusade somewhere out in the Holy Land.

This Crusader had, it seemed, brought the precious artefact back to his homeland where it had remained in his possession until he lay mortally wounded on a French battlefield. At this point he had entrusted the stave to his companion, the powerful Norman baron, Robert Fitzhamon, who lived in Britain. He brought it into this country where it was held as a financial asset, without Fitzhamon ever really comprehending its great religious value. He requested that, upon his death, the stave should be placed with him in his tomb in Tewkesbury Abbey. However, his last wish was never to be fulfilled, as the great treasure was stolen by the 'bastard' sons of a man named 'Robert of Montaigne' and entrusted to the monks of a priory at a place named Wilmington, which he sensed was somewhere in Sussex.

Why the Stave of Nizar should have been given to this particular priory, Bernard could only guess. However, he was convinced that the monks there were French and had practised a somewhat unorthodox form of Christian monastic discipline. For some reason, they had attached great religious significance to the Stave of Nizar and yet had kept its presence at the priory a complete secret. On ceremonial occasions it would be brought out and paraded as a ritual object; and at such times the relatively small community would be joined by special visitors from France. However, despite the secrecy surrounding the stave's presence at the priory, it appeared that certain individuals in very high places *had* been aware of its existence; a situation which had afforded this French 'alien house' special immunity from outside interference by both ecclesiastical and secular authorities.

In addition to all this, it appeared — from the psychic information — that the monks' influence had extended beyond the boundaries of the priory's own lands to other sacred sites within the countryside around Wilmington. These, he felt, had included a grass-covered 'castle mound,' known as 'Burghlee,' and a small church or chapel on a hill enclosed by a small wood or copse. This chapel may or may not have been synonymous with another location he had been shown where, it appeared, a man named 'Paganus' had been instructed to build a small chapel by the monks of the priory. At each of these sites the monks had apparently carried out ceremonies involving the use of the stave.

This, it seemed, was the web of intrigue surrounding the Stave of Nizar's colourful history.

But what did it all mean? Why had he been given all this information? Was it to enable him to track down the whereabouts of this rather valuable treasure of the past?

Leaning back in his chair, he took off his reading glasses and lit another cigarette. Something inside was telling him that there was more to this stave business than met the eye. Some sort of far reaching implication which would only become apparent as time progressed. Though what, he could not say.

The next step, however, was to tell his friend, Andy Collins, to see what he had to say on the matter.

Two
Wilmington

Thursday, 9th May, 1985. Leaving my duties as a sales representative and writer on the *Leigh Times* newspaper for a few minutes that afternoon, I decided to telephone Bernard. Not having spoken to him for a while, I needed to confirm our meeting arranged for the following week at our usual haunt, The Griffin pub in Danbury.

Cruising the streets of Leigh-on-Sea, I glanced out across the Thames Estuary from Essex into Kent, in between looking for a call box that worked. On a fine day you could see the North Downs; but not today. The weather was far too misty, and it looked as if it was going to rain later.

From a call box outside the main post office, I rang the psychic who immediately began to reveal details of some new material he had picked up a few days earlier in Tewkesbury Abbey; and it sounded interesting.

'Do you know of a Sussex village called Wilmington?' he asked, concluding his story. 'I think there's a priory there with a crypt.'

As I tried to scribble down a few notes, I thought for a moment. Wasn't that the name of the Sussex village in *Dad's Army*, the TV comedy series about a battalion of Home Guard volunteers during the Second World War? No, hold on, that was Warmington-on-Sea!

Bernard laughed. He, like me, had forgotten the most obvious landmark associated with a Sussex village of this name.

But then I remembered. Of course, it was *that* Wilmington — the one which gave its name to the Long Man of

Wilmington, the famous hill figure marked in outline upon the slopes of nearby Windover Hill. Its image came to mind — a huge effigy of a man, some 230 feet in height, with its arms outstretched, and holding in each hand a long staff or spear. No one rightly knew its true age or significance, although some scholars believed it to date back to the same period as the 4,000 year old Bronze Age burial mounds which lined the apex of the hill.

I had visited the Long Man of Wilmington on at least a couple of occasions and knew very well that there *was* a priory there, close to the base of the hill and in full view of the Long Man. However, I had never actually been into the priory which, I seemed to recall, possessed a small museum. I had no idea whether it contained any sort of underground crypt. But that could easily be checked out.

Friday, 10th May. By the time the caretaker came around to throw everyone out of Southend Central Library at seven o'clock, I had been able to confirm and piece together much of the story Bernard had been given concerning the so-called Stave of Nizar and its eventual journey to Wilmington.

The 'Nizar,' who had seemingly given his name to the gold ceremonial staff, turned out to be one of the two sons of a Moslim leader, or caliph, as they were known, named Al-Mustansir, who reigned as head of the Egypt-based Fatimud Dynasty in the years prior to 1094 AD. Upon Al-Mustansir's death in that year, a civil war had erupted between the supporters of Nizar and his brother Ahmad for supremecy of the caliphate. Nizar was defeated and murdered, and so Ahmad began his reign using the name Al-Mustabi. He had lasted until 1101 AD. However, it had been during his disastrous reign that the Fatimud Moslims had finally lost Jerusalem to the European crusading armies at the end of the First Crusade in 1099 AD.

So far so good. It seemed reasonable to conceive of Nizar coming across a gold stave which had originally been fashioned in the very same country in which he lived. And then, upon his death at the hands of his brother's supporters in 1094, perhaps the rod had been stolen and kept by a Fatimud Moslim until Al-Mustabi and his armies were defeated when Jerusalem had fallen to the Crusaders five years later. History tells us that many of the captive Moslims bargained for their lives by handing over vast quantities of Islamic and Judaic treasures, much of which found its way back to Europe, especially France. Perhaps the Stave of Nizar had been among these treasures.

Turning my attentions to the next piece of the jigsaw — Robert Fitzhamon — I found that in 1100 AD, just one year after the completion of the First Crusade, he had been in France participating in battles to quell the baronial uprisings which had been plaguing Britain's Norman monarchs. Indeed, it was during one of these skirmishes, in support of King Henry I, that Fitzhamon had received a head wound which had left him with mental disorientation and had contributed to his eventual death in 1107.

Once again, it was reasonable to suppose that one of Fitzhamon's French companions may have brought the Stave of Nizar back from the First Crusade in 1099 AD and then, as he lay mortally wounded on a battlefield in France, just one year later in 1100, he had bequeathed it to his fighting companion.

Next, I attempted to find reference to the 'half-wit Robert of Montaigne' and his apparent involvement with Wilmington Priory which, I soon found, *had* been a French alien house. Its *mother* foundation had been the Benedictine abbey of *Grestain* — not 'Gristaigne', as Bernard had spelt it — which was founded in 1050 AD by Herluin de *Contaville*, near a place named *Honfleur*, on the banks of the River Seine.

Following the Norman Conquest, the manor of Wilmington had been given, along with lands in nearby Pevensey, to Herluin de Contaville's *'dim-witted'* son, *Robert of Mortain* — as it was more popularly spelt — the half-brother of William the Conqueror. Robert, I found, had fathered *two sons* — William, his heir, who eventually became the Count of

Robert Fitzhamon, the powerful Norman baron who allegedly brought the magnificent Stave of Nizar back to England around 1100 AD, seen here with his wife Sibilla (Photo: Oxford, Bodleian Library, MS. Top. Glouc. d. 2, fol. 13r.).

Mortain, and another named Nigel.

It had been Robert of Mortain, the Earl of Cornwall, who had given Wilmington to Grestain Abbey. Once in their hands, the abbey had begun to use this Sussex coastal manor as a stop-over point for its representatives in England. Yet by the end of the twelfth century, some sort of priory had been established at Wilmington. However, nothing was known of its history until the first references to the various priors of Wilmington started appearing in ancient charters during the thirteenth century. The first mentioned was a Master *Samson*, circa 1200. A Prior *John* appeared in records for 1243, and among those which followed was a Prior *William de Gymeges* in 1268.

Despite the fact that the priory supported only a very small community of monks, its influence extended to controlling the local agricultural system over an extensive area. Yet, as a French alien house, Wilmington Priory should have come under a very rigid control from both ecclesiastical and secular authorities. Yet, just as Bernard had predicted, Wilmington appeared to have possessed an unprecedented diplomatic immunity. This had been most noticeable at times of military unrest between France and England when other alien houses were always seized by the Crown. Wilmington, however, appeared to have been left unsullied.[1]

But this special immunity had only lasted until 1360, for in that year the priory had been seized like any other French monastic house. It had again been seized in 1370, and in 1414 it was taken out of Grestain's French control completely. After this date it passed into the hands of the Dean and Chapter of Chichester who, for a century and a half, had run the priory as a farm and vicarage. It had finally fallen into private hands in 1565, some years after Henry VIII's Dissolution of the Monastaries.

I also found that the Benedictine monks of Wilmington Priory were thought to have practised an unorthodox form of monastic discipline. This was likely to have included aspects of the Cabala, a medieval mystical Hebrew doctrine, as well as other unusual ceremonies which had been attended by clandestine visitors from over the water.[2]

Everything Bernard had disclosed to me over the telephone seemed to be checking out, yet there was still more to come. The 'castle mound' named 'Burghlee,' which Bernard had felt was somewhere quite close to Wilmington, turned out to be a large grassy mound named *Burlough Castle* set on the apex of a hill about half a mile to the west of Wilmington. Very little was known about this strange mound. However, some scholars believed it to be the remains of a Norman mote and bailey, even though no such place existed in historical records. A stronger tradition suggested that it was once the abode of the fairy folk, possibly indicating its great age and past ritual use in pre-Christian times.

The little church, mentioned by Bernard as being set on a hill within a wooded grove, was also located. That appeared to be the tiny church of Lullington, situated on the top of a hill, lost in trees, about a mile south of the priory. It apparently measured a mere 16 feet square and had seating for just 20 people. Some historians even believed it to be the smallest church in England, although that was not quite correct, as what remained today was merely the chancel of a much larger edifice which had fallen into ruins long ago.

I could not, unfortunately, find any reference to a man named 'Paganus' who, Bernard believed, had been instructed by the monks of the priory to build a chapel in the area. That would have to wait until we visited the area.

Bernard certainly seemed to be on to something. Yet despite not having found any reference to a golden rod known as the Stave of Nizar, there was enough circumstantial evidence to suggest that the rest of his psychic information might turn out to be correct.

Yet he was convinced that the Stave of Nizar *did still exist* and that, for some reason, it was up to us to locate it. He did not know where it would be found, but he did know how we could find out. The clue appeared to lie within the medieval crypt below Wilmington Priory; and it would therefore have to be in here that our quest would begin.

Three
The Guardian

Thursday, 30th May, 1985. It was a fine day. The sun was shining and a coat was not needed. Inside the car park next to Wilmington Priory, we paused for a few minutes to enjoy a few sandwiches and a cup of coffee.

A clear view of the Long Man hill figure, reclining into a hollow upon the slopes of Windover Hill, dominated our gaze whenever we glanced across the fields to the south-east.

Nobody rightly knew what the figure represented. Some scholars believed it to have been carved by the monks of the priory as a representation of Samson, the Biblical strongman who brought down the house of the Philistines by dislodging its pillars with his arms. Others believed it to represent a pagan horned god, or possibly even a god of the underworld.

'Looks like someone trying to keep open a doorway to me,' Bernard announced, with a smile.

I hoped I would get more sense out of him within the priory.

The museum was not all that interesting — probably because our minds were on other things — so we moved swiftly on and soon discovered the priory's medieval crypt. So it *did* exist, and it was exactly as Bernard had described: dark, damp and lifeless.

For a while, we just paced about inside, studying every dark corner of the underground room. He appeared to be getting nothing at all, which was a bad sign. A quick decision was obviously needed to enable him to more easily attune to the site's inherent place memories, impregnated into the fabric of the walls by over 300 years of monastic devotion. I therefore decided to leave him on his own for a while to see if

A silhouetted Bernard posed for the camera in front of the Long Man of Wilmington before the fateful journey to nearby Burlough Castle.

that might help the situation.

Bernard agreed, so, handing him my notepad and pen, I stepped out into the sun, sat down on the lawn in front of the crypt and contemplated the thought of actually finding the Stave of Nizar.

Twenty minutes passed before my romancing was broken by the sight of Bernard emerging out of the darkness with a smile on his face. Lighting up a cigarette, he handed me the notepad which now contained a page of scribbled automatic writing.

I read it out aloud before even beginning to interpret its possible relevance to our quest.

> **Mortagne's son. Nigel. Stave here for long time. Prior, Will' de Gymieges. 1266? We used (the stave) in ritual, also in countryside. Prior Will. Milton Court. Lord of. Paganus. Small chapel in woods. We told him to build.**

At this point in the text, Bernard had written: 'What for?' To which his hand had scribbled:

> **We knew of the Rod's yesterdays. It gave us the feelings of**

God. We did not say of its existence. Guilliamus de Pykard. I priori here. Petrus de Savoy. Amadeus.

The direct references to the Stave of Nizar needed no explanation. However, the text indicated that it had been Robert of Mortain's son, Nigel, who had given the stave to the priory, and not his other son, William. Again, there was mention of a man named 'Paganus', apparently the lord of a place called 'Milton Court' which, I assumed, had to be somewhere near the tiny village of Milton Street, just a mile or so away from Wilmington. He, it seemed, had been instructed by a prior named William to build a small chapel in some woods. With this had come the name 'Prior William de Gymieges' and the date 1266. Records I had already uncovered confirmed the existence of this particular prior and yet associated him with the date 1268. Still, it was close enough.

After this had come the name of another prior, 'Guilliamus de Pykard' or, in English, William of Pykard. It was from this long-dead prior that the psychic communication appeared to have originated. This had been followed by the name 'Petrus of Savoy'; Petrus being the Latin rendering of Peter, someone who Bernard sensed was an Italian associated with the nearby castle of Pevensey. Bernard believed that Prior William de Pykard had worked together with Peter of Savoy to repair the castle's defences at some stage in its history. The name Amadeus mentioned was, he believed, Peter of Savoy's brother.

Pevensey Castle, I soon discovered, had been built by Robert of Mortain on the ruins of a Roman fort shortly after the Norman Conquest.[1] In 1101 AD, Robert's son and heir, William, the Count of Mortain, had unsuccessfully rebelled against King Henry I and, in consequence, his family had forfeited Pevensey. After this, the castle had passed through various hands, until it was eventually given to Peter of Savoy who — in 1254 — had shared the task of repairing the ramparts of the castle with a coven of twelve other men, one of whom had been the current prior of Wilmington. However, I was unable to establish which particular prior this referred to. I also discovered that Peter of Savoy's brother had been named Amadeus.

What the automatic writing had to do with our quest to find the Stave of Nizar, I had no idea at all. But it was interesting nevertheless and appeared to be snippets of historical fact associated with the various ancient sites of the area.

Yet no leading clue had been given concerning the present location of the stave. So, only a little despondent, we decided to visit the two outlying sites where Bernard had picked up the stave had been used in religious ceremonies. Perhaps one of these would hold some clue as to its eventual destiny.

As we drove south along a narrow country lane, I kept one eye out for a signpost which would direct us to Lullington church. I had worked out that it was situated somewhere in the woods off to the right-hand side of the road, so slowed the car down as much as I could.

Then the sign appeared, but quickly vanished before I had a chance to react. It had said something about 'To the church', and appeared to be pointing towards a narrow path leading into the trees. With cars close behind, there was no way that I could stop and turn around.

'Shall we carry on to Burlough?' Bernard suggested, as I vehemently cursed our predicament. 'We can do Lullington afterwards.'

I was not happy. What if we had been meant to go to Lullington first? It could foul up the whole quest. Anyway, it was too late to turn back now, so I turned right at the next junction and headed towards Alfriston, the nearest village to Burlough Castle.

With a little help from a man on a bicycle, we finally located Burlough Castle. Leaving the car at the bottom of a farm track, the pair of us strolled past the growling dogs behind the restraints of the nearby farmhouse's garden gate and eventually entered the field adjacent to the ancient site.

Once in view, we could see that the mound was, in fact, a large wedge-shaped plateau on the top of a ridge, about 100 yards or so in length and some 30 yards in width. Although the plateau had been cultivated into a long strip for agricultural purposes, tall grass and weeds still covered its banks.

Bernard and I climbed up the bank to the top of the mound, but the strong southerly winds were so distracting that we decided to move into the relative shelter of the trees and undergrowth by a stream which meandered its way past the base of the mound.

The psychic then began to stare intently back towards the grassy bank, yet for a moment remained silent. I noticed this but said nothing, although it was obvious that he could see something quite out of place. But what?

'You are not going to believe this,' he began, glancing back to me, 'but sitting cross-legged on the edge of that plateau is a curious-looking dwarf. A guardian figure or elemental of some sort. He's looking at us and laughing.'

Questing lore spoke of ethereal thought forms, created by

Hands in pockets, Bernard made his way towards the banks of Burlough Castle, the mysterious mound close to Wilmington Priory.

priest magicians of the past, who guard sacred places and hidden treasure. They may take any form, either human, animal or mythical which a good psychic would be able to see and communicate with clairaudiently. So what did this one look like?

'He's about four feet tall, with long bushy hair and a long beard,' Bernard said, rather hesitantly. 'He's wearing a leather tunic of sorts, with leather thongs around his feet and ankles. In his hand is a wooden staff, raised upright, and I would say that he appears to be associated with a very early period of the site's history, possibly Iron Age or even earlier.'

He sounded like something straight out of the pages of a Tolkien novel. Did he have a name?

'He says his name is "Ogmor," and he is laughing because we have "come up the wrong way" for some reason. I get the impression that this plateau was once covered with a huge turf maze and that during religious ceremonies there would have been a right and a wrong way to approach the site. It seems that we inadvertently entered the site from the wrong direction, and so he deliberately made us leave the bank and come down here.'

What was he doing at Burlough Castle?

'He says he's here to keep people off the mound and that many have visited the site before us.'

I felt it was time to tell the guardian figure about our quest to locate the Stave of Nizar. Was he aware of its existence?

'He has now erected a great wall around himself and the entire plateau,' Bernard revealed, still staring into thin air. 'When you mentioned the stave he seemed angered and so erected this wall.'

It was obvious that he knew of this artefact, but why the sudden hostile reaction?

'He says that the monks came here and interfered with the mound for many centuries and he now wants me to write something down.'

Sitting with my notepad on his lap, Bernard concentrated his mind upon the dwarf-like figure and soon his hand began to scribble a message.

It read:

> **They came and pierced my heart with the rod. They make signs in sky and earth. They cause me much pain. They heed not my warnings to depart. I sorry at my loss of strength.**

By this it appeared that the monks of Wilmington had visited Burlough Castle and carried out some sort of ritual during which they had pierced the ground with the Stave of Nizar.

'And I feel this ritual involved the use of Hebrew words,' Bernard added to my summary of the situation. 'And some kind of reverence to the sun, I think. I'm not sure in what way.'

Yet the presence of the stave had apparently drained the site of its inherent energies, leaving it weak and unable to function properly as a place of psychic or spiritual power. And the statement: 'They came and pierced *my* heart . . .' and 'I sorry at *my* loss of strength' implied that the guardian figure of Ogmor, and Burlough Castle, were one and the same. We were, in effect, speaking to the collective personification of the site itself!

Bernard decided that he would walk back up the grassy bank and confront the little man's psychic wall.

Following him, I diplomatically tried to convince Ogmor that we meant him no harm and that if he could help us in our quest, then we might be able to help him regain some of his lost strength.

'The wall has now been removed,' Bernard revealed, as he still stared intently at the invisible form. 'He seems to know of our quest and says that he might be able to tell us certain things about the stave.'

Once again, I tried, via Bernard, to engage the clairvoyant apparition in conversation and began by asking him how long he had guarded the mound.

'"Since time began",' he says. There was a pause before Bernard spoke again. 'Now he's saying that this place has always been sacred to nature and surrounded by waters.'

Having heard enough, I decided to try and help Ogmor regain his 'lost strength' by carrying out a simple visualisation ritual. To achieve this I would have to see and feel energies passing from my own aura, or energy field, into those already present at the site itself. In questing lore it was believed that the human mind could cause a very subtle effect upon natural energy fields of the landscape by producing a very mild form of psychokinesis, or mind-over-matter, purely by picturing or visualising your intentions.

So, raising my arms, I closed my eyes and mentally pictured streams of golden light pouring out of my body and forming into a huge spiral that encircled the mound in an ever-decreasing circle.

Bernard stood by and watched in utter amazement. With his eyes wide open, he began to *actually see* a mass of golden light — the visual form of subtle energies — spiralling up and encircling the site, like a luminous tornado focused upon Burlough Castle. And Ogmor seemed pleased as well. Jumping up, the little man ran into the centre of his home — its 'heart' — and stood with his arms and staff raised aloft, quite enamoured at what was taking place around him.

Opening my eyes at the completion of the visualisation ritual, I saw Bernard writing. It was another psychic message. So, was Ogmor pleased with my actions?

Bernard handed me the scribbled message and I read it out aloud.

> **Do you know of the legend of Peredur? This is the Castle of the Chessboard. He plays, loses, is told to hunt white stag in small wood. Remove head.**

It was seemingly our reward for having helped the guardian figure regain his lost strength. Had we not done this, then we would probably not have been given the message. But what did it mean? Peredur was a character from Welsh Arthurian literature, yet other than this it meant very little to either of us. The mention of a 'small wood' was, I felt, a reference to the wooded grove that surrounded Lullington churchyard. Was this correct?

Bernard nodded as he received the affirmative from Ogmor.

The message therefore implied that we were to now go to Lullington church and remove a 'head' of some sort. Perhaps the church's architecture included a removable stone stag's head, behind which the golden stave lay secreted in a cavity. I knew it was a wild idea, but in questing you are taught to expect the unexpected; so it might be correct.

As Ogmor appeared to have no more to say, we mentally thanked him for his assistance and began to retrace our steps back across the ploughed field towards the car.

Strolling across the hard, uneven earth, I had a curious thought. What if we had visited Lullington *before* going on to Burlough Castle, as we had originally planned to do? We would not have encountered Ogmor and would not have been given the clue about removing the stag's head. Had fate therefore intervened to make us skip Lullington and go straight to Burlough Castle? It was an interesting thought.

As Bernard clambered over the gate and stepped back on to the track, he stopped for a moment to compose his thoughts. 'Was Peredur the son of a man named Evawk, or some name like that?' he asked, quite out of the blue.

I had no idea. Why?

'Oh, nothing really,' he said, as if dismissing the entire question. 'It was just something which came to mind.'

Four
The Unintentional Quest

Ten minutes later our car pulled up behind another which had just come to a halt below the signpost pointing the way to Lullington Church. Leaving their vehicle, the party acknowledged our presence before beginning the slow ascent along the narrow path which led through a wooded area to the secluded churchyard crowning the top of the hill.

We followed close behind and, as the tiny church came into view, with its white slatted bellcote, another party of visitors was about to leave.

Despite their presence, I strolled casually around the church exterior looking for any gargoyle-like stag's heads affixed to its stone walls. One revolution of the building revealed nothing, so I made my way back across the sun-kissed churchyard.

Bernard wandered thoughtfully among the few remaining gravestones scattered about within the grass-covered churchyard, a concerned expression upon his face. 'I get the feeling that black magic has been going on here,' he revealed, shaking his head.

As there was no explanation, I simply accepted his word, but felt it unconnected with our own particular quest to find the Stave of Nizar. Moving away, I searched the wooded area surrounding the entire churchyard. It revealed no clues; neither did the tiny church interior. Something was wrong. There was definitely no stag's head either on, or around, Lullington church, I concluded, as I signed the visitors' book and rejoined Bernard out in the open. I found him sitting peacefully upon a wooden bench on the western edge of the churchyard, enjoying the cool shade offered by the tree cover.

The tiny church of Lullington, set within a secluded, wooded grove, where Ogmor, the guardian of Burlough Castle, claimed the 'head' would be located.

As visitors came and went, Bernard just sat in the shade, complaining of a growing headache, as I continued to pace about. A couple of times he got up to study a conglomerate of stone and mortar foundations close to where he was sitting. They appeared to be the last remnants of the old church nave which had been pulled down and removed long ago. Inquisitive, I asked him what he was doing.

'I keep getting the feeling that there's something down by those foundations,' he replied, getting up again to look at the block of stone about five foot square and some three feet in height: 'It's nothing definite. Only a vague feeling.'

Giving up, he sat back down and once more complained about his headache. Obviously, the bright sunlight was getting to him.

The final group of visitors then left, giving us the site to ourselves for the very first time. Taking advantage of the situation, I walked briskly into the church and knelt down in

The clod of stone and mortar foundations in Lullington churchyard, below which Bernard felt something lay secreted.

front of the altar, leaving the door open on Bernard's instructions, so that he could see what I was doing. Closing my eyes, I tried to mentally open up my mind to the site and began to ask for help with our quest. *Could anyone tell me why we had been led to this site?*

For five minutes I silently contemplated the situation hoping that Bernard would now be given some sort of message. Suddenly, there were footsteps behind me.

'Come on. Let's go,' Bernard said, his voice echoing as he stood in the doorway. 'There's another group of visitors coming up the path, but I think I know what's going on. Here, take this.'

Opening my eyes, I turned around and took hold of a muddy length of polished grey stone, about eight inches long, clearly shaped to look like a spearhead. Along two of its three faces were a series of, what appeared to be, occult symbols. So where had this come from?

'By those stone foundations, over there,' he explained,

Inscribed on the stone spearhead found in Lullington churchyard were curious magical symbols which could not be identified in any available occult books.

pointing towards the block of stone, some fifteen or so yards away, where he had earlier felt that something might be concealed. 'After you knelt down and started attuning I appeared to receive a boost of energy which allowed me to pinpoint exactly where it was hidden. I found it just below the earth on its western side.'

He stopped to touch and rub his forehead. 'Come on, let's get out of here. I don't feel so good. Anyway, we've got all that we came for here.'

Did the group who carried out this black magic ritual bury the spearhead?

'Yes, but I'll tell you what else I picked up as I touched the stone once we're away from here.'

But hold on. There was no way that I was going to leave the site until he had shown me exactly where the spearhead had been found.

Bernard reluctantly agreed, and so, only after a further fifteen or more minutes of getting out cameras, posing for shots and focusing the lenses, were we finally able to leave the site after having been in Lullington churchyard for well over an hour.

'I don't feel very well,' Bernard groaned, as we began the short drive back to Wilmington Priory.

I suggested that he let me know if he wanted to be sick.

Five minutes down the road he asked me to stop the car. As I jammed on the brakes, he opened the car door, leapt out quickly and vomited on the roadside.

I felt somewhat guilty. It was my fault that he was now in this state. We should have left right away, as he had rightly requested, and not remained there to take petty photographs. I also realised that we should perhaps have carried out some form of psychic protection ritual. This type of simple act would, I knew, give a psychic like Bernard, adequate mental protection from most external psychic influences of an undesirable nature.

As Bernard staggered back into the car, and the journey continued in silence, I suddenly realised something rather significant. The stone spearhead Bernard had discovered *was* the 'head' we had been told to remove by Ogmor. However, it was not a stag's head, as I had assumed, but a *spear*head. So we *were* meant to have found it. But for what reason?

The answer seemed to lie in the fact that the spearhead had been placed in the ground as a fixing marker to, in some way, seal the intentions of a black magic ritual which appeared to have left a rather nasty atmosphere at Lullington. An atmosphere which had been picked up by Bernard as soon as we had arrived at the site. Ogmor had therefore asked us to remove this offending artefact because it was, in some way, blackening or imbalancing the inherent energy matrix present at the site.

Yet how did all this relate to Peredur, the Castle of the Chessboard and the white stag? And what about our quest to find the Stave of Nizar? That morning we had journeyed to Sussex in an attempt to locate an Ancient Egyptian ceremonial staff which had once been in the hands of the monks of Wilmington Priory. Instead, we end up getting involved in a domestic quest to remove a piece of stone from a nearby churchyard.

It did not make sense.

Back in the priory car park Bernard strolled off to clean himself up in the toilets. When he returned I made him go through a visualisation meditation in an attempt to help him regain some of his lost vital energy; otherwise he might have been ill for days. It seemed to work to some degree so, sitting out on the grass in the late afternoon sun, he decided, at last, to reveal the images and impressions he had received as his hand had made contact with the inscribed stone spearhead.

It had been placed there, he believed, by just one man, working on his own, who had carried out a ritual at the site at either sunrise or sunset, as the low sun in the vision was casting long shadows across the churchyard. He had worn a black cowled robe, with the hood over his head. Then, using the stone foundations as a kind of makeshift altar, he had removed a cord from around his waist and tied one end to a dagger, and the other to a short wooden stake, which he had then pushed into the ground. Pulling taut the cord, he had then used the dagger's sharp blade to scratch a large circle into the soft earth. After this he had shortened the length of the cord and cut a concentric ring about nine inches inside the outer circle. This, Bernard felt, had then acted as his magical circle of protection.

It was at this point that the spearhead had been thrust into the ground to seal and intensify the ritual's power and intentions. Why exactly this man should have wanted to carry out a ritual in Lullington churchyard, he could not say. All he knew was that, on a psychic level, it had left a very sour taste at the site; so the man had to be classed as a practitioner of black or warped magic.

But when had this act been carried out? Was it recent?

Bernard was not sure. 'Some time ago,' was his only answer.

As to the identity of the occultist, he could not say. He felt too drained to even think about the matter, let alone continue our own quest to find the Stave of Nizar.

Reluctantly, I had to accept that our questing activities were over for the day. Maybe we could return some other time; that was, if he could face coming back to the area again.

Five
The First Matter

Saturday, 1st June, 1985. A howling wind tore violently through a copse of tall, spindly trees on the top of the mound-like hillock on which Bernard now found himself in a state of confusion and fear. The pitch darkness concealed the location. There was a clearing there and it looked like Lullington again, although he could not be sure.

Glancing towards the ground, his eyes beheld a disturbing sight — hundreds of large, black scavenger birds were desperately flapping their wings in a state of chaotic frenzy, unable to fly. Then an even more obscene sight assailed him — three silhouetted figures in black cowled robes stood silent and motionless in the centre of the clearing. In the hands of the middle figure was a huge, black Calvary cross, some six feet in height, held before him the correct way up; as if to mock and mimic the very symbol of the Christian faith.

The whole scene reeked of evil and Bernard was not going to stay. He *had* to return to the security and protection of his own home before he was drawn any deeper into their black ritual. His mind's eye lifted from the mound before darkness enveloped him.

Twisting and turning in his sleep, Bernard regained consciousness and opened his eyes. The more familiar surroundings of the bedroom ceiling calmed him down. Yet the imagery and feelings of the curious dream were too strong to ignore. He would only be drawn back; back to that place. No, he could not return to sleep. He would have to get up. It was the only way.

Trying not to wake his wife, he slid out of bed and crept quietly out of the room. Downstairs, he lit a cigarette and put the kettle on for an intended cup of coffee. His nerves needed calming, he convinced himself.

Where was this mound he had witnessed? He knew it was situated within a copse of tall, spindly trees. It felt like Lullington. But he had not seen the church. So was it there? Possible . . . but no. Something now told him that the disturbing sight of the large black birds was a symbolic clue. They were rooks, he believed, and he was sure that the mound in the dream was actually called *the Rookery*. Perhaps Andy would be able to find out if such a place existed.

Pouring out the boiling water, he thought about the three men in the black cowled robes. Just who were they? Could one of them have been the black magician who had planted the inscribed spearhead in the churchyard at Lullington? It was possible. Yet, if so, then who were the other two? He could not give himself any answers. In fact, he was not even sure if he had witnessed a real event taking place at that time, or whether it was purely a symbolic dream; a portent of things to come.

Baffled, tired and confused, Bernard stubbed out his cigarette and scribbled down a few notes, before finishing his coffee and tiptoeing his way back upstairs. Climbing into bed, he noted the time. It was now 4.25 am.

Tuesday, 4th June. It was now over five days since Bernard and I had discovered the inscribed shale spearhead; yet the meaning of its unique magical symbols still eluded me. Nowhere had I been able to find any similar characters used in magical practices. However, somebody would surely recognise them. But who?

I had an idea. If anyone would be able to decipher them, it would be Nigel Pennick, the Cambridge-based author of a number of books on ancient mysteries. Nigel had been studying magical alphabets for many years, so perhaps he had come across similar symbols before.

From a local call box I briefly explained to Nigel what was going on and he agreed to see me later that evening.

Within the hour I was travelling at great speed along the M11 motorway towards Nigel's Cambridge home with the precious artefact by my side.

For the meeting we were joined by Nigel's close friend, Prudence Jones. Together, they listened patiently as I related the extraordinary tale of how the spearhead had come into my possession. I was not sure whether either of them actually believed the story. However, both studied the fashioned spearhead and attempted to associate its strange symbols with any of the magical alphabets already known to them.

So, *were* they familiar?

'I'm not sure,' was Nigel's initial response to my nagging question. Shaking his head, he drew a small booklet towards him. 'Some of the characters closely resemble various letters used in one of the Bardic alphabets; a magical system allegedly inherited by the pseudo-Druids of the eighteenth century.'

He pointed out similar letters in a booklet which he himself had penned. They certainly looked quite similar. So what did the inscription say?

'I'm afraid that not enough of the characters match to allow any sort of translation,' Nigel pointed out, reaching for a piece of paper. 'However, we shall see what we've got.'

I watched with bated breath as Nigel jotted down peculiar-looking letters between a few broken lines, where the letter could not be interpreted, almost like a game of hangman. Yet, in conclusion, none of it made any sense. Only a few letters matched; no real words. So I felt a little despondent.

But Nigel seemed concerned. He kept referring to a book he was sure he possessed which mentioned many of the sites I had been speaking about. Eventually, his curiosity overtook him and he left the room in search of the book in question. Minutes later he returned clutching a flimsy cover book entitled *The Wilmington Giant*, written by a man named Rodney Castleden.

'I knew I had it somewhere,' he said, beginning to flick through its pages. 'The book is about the mysteries surrounding the Long Man of Wilmington and I'm sure it mentions Lullington in it somewhere.'

I looked on patiently as he scanned its index for any references relevent to our quest.

'Ah, here we are,' he announced, handing the book to me. 'Lots of references to Lullington and Burlough Castle. See what they say.'

Most of the entries were to be found in one particular chapter, coincidently entitled 'The Quest'. It began with a history of Wilmington Priory which, I soon discovered, included an account of its rather unorthodox religious practices. It also mentioned the special immunity afforded to the French monks at times when other medieval alien houses had been seized by the Crown. The author even hinted at the possibility that the priory's monks had followed a form of Hebrew mystical doctrine known as the Cabala — all just as Bernard had suggested.

Yet it was Rodney Castleden's reference to an extraordinary article entitled 'The Long Man of Wilmington', published in a 1932 issue of the *Sussex County Magazine*, which instantly grabbed our attention. Written by a man named S.F. Annett, it had linked the landscape around Wilmington with an episode in the Welsh medieval romance known simply as *Peredur*, in particular, his *visit to the Castle of the Chessboard.*

Apparently, on his journeys, Peredur comes upon the Castle of the Chessboard and takes sides with a board playing a game on its own. It loses, so he throws the board into the water. Peredur is then told to make good his injury by going to a 'nearby wood' and beheading a white stag, or hart, that frequents this place. The Welsh hero then hunts, kills and *beheads* the stag in the wood, following which, a *mysterious knight*, or a lady in some accounts, then seizes the head and carries it off. As a punishment for his failure, Peredur is then sent to a mound 'beneath which is a carved man' and, once there, he recites a spell. A huge black man then appears ready to do battle. The hero defeats this black man who then disappears back into the mound.

Even more remarkable had been Annett's suggestion that

the Castle of the Chessboard was, in fact, Burlough Castle, and the 'nearby wood', where Peredur hunts, kills and beheads the white stag, was the wooded grove surrounding Lullington church!

Why the author of this article should have wished to link his own local landscape with an episode in a clearly Welsh medieval romance, seemed a complete mystery. Perhaps Annett had been a keen admirer of the Peredur story and had wanted to place some sort of mythical significance upon the area in which he lived. Whatever the answer, the fact remained that both S.F. Annett and Rodney Castleden had echoed Ogmor's psychic message associating Burlough Castle and Lullington church with the Peredur episode involving the Castle of the Chessboard and the beheading of a white stag. This incredible coincidence could not be ignored. Had Annett therefore been inspired to write his article? Or had Bernard merely picked up on the ideas contained within its pages? I hoped it was the former.

Yet there was another, more disconcerting answer to this riddle. Was it possible that our occultist friend had deliberately chosen to use Lullington churchyard as the site of his black magic ritual because he himself had read Annett's 1932 article? Perhaps he had seen the reference to the beheading of the white stag and the releasing of a 'black man', and had then decided to use the sites concerned because of their association with the Peredur story? Was it also possible that he had substituted the stag's head for a spearhead for this very reason?[1]

If this was so, then it brought to mind another disturbing implication. In the Peredur story, the hero beheads a white stag. A mysterious knight then appears who seizes the head and carries it off. Could the occultist have therefore carried out his dark ritual in the belief that, by some strange quirk of fate, someone would come along — some sort of 'mysterious knight' — who would likewise seize the spearhead and make off with it, enabling the black man to then rise up from the mound, like some sort of dark apparition rising from the grave?

It was an eerie thought, but for some reason it appeared to

make sense.

The index to *The Wilmington Giant* showed that on page 45 there was a reference to a place called the Rookery. Turning to the page concerned, I found the location of Bernard's strange dream. It was described as a 'strange wooded mound' just to the south of Burlough Castle. And, like Burlough, very little was known about its age and past purpose. However, it seemed that some local historians, Rodney Castleden included, believed it to be the site of a small chapel built in 1315 under the instructions of the Prior of Wilmington by a man named *Paganus*, the Lord of Milton Court, on whose land the mound was situated; thus confirming the psychic information Bernard had received whilst in the crypt at Wilmington Priory. It appeared that this possible tumulus *had* once been used as a rookery, although the birds had departed when a past owner of the Milton Court estate had decided to cut down the trees on the top of the mound. New ones now grew on the Rookery, although the rooks have never returned.

Monday, 10th June. In the busy, but somewhat homely surroundings of The Griffin pub in Danbury, Bernard joined me clasping two pints of beer; bitter for me and Guinness for him. It was our regular haunt and it was also our first get together since the Lullington sketch the previous month.

Our conversation quickly turned to the disturbing events of that fateful day and, hoping that he might consent to psychometrising the shale spearhead, I brought out and placed the stone on the table in front of us.

The last time Bernard had touched the inscribed spearhead, in Lullington churchyard, he had picked up a considerable amount about the mysterious black-robed figure who had concealed it as part of his dark ritual. Even though I had since doused the spearhead with holy water to dissipate its ritualistic charge, I hoped it might still contain enough vibrations for him to be able to tell me a little more about the man.

As if to accept my suggestion, he picked up the length of

shale and held it loosely in his hand. After rolling it around in his fingers for a minute or two, he looked up. 'Well, it still contains a very mild negative charge. Do you want any scribbles?' he asked, pulling his notepad across the table. Scribbles was his term for automatic writing.

Naturally I did, so handed him a pen and waited for a response. Sitting quietly amid the hustle and bustle of the comfortable, yet noisy pub surrounds, he cleared his mind and waited. A few moments later words began to appear on his notepad. I read them upside down:

Great magistry not correct. Re-work. Fuse.

They made little sense to me, but at least the line was open, so to speak. I asked him to see if he could find out when the ritual had taken place at Lullington.

'1985', was the prompt reply.

1985? It had taken place that very year? This was a surprise to me as I had assumed that the ritual had taken place some years back. So, this man *was still around!* My next question was inevitable: who carried out the ritual?

Bernard's hand wrote again.

Magister magnus in igne. White stone not correct. Re-work. Re-fuse. Re-live. Heat vessel hot. Black substance is right.

Yes, but *who* put it there?

His hand responded with more words.

It comes. Use. Skulls. Black blood. Dying into flame. Re-live. Re-birth. Soul. Michael Mayer. Kalsination is good. Black. Re-live. Bring to life. Zozzimoz. Place. Re-work. Re-live. Heat.

It was still not an answer. I wanted to know who buried the spearhead?

His hand scribbled again.

Enclosed power. Worked alone in house. Dark. Heat. Relight flame. Sulphur.

That was it. Bernard got no more from the spearhead. Putting it down in front of him, he lit a cigarette and swallowed a mouthful of Guinness. 'Well, whoever it was who planted that spearhead, they are very strong on a psychic level and are quite capable of blocking out anyone who tries to attune to them, or their home.'

He stopped to crystallise his feelings. As I was writing I could see a man in a darkened room. Around him were old benches, skulls, things being burnt in glass bottles and more black birds.'

More black birds? What, in the room?

'No, I think it was a symbolic image to show me that he is surrounded by very negative energies and emanations for some reason.'

In questing lore large black birds were omens of ill fortune, death and black magic. They were not a good symbol at all. Yet the rest of the imagery and the automatic writing appeared to indicate that our occultist friend was *an alchemist;* a person who, through complex and tedious magical operations and experiments, was trying to achieve an alchemical transmutation — the changing of base matter into a pure state; usually a base metal into gold.

Words and statements such as 'Dying into the flame', 'Bring to life', 'Heat' and 'Sulphur' all seemed to confirm this fact. The man was into alchemy which concerned, not only the transmutation of base matter into a pure state, but also the transition of the alchemist's own 'base' mind into a higher state of perfection.

'That may be so,' he admitted. 'However, whatever this man is into, he is warping and distorting the process to his own ends, hence the negative energies which resulted from his use of Lullington churchyard. I therefore feel that he is currently involved in a bizarre magical operation, using the principles of alchemy in some way.'

So the man was still around. But who was he? Where did he live? And was he aware that we had wrecked his warped ritual?

'I'm not sure. But I'll tell you one thing. I get the feeling that when he does find out that his spearhead is missing, he will replace it with another one.'

At the same place?

'Very possibly, yes. I also get the feeling that we have not seen the last of him yet.'

On arrival home that night I scanned my bookshelves for anything on alchemy. I soon found that Michael Mayer — or Maier as it was sometimes spelt — had been a seventeenth century German exponent of a mystical doctrine known as Rosicrucianism. He had also been an important alchemist of his age.

I also found that the name 'Zozzimoz' appeared to be a reference to a man named Zosimos of Panopolis. He had been a very influential alchemist, writer and visionary who had lived in the town of Panopolis — the modern Akhmin — in Egypt, around the beginning of the fourth century AD. He had also been a Coptic Christian.

In Egyptian history, the first few centuries after the time of Christ were referred to by classical scholars as the Graeco-Egyptian period. This was due to the fact that, although the country was under Roman occupation, its culture and religion was still being heavily influenced by the Greeks. Therefore, Zosimos was referred to as a Graeco-Egyptian alchemist.

Zosimos was most remembered for one particular account of a complicated, and obviously symbolic, series of dreams which were considered to contain the keys to the ultimate alchemical transmutation — the release of the soul to become a free spirit, at one with the God-head, and free from the laws of reincarnation.

From the automatic writing Bernard had received that evening, it looked as if our alchemist friend had achieved what was known in alchemy as the First Matter, or Black Stage, in his transmutation; which was also known as the Negredo, the Black Crow, the *Crow's Head,* the *Raven's Head* or the *Black*

Man. It was a stage reached — if using the Zosimos system — by mixing flesh, blood and bones with sulphur and then heating them within a bowl, called the 'bath of rebirth,' to attain a black substance. This would then be re-heated, or calcined — Bernard had picked up the word 'Kalsination' — until it eventually became a powder. Then, after further liquid had been added, the heating would be continued for one whole year before the resulting mess would be mixed with the alchemist's own moisture. It would then be slowly calcined once again until the so-called 'divine spark' was released from the mixture in a glowing form.

I also discovered that, in alchemical tradition, the white stag represented the soul of the alchemist. So, perhaps our alchemist friend had been aware of this association when he chose to use Lullington as the site of his ritual. Not only this, but it seemed difficult not to see the obvious links between alchemy and the other aspects of the Peredur story and Bernard's Rookery dream. The black man, the removal of the stag's head and the large black birds — they were all present in some form or another.[2]

So what were we to do next? Bernard had temporarily lost interest in the quest to find the Stave of Nizar and wanted only to forget the whole episode. Yet he still retained the feeling that the corrupt alchemist *would* replace the stone spearhead we had unearthed and that, at some time in the not too distant future, our paths would again cross.

However, for the moment all Bernard hoped was that he was wrong . . .

Six
The House

Tuesday, 25th June, 1985. In front of them lay their destination — a two-storey, red-brick, Victorian-style terraced house with double-bay windows either side of a recessed green front door. Black-painted, wrought iron railings held back an unruly privet hedge which divided the kerb from an overgrown garden of sorts. There was no gate, only an opening on to a path of chequered red and black tiles leading up to the door step, some four to five paces from the road.

Bernard, Andy and their two companions stared with definite apprehension at the uninspiring building. It hardly seemed like the magical stronghold of a warped black alchemist who, only the previous month, had caused them so much anguish in Lullington churchyard. And yet, as had been predicted, he had now gone too far. His own sickening brand of black magic had rebounded upon him, destroying both his mind and his body; and leaving his home an uncontrollable psychic mess. Only now would they be able to uncover his true identity. That was, if they could combat the psychic attack which would surely result from their entry into the empty building.

Hesitantly, the four walked up to the recessed front door and, glancing around to make sure that no one was watching, they turned the round door knob. As expected, the door swung open. Swiftly, they stepped into the hallway.

Everywhere was in a terrible state of disrepair with paint and wallpaper peeling off the walls to reveal damp and mould. Surely all of this could not have happened in the past few days. He must have lived in this squalor even before his death,

Bernard said to himself, as he carried on along the passageway.

'The whole place is completely saturated in negative energy,' the psychic revealed to the rest of the group, as they pushed open each of the ground floor doors.

They stopped and stared in absolute amazement at the scene in one of the rooms, off to the left of the hallway. Books, shelves, the contents of open cupboards and broken ornaments lay strewn across the floor.

Yet then a strange, unnerving sound reached Bernard's psychic ears, a low vibratory drone which appeared to combine more than one tone. It filled the air and gradually grew with intensity. Turning around, an extraordinary sight greeted the group — several balls of electric-blue light, about the size of footballs, hung motionless a few feet above the ground at the far end of the room. They were, Bernard felt, in some way linked with the peculiar humming noise, for they were growing in brightness the more the sound increased. But what were they?

'Manifestations of extremely imbalanced psychic energy,' he announced, after having been passed the answer from an unseen source. 'They will have to be dealt with, and fast.'

'A Christian banishment,' someone shouted, as Andy quickly bent down and picked up a length of scrap wood, which he then snapped in two and brought together to form the sign of the Cross. The others, upon realising what he was doing, likewise constructed crude wooden crosses with pieces of wood which, they too, held out between them and the visible manifestations.

'I command thee in the name of the Father, the Son and the Holy Ghost to leave this place,' Andy shouted, in virtual desperation. Nothing happened. Several more times the command was given before the balls of light eventually began to fade away. It looked like they were winning.

Suddenly, a light bulb exploded overhead, sending everyone scurrying for cover. Luckily, no one was hurt. But then another bulb exploded in a separate room. Then another, and another. The dissipation of the psychic energy was somehow disturbing the house's electrical circuit. Odd cracking sounds within the room completed the eerie spectacle, which was by now unsettling each and every member of the group. Never had they seen anything like this before.

With the glowing orbs out of the way, yet with the low humming sound still detectable, they promptly left the room and decided to go upstairs to the first floor where *he* had practised his degenerate brand of alchemy and magic.

The doors on the landing were systematically pushed open to reveal further rooms in a state of chaotic mayhem. Everywhere personal effects of every kind littered the floor. He had certainly made a good job of wrecking his home before his death, Bernard thought. But for what reason? Had he gone mad?

But then an out of place creaking noise begged their attention. Turning around, they beheld a disconcerting sight: a door leading into one of the rooms at the end of the landing was bulging outwards, as if something of immense strength was pushing it from the inside. But no one else was in the house. So what lay behind that door?

A powerful boot to the door by Andy not only stopped the unnatural bulging effect, it also sent it flying on to the floor inside the room. And the scene inside was simply bizarre — ancient leather and skin-bound manuscripts and books of all sizes lay scattered across the filthy carpet, their covers and pages opening, shutting and flapping about completely of their own volition. It was a mesmerising sight.

'I baptise you in the name of Jesus Christ,' one of the group bellowed out, as Bernard turned around to see him grabbing two forks, all he could find suitable, to make the sign of the Cross.

And then darkness . . .

Bernard awoke from his lurid nightmare and was almost sick. To make sure he did not lapse back into the same imagery, he sat up in bed. The time, he could see, was 4.25 am.

His head could not take any more. Yet questions begging

answers already danced around his mind. What the hell was going on? Why had he experienced such a thing? And what did it mean? Was the Black Alchemist really dead?

He did not want to know. The ill-effects which had followed the discovery of the inscribed stone spearhead at Lullington had been enough. He did not want any more trouble; especially the sort of hassle implied within the unnerving dream. And what was he to tell Andy? He did not like it one little bit.

Even though he wanted to disown them, psychic impressions now began to fill his mind. The Black Alchemist *was* still alive. The dream had been a symbolic representation of things to come; a portent perhaps. For it seemed that the man was going too far in what he was up to on a magical level and, in consequence, it would destroy him both in body and in mind.

Tired, Bernard looked across to his wife, still asleep, and decided to try and get some rest himself. Hopefully, this time his dreams would not be tainted, he muttered to himself, as he slid down into the sheets and closed his eyes.

Later that morning Bernard paused from his chores at work to consider the implications of his disturbing nightmare the previous night. Was he to tell Andy or not? If he did, then he would only want him to pick up further information about the matter; like the man's name, address and telephone number for starters! He would then immediately rush off to find the house; wherever it was.

Sussex. The thought came into his mind as if in answer to that last question. In fact, to be more precise, a seaside town somewhere on the Sussex coast. Which one though, he was not told. This was where they would find the house seen in the dream. So at least it existed.

On the other hand, if he did not tell Andy then the memory of the nightmare would only play on his mind for weeks to come; and what if it *was* to come true and the Black Alchemist did destroy himself? No, he would have to tell him; although not for the moment. In a week or so; when they next met.

For the time being he decided to not even record the contents of the dream, just in case it opened up any unwanted psychic channels with the man which might lead to further physical and mental torment. This he could do without, as it had taken him nearly two weeks to fully recover from the ill-effects that had resulted from their trip to the Sussex Downs the previous month.

Monday, 8th July. He had given Andy a basic outline of the lurid dream the next time they met, out on the small triangular-shaped green in front of Danbury church in the hot, afternoon sun the previous day. However, he had decided to save the full contents for a letter which he intended writing that evening.

The chance came later that night so, slipping into the peace and quiet of the dining room, he sat down at the table with a notepad in front of him. Picking up a pen, he wrote first the date before commencing the letter with a brief outline of a recent dream he had experienced concerning the Stave of Nizar. Only after this did he move on to the dream about the Black Alchemist's house.

After confirming its date, he paused for a moment to recall the imagery of the nightmare. Bringing this to mind, he began to scribble down what he could remember:-

> **. . . red-brick Victorian style. Double-bayed, at least downstairs. It is quite close to the road. Approx 4/6 paces. Front is black railings and old privet hedge. Path to door is black and red tiles. Front door is green.**

He stopped writing. It would be far easier to just sketch the house, he realised.

A rough drawing soon appeared below his written words. He then resumed his letter.

> **We entered hallway. No one let us in??? The whole house is –**

Writing his letter, Bernard sketched the red brick, Victorian-style house visited in his dream.

> **totally saturated with negative energy.**

At this point he felt a sudden headache enter his mind. It was exactly the same feeling as he had experienced when the spearhead had been unearthed at Lullington. Recalling the precise imagery of the Black Alchemist's house was opening up a telepathic link with the man's imbalanced vibrations. He would have to take things more carefully.

'I'm getting a headache', he noted down on paper before continuing his account of the dream:

> **One room downstairs — on left — was in very bad state. Books, shelves, contents of cupboards, ornaments, etc., all strewn over floor.**

He stopped again. Something was happening. Not only did he now have a headache, he could also feel and see his handwriting becoming more fluent and illegible, almost as if he was about to launch into a bout of automatic writing. An exterior force — associated with the Black Alchemist — appeared to be influencing him to some degree, so he decided to break off the link for a while to make a cup of coffee, have a cigarette and return later to the matter. For the record, he wrote: 'My writing is becoming very bad. Stopping for while.'

Twenty minutes later, in a revitalised state of mind, he sat back down at the dining room table to resume his dream account. Everything went without a hitch for the next few lines, but then the psychic interference resumed. His headache returned and, in place of the memory of the empty house in a state of chaotic mayhem, his psychic eye now perceived the clairvoyant image of a man —seemingly the Black Alchemist himself — working in a darkened room and apparently aware of a foreign presence invading his privacy.

Leaving the account of the dream, he began to write down his new feelings and impressions:

Someone knows of my presence now. Man in back room. In large room. Benches, bottles, sulphur, books, bunsen burners, glass.

Then came his first clear picture of the man:

Tall. Brown sweater. No sleeves. Grey trousers. Short grey hair. Close cropped. Can't get name. He's looking round . . . at me. Something being thrown. Powder from crucible.

He flinched backwards with a sudden stabbing pain in his head. It broke the contact between the two minds. He felt weak and had to stop. The powder thrown at him from the crucible had been some sort of ash, he felt. Something the man used to dissipate unwanted psychic influences.

The room itself was set out like a kind of home-made alchemical laboratory, with bottles and apparatus laying about all over the place. Bernard believed that his presence had actually been felt by the Black Alchemist, almost as if the man had known that he was sharing the room with an unseen force.

Another break was in order. So, after more coffee, more cigarettes and a few mental diversions, he settled down at his dining room table for the third time that evening.

'I'm beginning to wonder if I'll ever get this finished,' he recorded, before quickly finishing off the account of the dream.

This time there were no further psychic interruptions, and with the account now out of the way, Bernard ended the curious letter with some very significant feelings which were milling about in his mind concerning the whole Black Alchemist affair. Points which he was not at all happy about.

I don't know what to make of all this. I do not like it at all. The man can obviously 'pick up' the interference, and I hope he doesn't track the source — me.

General impressions are that he is, I feel, an academic. Used to working on his own. Probably holds a position of trust, in a quiet environment, ie. library, college, etc.

Has access to equipment and books. Is working on his own and living on his own.

Has enough knowledge to 'block' his name and address, but he is going too far in what he's into. Almost, no, most certainly an obsession of re-working ancient texts. It *will* be his downfall. He is not heeding the signs of imbalance. The energies he is building *will* destroy him.

I will not attempt a name and will not attempt the address. It is too dangerous for me at the moment. Any strange occurrences and I will ring you immediately.

In the months which followed, only one — rather vital — piece of information was to be added to our knowledge of the Black Alchemist saga. His two-storey, Victorian-style, terraced house — as seen by Bernard during his extraordinary dream — was somewhere within the Sussex seaside town of Eastbourne, just five miles south-east of the enclosed, hilltop church of Lullington.

Seven
The Dome of Kent

Saturday, 3rd May, 1986. The very first red glow of the coming dawn picked out the silhouetted image of a lone church perched high on a tree-lined hill. Dozens of large black scavenger birds — rooks perhaps — were circling the Christian edifice in an anti-clockwise motion, gliding, climbing and swooping, but never landing.

The sight was out of place. Something untoward was happening at the church. The birds were, Bernard realised, symbolic representations of powerful dark energies, building up and originating from a point somewhere *within* this house of God.

Bernard knew that it had been no ordinary dream. Although he had no idea of the church's location, he felt sure it existed and that something evil was going on there. However, as to why he should have been granted a glimpse of this scene, he did not know. It just appeared to be one of those psychically-inspired dreams he occasionally experienced from time to time. For this reason, he decided to forget the matter and carry on with his usual Saturday morning chores; starting with taking his wife shopping.

Yet despite trying to take his mind away from the simple contents of the curious dream, a vivid image of the hilltop church stayed with him throughout the day. By the early evening the imagery had become so strong that he decided to retire to the relative stillness of his dining room to sit and concentrate on the haunting image to see what else he could discover. Quite obviously, there was a church somewhere exuding dark, unwelcoming energies strong enough for him to pick up and register as a psychic. So could he find out its location?

Intrigued, but not over enamoured by the prospect, Bernard closed his eyes. He could still see the scavenger birds circling the church, but then he began to make out further details about the location.

The church appeared to be on a hill which was capped by a copse of tall trees. Its architectural design suggested that it was not very old, probably only Victorian. Despite this, he could see that the huge stone blocks used to construct its walls were slightly weathered with age. An avenue of trees — conifers he believed — led through the churchyard to the church porch.

As no further imagery or impressions came to mind, he broke off his concentration, opened his eyes and scribbled down a few points of interest before leaving the room.

Sunday, 4th May. For the second day running Bernard continued to see the swirling black bird-like energy forms circling endlessly around the unidentified hilltop church. The feeling was that a black ritual had been carried out inside the building and, whatever it was, it was still in progress and growing with intensity.

Yet then, shortly after lunch, a rather chilling impression was unexpectedly added to Bernard's knowledge of the situation. Something now told him that this ritual had been carried out by the Black Alchemist from Eastbourne, in Sussex. But if this was so, then where was the church? And what was he up to this time? Furthermore, what had all this to do with him?

No immediate answers came to mind, aside from the impression that the church was situated somewhere in the southern counties, for what it was worth. Probably somewhere on the Sussex Downs, he presumed, close to the Black

Alchemist's own home.

I arose that morning with a strong compulsion to return to the Sussex Downs as I had a sneaky feeling that the Black Alchemist was on the move again.

I had not spoken to Bernard for several days and, although we had arranged to meet at The Griffin pub in Danbury the following Tuesday, I wanted to speak to him about my feelings. The Black Alchemist affair, which had long been dropped, even from casual conversation, kept coming to mind, especially Bernard's statement that one day our paths would once again cross with his, and that he would eventually replace the inscribed stone spearhead we had removed from Lullington churchyard almost exactly a year before.

Lullington itself kept playing on my mind, so I wondered whether the Black Alchemist had returned to the site and replaced the original spearhead. A gut feeling said yes. So, on the spur of the moment, and without ringing Bernard, I decided to revisit the Sussex Downs for the first time since the discovery of the spearhead the previous May.

However, a thorough search of Lullington churchyard revealed nothing; so I gave up and returned to Essex.

Monday, 5th May. No, the church was not in Sussex, it was in West Kent; that was the feeling in Bernard's mind now. Where exactly, he had still not been told. However, it was beginning to dawn on him that he was about to be thrust into a second confrontation with the activities of the Black Alchemist; a thought he did not relish. In readiness, he purchased a copy of the Ordnance Survey one inch to the mile map of the West Kent area. He had no idea exactly what was going on, or why the occultist should suddenly want to make a reappearance in West Kent exactly a year after they had ruined his ritual in Lullington churchyard. All he did know was that something out of order was gradually building up inside that church, and it would have to be dealt with before the matter got out of hand.

Tuesday, 6th May. Bernard strolled into The Griffin and bought himself a Guinness before joining me in the corner of the crowded bar. From his jacket pocket he produced a collection of notes which he handed across the table. 'You'd better read these. See what you think.'

They concerned a series of images and impressions he had received over the past few days concerning a church on a hill in West Kent.

I read them with great interest before revealing details of my own visit to the Sussex Downs only two days before.

Something was undoubtedly going on — that we had both picked up — and, unusually for Bernard, he seemed eager to find out more about the matter.

So, once again, he began to concentrate on the image of the hilltop church as we sat supping our drinks amid the noisy background din emanating from the groups of local youths crowded around nearby tables.

With his eyes still open, he fixed his mind on the now familiar image of the church.

'The scavenger birds are still circling the hilltop,' he revealed. Yet with this came a further disturbing image. 'I can now see grotesque demon or gargoyle-like creatures crawling about at the foot of the church walls, hopping in and out of reality. They appear to be yet another symbolic representation of the chaotic force building up there.'

Carefully, I jotted down his words.

'I now see more of the church. There is an outer and an inner door within the porch. The last leads into the church itself. There is also a kind of funny-looking bell tower on the south side of the building, next to a protruding piece of gabled architecture.'

But what's been going on there?

'I feel that the Black Alchemist has walked around the

outside of the church and somehow closed off its energies . . . like creating some sort of barrier, as I can't seem to break through this to get into the church itself.'

Why should he want to do this?

'I suppose he has set up some kind of psychic barrier or wall to prevent anyone from entering inside its interior on a psychic level,' he suggested. 'I don't know why.'

So where was the church?

Bernard broke off his concentration and look towards me. 'I'm going to have to stop,' he stated, lighting another cigarette. 'I'm beginning to feel headachey and sick. In fact, I get the feeling that, if I don't stop, then I'll slip into a trance and something rather nasty will come through. I could hear this gutteral voice in my head which seemed poised to overshadow me.'

And I knew from past experience what that could mean — he would fall into a trance and become possessed. Quite obviously, a strange gutteral voice issuing forth from Bernard's mouth would have been dangerous to his well-being and rather embarrassing in front of the crowds of youths sitting at the tables around us.

As I wanted to use the toilet, I took this opportunity to disappear for a moment or two. When I returned, I found Bernard scribbling in his notepad.

As I sat down, he pushed it in my direction.

He had written the words *'Remien vigilia'* and *'Ratio experimentia',* which appeared to be Latin. As neither of us could read Latin, we were stumped for an instant translation.[1] Beneath this he had sketched the image of a huge cave, with steps leading into it, which he said he had seen in his mind. Below this he had written, in an automatic script:

I am the priest of the sanctuary. He has cut my head from my body. It comes as the sun, as the spring of crystal waters.

It meant nothing to either of us. However, I should have remembered that I had seen similar words the previous year when I had studied the history of Zosimos of Panopolis, the fourth century, Graeco-Egyptian alchemist.

'Come on. Let's go into the churchyard. The atmosphere will be different out there,' he said, standing up.

It was a good idea. As it was still light, it would make an ideal setting for carrying on the psychic work without any interference.

Standing beneath a large horse chestnut tree, which Bernard had always felt drawn to, for some reason, he began to receive further images and impressions concerning the situation.

'As it's in my mind,' he said, beginning to pace about beneath the tree, 'I get St Mary's. Write it down. It's the dedication of the church, which I can now see is next to a village green, a big one, with houses beyond that; quite old, eighteenth or nineteenth century buildings, I should think. The Black Alchemist has walked around the church with his arms up in the air.'

Rapidly, I scribbled down Bernard's words.

'Write this down,' he continued, stopping to point towards my notepad. '*The True Glass of Alchemy*[2] . . . It's a book.' He turned away and continued to pace about. 'Ion is the name of the priest of the sanctuary I mentioned in the pub. It's a vision that the Black Alchemist twists . . . *Amphitheatre of Eternal Wisdom* . . . another book. And also the name "Bacon."'

'I now see the imagery associated with alchemy I first saw last year when I psychometrised the stone spearhead,' he continued, breaking his concentration and looking towards me. 'Things being burnt, laboratory apparatus and ancient manuscripts, and also someone's head being cut off and mangled with flesh and blood. Very nasty.'

But then the headache and nausea returned.

Realising that he was getting into difficult territory, I begged him to stop his attunement and rest for a while. But he just continued.

'I feel a serpent or a dragon is connected in some way,' he added, as we both lit cigarettes and waited for a few minutes.

Bernard stood beneath the horse chestnut tree in the centre of Danbury churchyard and picked up further information about the church on the hill seen in his dream.

'The church is at "Ide Hill",' he revealed at last, 'wherever that is. Something's been placed in the church, and he's definitely sealed off the building on a psychic level.'

What exactly had he placed in the church?

'Same as before, I suppose.'

What? A spearhead?

'I assume so.'

So what was our job?

'Remove it,' he responded, before pausing once more to compose his thoughts. 'I feel that all this has got something to do with Zosimos again. This priest, Ion, is one of Zosimos' visions which the Black Alchemist warps for his own ends.'

I had not come across the name Ion before, even though I had read about Zosimos' dream in which the priest sacrifices himself at a dome-shaped altar. There had been no mention of the priest's actual name, so perhaps it had not been recorded.[3]

That appeared to be it. Bernard began to make his way back towards the church as if to signal an end to the psychic communication. However, we now had the location of the church of his dream and a rough idea of what had gone on there, so we could now act accordingly.

Back inside the pub we discussed the situation whilst attempting to find Ide Hill on the Ordnance Survey map. Almost immediately, I found it — a village of that name just a few miles outside the town of Sevenoaks, in West Kent. The local map contours showed that the village church was indeed on a hill and that, on its southern side, was a fair-sized green with houses beyond that. So far, so good. The rest I could check out later.

But when were we to go down there? Bernard could not make it on a weekday, so it would have to be during the coming weekend. However, our Sunday was already planned as I had arranged for Bernard to meet Colin and Gelly Paddon, a Milton Keynes couple who, during August the previous year, had been led to a wood, not far from their home, where they had psychically discovered two swords identical in every respect to the one found by Graham Phillips and I by a lake in Worcestershire during 1979. I had also invited along Caroline Wise and Alan Cleaver, two friends of ours. I therefore decided that the best thing was to combine this get together with our trip to Ide Hill and invite them all to accompany us on the quest. Anyway, we would probably need a little help.

So a time was set. I would inform all parties involved. After this we returned to the subject of the apparent ritual which the Black Alchemist had carried out at Ide Hill. So, what was he up to this time?

Bernard could not say.

Okay, when had he carried out this ritual? And to help him answer this question, I pointed out that if he had first begun to pick up the images of the church over the night of Friday/Saturday, 2/3rd May, since which time the negativity there had been on the increase, then it had probably been carried out on May Day, 1st May, one of the eight great pagan festival dates in the yearly calendar.

Bernard agreed.

If this was so, then perhaps the Black Alchemist had buried the inscribed stone spearhead at Lullington exactly one year before that, on May Day 1985; some three weeks before we had found it.

He shook his head. 'No, I feel it had been buried for a couple of months before we found it.'

I thought again. What about the spring equinox 1985, around 21st March, the main pagan festival date prior to May Day?

Bernard contemplated the idea for a moment. 'Yes, I think you're right. Anyway, I'm off now. Give me a ring to confirm times, etc.'

I nodded, as he got up to leave.

At home I ploughed through whatever books I possessed on the topography of Kent, looking for references to Ide Hill.

Unfortunately, I found very little information about the church because — as Bernard had predicted — it was a Victorian structure, only built in 1865. It *was* dedicated to St Mary and yes, a tree-lined path of evergreens *did* guide the visitor from a lychgate on the south side, through the churchyard to the church's south porch. The site *was* encircled by a copse of tall trees and there was a 'peculiar bell tower', or spirelet, attached to the south wall.

So Bernard's imagery had been accurate. But why use this site? The question still bugged me. Yet then, searching through one particular book on the Kent countryside, I discovered something which gave me a clue. For it appeared that Ide Hill was known as the Dome of Kent, due to the large group of beech trees which crowned the summit of the hill to form an unusual domed canopy which surrounded the church. The tops of these trees gave Ide Hill a height of around 800 feet above sea level and therefore formed one of the most picturesque high spots of Kent.

Now domes, I knew, were very important to the Zosimos system of alchemy. Richard Cavendish, in his book *The Black Arts* (Routledge and Kegan Paul, London, 1967), said that, in one of his visionary dreams, Zosimos had seen a priest sacrificing himself at a dome-shaped altar standing at the apex of fifteen steps, at which the priest announces: 'I have accomplished the action of descending the fifteen steps towards the darkness, and the action of ascending the steps towards the light. The sacrifice renews me, rejecting the dense nature of the body. Thus consecrated by necessity, I become a spirit.'

The priest then says that he has suffered unbearable violence. He has been decapitated with a sword and his bones have been mixed with his flesh and then burnt in the 'fire of the treatment'. So, 'through the transformation of the body', he becomes a free spirit. Of course, this peculiar form of alchemical transformation was both a physical and a symbolic spiritual process attempted by some people in the hope of achieving divine union with the God-head to become like a god themselves.

Much of this imagery appeared to confirm what Bernard

had seen in vision out in Danbury churchyard, and supported the idea that the Black Alchemist was using the Zosimos system of alchemy. I therefore felt he had chosen Ide Hill as his own 'dome-shaped altar' due to its topographical description and appearance as the so-called Dome of Kent. Yet, if so, then other facets of the Zosimos dream now appeared to fall into place. For, if someone intended to achieve the final stage in their alchemical transformation, Zosimos then suggests that they construct a temple '. . . as of white lead, as of alabaster, having neither commencement nor end in its construction. Let it have in its interior *a spring of pure water, sparkling like the sun',* virtually the same words that Bernard had picked up in the pub earlier that evening.

We already had our 'dome-shaped altar'. That was Ide Hill itself. In which case, the temple with 'neither commencement nor end in its construction' appeared to be the psychic wall or barrier put up around the church by the Black Alchemist. And with this realisation, I began to understand just exactly what he was doing. He was preparing the site for some kind of rebirth ritual, for, according to Richard Cavendish again, this temple represented the body and womb of a woman, containing within its perimeter the sparkling waters of life, the alleged source of the divine soul of man. So, in the mind of the Black Alchemist, could this divine female be associated with Ide Hill church's dedication to St Mary, the Virgin Mary, who gave divine birth? I thought so.

The next stop would therefore be to find out what exactly he was gestating inside that church.

Eight
Ide Hill

Sunday, 11th May, 1986. 'I hope that we're not walking into a trap of some sort,' Bernard laughed, as Ide Hill church came into view across the village green.

A trap? I hoped not. Anyway, what did he mean, a trap?

'Oh, it's nothing. Just a thought. Something I've been thinking about for a while.'

I let the matter go. Yet I knew from past experience that if Bernard dropped something out of place into casual conversation, then it was usually inspired in some way.

As we parked the cars, I kept a careful watch on Bernard, half expecting him to start experiencing headaches and nausea at any moment. However, as he climbed out of the car, he seemed relaxed and openly admitted that he was deliberately refraining from attuning to the site — for the time being at least.

Crossing the green, groups of people were walking past in every direction holding clipboards and studying certain buildings and features, as if looking for something.

Curious as to their actions, Gelly approached and spoke to one group and returned with an answer. 'The whole village is involved in a massive treasure hunt,' she revealed, with a smile. 'They've been given certain clues which will lead them to buried treasure of some sort.'

'Isn't that bizarre,' Colin remarked, looking towards the rest of the group. 'Here we are on a quest to find a hidden artefact and the whole of Ide Hill are on a quest of their own!'

'Perhaps they'll find the spearhead before us,' Alan quipped, concluding the conversation.

Caroline, Bernard, Colin and Gelly Paddon, and Alan Cleaver made their way across the green to Ide Hill church.

It was a thought. However, it was a bizarre synchronicity, if nothing else.

Approaching the Victorian church, I could see its peculiar bell tower and the avenue of trees leading from the lychgate to the south porch, all just as Bernard had described the previous week. Casually, the group moved into the churchyard and followed the worn path which wound its way around the building. Quietly turning to Bernard, I asked him if he was picking anything up.

'He took this path around the church, in an anti-clockwise direction,' he responded, looking up at the stonework and composing his thoughts for a moment.

'The psychic barrier is between us and the wall. I see him walking around with his arms up in the air, touching the stone walls.

'Each time he came upon a doorway, he followed its edge with one hand, before returning it to the top of the door and then lowering it to the ground, as if to symbolically seal off the door to the outside world.'

Accepting his word, we continued to stroll about.

Unexpectedly, a sudden wind then whipped through the tree-lined hilltop. Taking this as an omen that something was beginning to build up on a psychic level within the churchyard, I called the group together. In a corner, beneath the overhanging branches of a tree, we conducted an appropriate protection ritual before attempting to go any further.

Walking around the church, using a visualisation ritual, the Black Alchemist's psychic wall was then safely dismantled, leaving us free to enter the church. Inside, the group carefully looked around, not knowing quite what to expect or find. I kept an eye on Bernard, just in case he started to get into any trouble. Memories of the problems he had experienced at Lullington the previous year filled my mind. Yet he seemed to be okay; smiling and joking in his usual way.

Then, at precisely 3.20 pm, Bernard announced: 'The spearhead is beneath the altar.'

Only I heard his words, so, without further word, as Bernard left the church for his own safety, I walked briskly into the chancel and got down on to my hands and knees. Pulling up the rear of the altar draping, I tried to locate the hidden artefact. However, it was too dark to see anything within the altar's wooden frame. Striking a match, I held it out towards one of the corners. Nothing. The match went out. Lighting another, I held it towards one of the other corners. Still nothing.

By this time the others had joined me, so I revealed Bernard's words. Suddenly, the psychic reappeared from around the south door.

'Whatever you do, don't touch it,' he yelled.

Everybody looked up to await an explanation, but Bernard had gone again.

The search resumed. Several burnt matches later, I concluded that nothing lay concealed anywhere around the altar frame. If anything had been planted, then it was certainly not there now. Despondency and frustration overtook my senses almost instantly. What the hell was going on? I needed an explanation.

Frantically, I continued to search around the altar area in

every conceivable hiding place, but still nothing could be located. Bernard re-entered the church again and realised the predicament.

Where was the spearhead?

'I'm not sure,' he answered, seemingly just as confused as everyone else. 'I certainly picked up that it was under the altar. It should be there. Perhaps I was just picking up on the negative vibrations it has left at the spot.'

I wanted to think so. The Black Alchemist must have realised that somebody was on to him and had therefore returned during the week to retrieve his inscribed stone. It was the only answer; other than to admit that Bernard was wrong. No, that was silly. Why should he pick up so many vivid images and impressions concerning an obscure Kentish church just to be wrong? It did not make sense. The Black Alchemist *must* have retrieved it.

Yet all this implied that the man was also a very adept psychic who was acute enough to have realised that someone was now on to him. We should have retrieved the spearhead as soon as we had sussed it was at Ide Hill. If so, then it would have been in our possession by now.

'Oh, don't worry, its been a good day out' Gelly said, as she continued to search behind each of the rows of wooden pews.

This made me even more annoyed. It should not have been just 'a good day out.' The whole thing made Bernard and I look foolish.

Colin conducted a simple Cabalistic banishment ritual in the nave to clear the atmosphere of any possible psychic residue left by the Black Alchemist's imbalanced activities.

At the same time Bernard sat in a pew and wrote.

Moving over to the psychic, I looked into his notepad, which he quietly turned towards my direction. On it was, what I took to be, a sketch of an inscribed stone spearhead. Below this —and arrowed to the stone itself — was a strange magical symbol composed of a spiral and the astrological signs for the planets Mercury and Venus.

What was this?

He looked back at his drawing. 'As Colin was carrying out

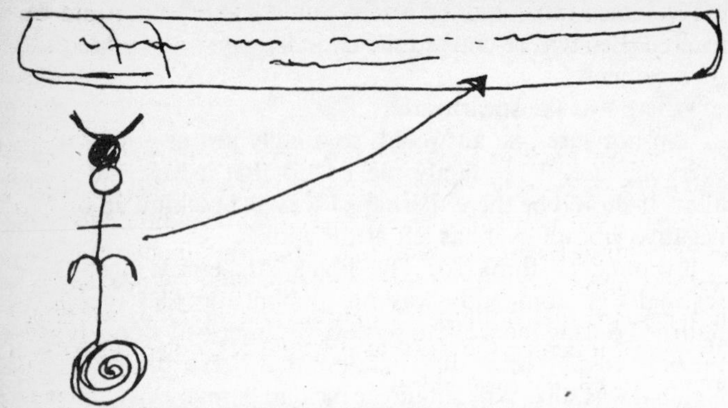

Sitting inside Ide Hill church, Bernard clairvoyantly saw the symbols on the spearhead supposedly concealed beneath the altar.

his banishment, I got an image of someone removing this stone; presumably the one which was below the altar. On it were similar magical characters to the spearhead we discovered at Lullington, along with this symbol, which I drew.'

So, had the Black Alchemist taken away his inscribed stone; or was it just wishful thinking on Bernard's part?

Moving out into the churchyard, I showed Caroline Bernard's sketch of the inscribed stone with its curious symbol.

'It looks like John Dee's *Monas Hieroglyphica* symbol,' she said, confidently.

The *Monas Hieroglyphica.* Dr John Dee had been an English astronomer, mathematician, scientist and ritual occultist of the sixteenth century who, among many other things, had decided the date for Queen Elizabeth I's coronation by composing her a favourable astrological chart. The *Monas Hieroglyphica* was a magical symbol he had devised and used, although I did not believe it was the symbol that Bernard had drawn that afternoon. This one appeared to be slightly different; a combination of other, more mundane occult symbols.

I told Caroline so, but she begged to differ with my

judgement. I did not listen, and Bernard was elsewhere, so he could not comment on the matter.

The journey back to Essex gave us an opportunity to review the day's non-event. Okay, so the Black Alchemist had apparently retrieved his own artefact, but where did that leave us? My mind turned to Bernard's earlier statement about us walking into some kind of trap. And then later, just before we had realised that nothing lay beneath the altar, his warning about not touching the stone as it would endanger our souls. What had all that been about?

'I'm not sure. Whilst I was outside in the churchyard I heard the words "Do not endanger your soul." They appeared to come from some sort of spirit guide; a man who told me that he had lived on this earth as an alchemist during the sixteenth century. He also told me that he would act as our guide to help us combat the workings of the Black Alchemist. Why he should want to help us, I don't know. Anyway, with this had come the distinct impression that if you touched the stone, then you would be in great danger.'

What sort of danger?

'Perhaps the stone was charged with some sort of self-defence mechanism,' he suggested. 'Something like a psychic booby trap which was meant to cause mental torment if somebody touched it.'

I wasn't sure. This would not explain his earlier statement that we might have been walking into a trap. A trap suggests something that has been set up on purpose to ensnare, not defend. Still, to be honest, it did not really matter anymore. The fact that the day had not produced a result was the only thing which concerned me at that moment.

Yet, for some inexplicable reason, we both felt sure that the Black Alchemist *would* strike again, and soon.

Tuesday, 20th May. Bernard was agitated. Lighting a cigarette, he stared out of his lounge window and watched the skies darken as the heavy storms grew nearer and nearer.

Soon after the Ide Hill sketch he had begun to feel that the Black Alchemist had, in some bizarre way, managed to monitor our visit to the church there. At first he had considered that he may actually have been present himself, hiding out of sight perhaps, or blending in with the groups of villagers taking part in the treasure hunt. However, he had eventually dismissed the idea in favour of the probability that he had tuned into our visit on a psychic level. Yet, even before this date, the man had realised that we were about to visit the church and had returned there to retrieve his inscribed stone, or so it seemed. It was an incredible solution, although it appeared to be the only logical assumption.

Then, a few days ago, he had received the distinct impression that the Black Alchemist had managed to psychically track them along a definite compass bearing into Essex, therefore giving him an idea of their approximate whereabouts in the county. Nothing specific; no names and no addresses, only vague, unconfirmed feelings.

The impression had remained with him, growing stronger and stronger as the days had gone by.

The hot, humid day had brought with it a peculiar psychic feeling; almost like an increase of static on a radio. It had grown with intensity throughout the afternoon until the thunderstorms had struck. Now the atmosphere was charged with a sense of foreboding, and as the storms passed overhead, a new impression overtook his mind. Peculiar thoughts entered his consciousness: a charged atmosphere was an ideal climate for psychic disguise; a time to travel and the right time to sow a seed.

There was no doubt. They were the thoughts of the Black Alchemist. Their minds were once again linking together. He was on the move, ready and poised for his next confrontation.

But what did he want with them? Was he annoyed at their interference; or was there something more to it than that? All he could do was patiently wait and see what would happen next.

Nine
Shenfield Common

Wednesday, 21st May, 1986. Gale force winds tore violently across the South of England throughout the day. Fences came down; trees were wrenched from their roots and seas churned and lashed over walled defences in coastal regions.

The fierce, elemental weather agitated Bernard even more. Something was going on and he had to find out what.

Returning home from work early that evening, he retired to the stillness of his dining room and contemplated his feelings of the previous day. Moments passed before an overwhelming feeling surged into his mind. Yes, someone, presumably the Black Alchemist, was on the move. There had been an encroachment from across the water. Someone had visited Essex in the past 24 hours. Billowing clouds of darkness, like searching black fingers, had sought, felt, sensed, before quickly retreating back.

The Black Alchemist had struck again. But where?

A peculiar atmosphere hung in the air throughout the day. A sense of expectation, restlessness and a churning in my stomach told me that I must do something, go somewhere, as the Black Alchemist was on the move once more. Should I return to Ide Hill? No, it was too far to go just to find nothing. Should I ring Bernard? No, he said he would ring me if anything further happened.

For the moment, all I could do was wait, and wonder.

Thursday, 22nd May. The expected call from Bernard came around seven o'clock as I sat down to watch *Top of the Pops* on television.

'Do you want to go for a little drive?' he asked, rather mysteriously.

Obviously. But why?

'I'm not sure. The air's thick, isn't it? I feel there's something going on in the Shenfield or Brentwood area, so I think we should take a look around.'

Shenfield or Brentwood. I tried to think of a convenient place we could meet. The car park of The Green Dragon pub in Shenfield at eight o'clock, and we could see what happened from there.

Bernard agreed.

Shenfield was a small town, adjoining the larger town of Brentwood, some eight miles west of Wickford. It normally took me about thirty minutes to get there, so I picked up a few items for the journey and left the house around 7.30 pm.

The two cars entered the car park of The Green Dragon simultanueously. After locking the car, I set off with Bernard towards our unknown destination.

So, what was going on?

'I'm still not sure,' he responded, as the car entered a built-up area on the outskirts of Brentwood. 'All I get is the impression of very black emanations coming from a wooded area somewhere around here. I suggest that we just cruise around for a while and see what happens.'

Unfolding the local Ordnance Survey map, I immediately noticed that to the south of Shenfield was a large wooded area marked as Hart Wood. A coincidence, I pointed out, when considering the links we had already assumed between harts, stags, alchemy, Lullington and the Peredur story.

Two roads bordered the edge of Hart Wood and yet, passing along each of these, Bernard said he felt nothing. I had obviously been wrong. But then, to the left, another wood came into view. This one was much smaller and was marked on the map as Shenfield Common. Without another word, Bernard pulled the car into a small, gravel-floored car park nestling just inside the wood. Neither of us were sure whether this was the correct place, but it seemed as good a place as any to stop for a while to see if he could tune into the epicentre of the apparent negativity.

Stretching our legs, I asked Bernard what he felt.

He pondered over the question for a moment before giving his reply. 'Let's go for a stroll.'

So, *was* there something in the wood?

Bernard moved around to the passenger side of the car and locked it before answering. 'Possibly. There's something around. I can feel it.'

Inside the wood, the atmosphere was one of peace and tranquility. Well, it was to me at least. And the evening itself was calm and relatively warm for May.

For a while we just walked in comparative silence, not really knowing where we were going, or what to expect. As the tree cover grew more dense, and the light gradually faded, we moved into the heart of the wood.

Whenever a path split in two, Bernard would pause for a moment before intuitively making a decision to carry on either one way or the other. Yet then he stopped and lit a cigarette.

I waited for his comments.

'Well,' he began, with a sigh. 'I feel we are being drawn towards something. We seem to be getting closer, so I suppose we should carry on.'

We continued to walk as I attempted to memorise the route taken.

Eventually, after some fifteen minutes in the wood, a large clearing loomed up ahead, some forty feet or more in diameter, and only about twenty yards from the railway cutting which ran between the stations of Shenfield and Brentwood.

Bernard came to a halt and cringed. 'Stop here,' he suggested, hesitating for a moment to contemplate the situation. 'In that clearing I see dark finger-like wisps of negative energy radiating out from its centre and rising up into the air, yet not going beyond its outer limits. They're like fingers of coldness, swirling around.'

Reaching for my notepad, I began to scribble down his words. To him at least, it appeared that something of a dark ritualistic nature had taken place inside that clearing. For the moment, we remained on the path and, as we both began to take a few photographs of the setting, Bernard tried to work out what to do next. I insisted that before we went any further we should both carry out a protection visualisation of some sort. He agreed, so, having done this, the pair of us moved cautiously along the path towards the clearing.

As we approached the open space, Bernard held out his hand as a gesture for me to remain still. 'It's too easy,' he whispered, as if someone might be listening to our conversation. 'No, it could be a trap. I suggest we approach it from another direction. From the undergrowth perhaps.'

Moving into the knee-height brambles and thorn bushes, we pushed our way around the outside of the clearing and moved closer to its edge.

Bernard stopped once again. 'It's like walking into a bullring,' he commented as we stared into the open space. 'Now I see and feel a flurry of feverish activity. Our presence is affecting something. Come on, let's carry on.'

Inside the clearing, his clairvoyant vision altered. 'The flickering dark fingers of energy have now withdrawn and disappeared into the centre. Something's happened. I think we've triggered something off. But what?'

We were both now fully within the clearing. He seemed okay; no ill-effects as yet. So, what else was he picking up?

'I can hear the thoughts of whoever it was who did this ritual,' he said, slowly opening up his psychic mind to the site.

'I can hear their words. The name "John". Who's "John"? Someone who wasn't right, but thought he was.'

I said I did not know.

'"John", who drew something which was wrong and has now been corrected. I feel that this person is pleased, as if someone has sussed something; put it right,' he added, pacing slowly about. 'I have an ache in my bones. There was a line with something.'

I did not even try to understand; just kept a watchful eye on the psychic in between scribbling down his curious statements.

Picking up a long stick, Bernard began scratching a line from one side of the clearing right across to the other. He then cut another line diagonally through the first one to form a cross. He did not look as if he knew what or why he was doing this and did not explain his actions.

'Someone keeps a diary,' he revealed, quite out of the blue, 'and all this has something to do with matey.'

Who? The Black Alchemist?

'Yes, and something's been buried.'

Pausing for a moment, he looked towards me. 'This has been set on purpose. *It's a trap,* and we have walked right into it. So, we have two choices, either find it, or leave it alone. What do we do then? Find it, I suppose.' Shrugging his shoulders, he continued to pace about.

What was buried?

'Another spearhead I should think; buried in or around the clearing. So where is it?' he queried, as if questioning his own

The author surveyed the spot in the clearing within Shenfield Common where the Black Alchemist had set up his ritual trap.

psychic faculty.

'Over here?' He moved across to a large tree in the centre of the clearing and used a stick to poke about in the earth and leaves around its roots.'No, not here. Then where?'

He studied another tree on the northern edge of the clearing. Using the stick again, he prodded about in the dirt between the exposed roots. The soil was soft. A piece of jagged glass came into view from below the ground, and then something else—a crude black spearhead clearly inscribed with magical symbols.

'Don't touch it,' Bernard yelled, as he stumbled backwards, retching.

Going into action, I quickly doused the spearhead with holy water. Flipping it over with a finger, I gave it a second soaking as I noticed a message running down its length, which warned: 'To touch is to enslave'. I could now see why Bernard had not wanted me to touch it.

After taking a couple of photographs of the stone *in situ,* I looked around for Bernard. My eyes found him sitting down on the opposite side of the clearing, staring out across the railway cutting.

Fearing for his safety, I rushed over to him. He looked as if he was oblivious to what had just happened. Slightly puzzled, I asked him if he was alright. In response, he simply nodded and then, in a rather complacent and sombre mood, began to relate a whole series of psychic images and impressions which appeared to be pouring through his mind.

'I see a black doorway,' he started. 'I'm going down a corridor . . . I'm now in a dark room. There's a smell of gas . . . He (BA) is there . . . "And so the vapours rise . . ."'

I could not write down the words quickly enough, so lost the next part of the message.

'It is to do with this stone spearhead. The symbol, which "John" drew and he has now corrected . . . it will give birth . . . interference will cease . . . others will come . . . name "John" again. It is the same symbol I saw at Ide Hill, which was incorrect and has now been altered. Who is "Khunrath"? I see a picture of a garden; with a maze and a single door.'

Then came a somewhat more disconcerting statement:

'There's something else here. I see blood dripping . . . blood blots . . . red stuff . . . numbers . . . centre of cross . . . something to do with travelling to the centre of the universe, a rebirth, transformation and sending back out in a changed state. Something sealed.'

At this, he stood up, virtually ignored my presence, and walked almost somnambulistically back across the clearing as if looking for something. Where the clearing met the path, he stopped to study a deep, rectangular pit, some three feet by two feet, which was full of rotting leaves. It seemed significant so, without a word between us, we began to pull away the leaves to see if anything lay concealed below them.

An out of place object soon revealed itself — a large, brown, cylindrical medicine bottle, its lid sealed with red sealing wax. Inside it were folded up pieces of paper stained with what appeared to be fresh blood.

Bernard began retching again as he doubled back and stumbled his way out of the clearing and on to the path. I

The author doused the black-painted stone spearhead as it lay between the roots of the tree inside the woods of Shenfield Common. On its face was the chilling warning: 'To touch is to enslave'.

abandoned everything and ran after him, pleading with him to stop attuning to what was going on for his own safety.

Reaching the point where we had stopped on the path to take photographs of the clearing, I waited in silence as Bernard recovered.

Several minutes and a cigarette later, he was almost back to his usual self. I suggested that we try to find out exactly what was happening.

Both of the artefacts were still *in situ.* So, should we leave them where they were? Or should we collect them up and deal with them elsewhere? The negative emanations coming from the stone spearhead should have been neutralised when I'd doused it with holy water. That, therefore, should give us no further problems. But what about the bottle? What were we to do with that? It almost certainly contained a psychic charge set up by the Black Alchemist which was to have popped out, like a genii from a bottle, the instant we had broken the seal and unscrewed the cap. Nevertheless, its contents would have no effect on us so long as the bottle remained sealed.

The author removed the sealed brown bottle from the pit inside the clearing within the woods of Shenfield Common.

So, how could we dissipate, or diffuse, the psychic charge the bottle contained? We could not douse it with holy water, as this would not affect the bottle's contents. We could not bury it, as this would only result in the psychic charge remaining dormant until some poor, unsuspecting person found and opened the bottle. So what *were* we to do with it?

Bernard did not want to know. Therefore, at a loss to know what to do next, I collected up the artefacts, slipped them into my black holdall, and began to move back to the car. We could go for a drink in The Green Dragon. Perhaps he would receive some psychic inspiration once we had left the area.

Walking away from the clearing, he broke his silence. 'Do you know,' he began, unexpectedly, 'although we may have outwitted the Black Alchemist on this occasion, and may continue to do so in the future, he's gathering together a group of dedicated followers who will be able to take over even if he departs from the scene.'

I requested further information, but he gave none.

Ten
The Green Dragon

The wooden-panelled lounge bar of The Green Dragon hung heavy with cigar smoke and joviality from the mostly male clientele. Groups of businessmen, some still sporting their city suits, stood in small groups laughing and chatting above the incessant noise of the jukebox in the corner.

As Bernard placed our drinks on to the table and took his seat, I suggested that we attempt to put the whole situation into some sort of perspective. I needed to go through the exact sequence of events in the clearing and find out exactly what was going on. Bringing out my notebook, I slipped it in front of me in anticipation of his response.

'I believe he slipped into Essex either under the cover of yesterday's gales, or during the violent thunderstorms the day before that,' he began, as he sipped from his straight glass full of Guinness. 'Then, having chosen his site, he set up his ritual trap before moving quietly back to Sussex.'

I remarked on just how close the area around Shenfield Common was to the M25 London Orbital ring road which he would have undoubtedly used, via the Dartford Tunnel, to enter into the county.

'But why use Shenfield Common?' Bernard queried. 'Why did he not use Hart Wood? Surely that would have been the most obvious choice.'

I thought for a moment. Why *had* he used Shenfield Common? A solution came to mind, although before I said a word, I consulted the Ordnance Survey map, just to make sure. Yes, I felt I had an answer. It looked very much as if before the railway line had been laid between London's Liverpool Street station and Shenfield during Victorian times, Shenfield Common formed part of the much larger Hart Wood. So, as well as dividing the wood with a deep cutting, the railway had symbolically severed the *head* of the *hart*. Indeed, my glance at the map appeared to visually confirm this supposition. Anyway, whether this was so or not, it was the sort of topographical association which, we knew from past experience, the Black Alchemist would have taken into consideration when deciding on an appropriate site to carry out his ritual. The presence of a Hart Wood would have been too much of an opportunity for him to have resisted utilising in some way.

'You could be right,' Bernard admitted, leaning back in his seat. 'So who was this "John" I picked up inside the clearing? The one who . . .,' he tried to recall his earlier words, '. . . had not been quite right, so a symbol had been changed and corrected by the Black Alchemist. I think it's the same symbol as the one on the inscribed spearhead I saw in Ide Hill church,' he explained, lighting up another cigarette and turning it slightly in his mouth as he drew in smoke.

Of course. The symbol at Ide Hill. Now I *knew* who this 'John' was. I should have realised before. Caroline *had* been right — the curious symbol seen by Bernard inside Ide Hill church was indeed the so-called *Monas Hieroglyphica,* the visual device devised by Dr John Dee, the Elizabethan alchemist, astrologer and ritual magician. This was the 'John' that Bernard had been picking up. In fact, on the other side of the inscribed stone spearhead found that very evening was the same symbol — Dee's *Monas Hieroglyphica.* And yet, as Bernard had suggested, it had been slightly altered, changed or updated by the Black Alchemist. I knew very little about the *Monas* symbol, but I could check it out when I got home later that night.

'Dr John Dee,' Bernard repeated the name. 'I've not came across him before. However, I feel that BA obviously believes that he didn't get this symbol quite right, so he's upgraded it in some way.'

BA! Our abbreviation for the Black Alchemist!

On the other side of the stone spearhead was the same curious symbol seen by Bernard on the Ide Hill stone.

He placed down his half-empty glass of Guinness. 'I will even go so far as to say that BA actually believes he corrected the design under the psychic guidance of Dee himself. The man thinks he's in contact with John Dee.'

That was an absurd belief. Why should the spirit of someone like Dee wish to communicate with a corrupt character like the Black Alchemist? The man was obviously deluding himself.

I moved on to other matters. What about the Ide Hill sketch; what had all that been about?

'I feel it was some sort of trap,' he admitted. 'It was an attempt to ensnare us for some reason. Ever since the Lullington sketch, when we first found the spearhead, I've had the feeling that there's more to this whole affair than we could ever have imagined. It's almost as if the Black Alchemist knew that someone would remove that stone from the churchyard. He didn't know who, or when, only that when somebody took it, he would know psychically.

'When we were at Ide Hill I actually felt that he was

physically there, watching us. I didn't say anything at the time because it seemed silly. Now I realise that it was a psychic thing. He *knew* what was going on. He'd been watching our movements on a psychic level. Nothing specific. Just snippets here and there. Feelings. That sort of thing.'

Why did he remove the inscribed stone from Ide Hill church before we got there? Obviously, it must have had something to do with the fact that we left it for too long before going down there.

'I'm not quite sure,' he said, frowning. 'Maybe it was because we went down there with a group, so the chances of the right person picking it up were greatly diminished. Someone else touching it would have sent confusing impressions back to him, so he removed it and waited for another opportunity to strike.'

So why did he appear to be setting up some sort of rebirth ritual in Ide Hill church using a corrupt form of the Zosimos ritual? How did that fit into it?

Bernard sighed as he took out a cigarette. 'Perhaps there's a link between what he's doing in alchemy and why he's having a go at us. He knew that whoever found that spearhead at Lullington would be a fair match for his own abilities and some sort of threat to his alchemical transmutation who would have to be dealt with. Since then he has been attempting to locate us. Nothing definite, only vague directions. From Sussex, into Kent, and now into Essex. I don't think he actually knows who we are — not yet at least.'

He obviously knew that we were on to him. But why set traps to ensnare us? Why was he trying to track us down? What did he have against us?

'He seems to think we are his opponents and is now trying to strengthen the mental link between his mind and ours. He believes that by touching his spearheads, or by opening that bottle, he will be able to bring us into his grasp. For what ultimate purpose, I don't know.' Bernard sat back and watched as a group of teenage girls came over and sat in a crowd on the table next to us, oblivious as to the peculiar nature of our conversation.

He carried on only after they had settled down. 'The trouble is that BA doesn't know who he's dealing with. He must, by now, have realised that we are not fools. Yet, in a way, that may give him the upper hand.'

We would have to see.

After getting up to buy another round of drinks, I pulled out the inscribed stone. Like the Lullington spearhead, it was a piece of shale crudely shaped to look like a spearhead. However, this one was shorter, wider, and had been painted black so that its inscribed symbols stood out clearly. On one side was the written warning: 'To touch is to enslave', and on its reverse was the modified *Monas* symbol and a line of the strange mystical characters like those on the Lullington stone. Yet missing from this one were the three words in the strange script which Nigel Pennick had felt were characters from a Bardic alphabet.

Putting down the spearhead, I turned our attentions to the disposal of the sealed brown medicine bottle. What were we to do with that? I suggested to Bernard that he seek the help and advice of the Elizabethan alchemist who had first made contact with him outside Ide Hill church earlier that month. He had apparently manifested himself to Bernard for the specific purpose of helping us with the Black Alchemist affair.

He agreed, so, with the noise of the crowds and the jukebox reaching a crescendo, I wrote down the guide's name on a clean sheet in my notebook and asked him to communicate with us in some way.

After a minute or so of silence, Bernard nodded. 'He's here. Ask what you want.'

What were we to do with the bottle? A simple question, and one which I hoped the spirit guide would be able to answer.

The man began by informing Bernard of his trials and tribulations during his own lifetime on earth. It was interesting information, which later checked out. But it was not what we wanted to hear on that particular evening.

'Now he speaks of someone called Count St Germain,' Bernard continued, with a smile.

Yes, but what about the bottle? !

'Okay, he says that inside the bottle are two pieces of paper with blood blots; each the shape of stars, I think.'

Now we were talking.

'Each of these pieces of paper,' Bernard tried to explain, as a bellow of deep laughter issued from a crowd of middle-aged men in front of us, '. . . has been imprinted with psychic interference. The bottle was sealed to contain a message that was meant to instantly affect our minds. It was to have given him images of us. It would have acted like a drug hallucination, causing the appearance of supernatural manifestations.'

I jotted down his words beneath the guide's name, trying not to miss anything out. So what should we do with it?

'He says: "Use Catholic incense." You must open it enclosed in this, with four bowls of holy water, one at each of the points.'

At each point. Did he mean each of the four cardinal points, the four quarters — north, south, east and west — which, in magical terms, represented the directions from which the four elemental forces of Earth, Air, Fire and Water originated from and returned to during a ritual?

'He says yes,' Bernard responded, still miles away from the hearty activities surrounding us in the pub. 'He also says that it was him who influenced me to pick up the stick and quarter the clearing in the same way. It drained the energies away to the four quarters. The same thing will happen once the negative energies are released from the bottle.'

Now I knew what to do. But whilst the guide was still on the line, so to speak, I asked him whether he could tell us why the Black Alchemist had set up the trap in Shenfield Common?

'He says it was an attempt to get near us before any final action is to be taken.' He paused for a moment. 'Do not treat other worlds too lightly,' he said, turning at me. 'Well, that appears to be his parting message.'

I passed the time waiting for my parents to go to bed by taking photographs of the inscribed stone spearhead and the sealed medicine bottle. After this, I scoured my bookshelves for any

The curious symbol first seen at Ide Hill, and found on the inscribed stone located in Shenfield Common — pictured left — turned out to be the so-called *Monas Hieroglyphica* symbol of Dr John Dee, the Elizabethan occultist — pictured right.

books which might contain information concerning Dr John Dee and his so-called *Monas Hieroglyphica* symbol.

In one book, entitled *The Rosicrucian Enlightenment,* written by a lady named Frances Yates (Paladin, London, 1975), I found what I wanted. For on pages 22 and 23, it said that Dee had written a whole book about this one particular symbol which he called, quite simply, *Monas Hieroglyphica.* It was first published in 1564, and within it, Dee had outlined his belief that this particular symbol contained the ultimate formula for a combined Cabalistic, alchemical and mathematical science which, he believed, would enable its possessor to climb up and down the scales of being from the lowest to the highest realms of the ethereal universe. No wonder the Black Alchemist had shown so much interest in this symbol.

Frances Yates went on to say that the seventeenth century Rosicrucian architect, Elias Ashmole, wrote that on 27th June, 1589, Dee, when in the German town of Bremen, had been visited by one Dr Henricus *Khunrath,* a great German alchemist and philosopher. Apparently, this meeting had heavily influenced Khunrath's 'extraordinary work' entitled *The Amphitheatre of Eternal Wisdom,* published in Hanover during 1609. This was, I realised, the book title that Bernard had first mentioned as we had stood beneath the old tree in Danbury churchyard on Tuesday, 6th May, just prior to the Ide Hill sketch. So a book of this title did exist, as did someone called Khunrath, the name he had picked up earlier that evening inside the clearing.

Interestingly enough, *The Amphitheatre* made reference to such things as sacred gardens, long tunnels and a single doorway — all images that Bernard had clairvoyantly seen out in the clearing that very evening.

It looked very much as if the Black Alchemist had studied the works of Zosimos, Dee, Khunrath, and possibly even those of the thirteenth century alchemist and philosopher named Roger Bacon, as the name 'Bacon' had also cropped up as we had stood beneath the old tree in Danbury churchyard on Tuesday, 6th May.

He must have come to the conclusion that the *Monas* symbol was the visual key he required to achieve his alchemical transmutation. However, in the mind of the Black Alchemist, Dee had incorrectly drawn the symbol, so he had corrected it to his own and, seemingly, to Dee's own satisfaction.

However, I still could not understand what exactly he had been up to inside Ide Hill church. All that business about Zosimos' Priest of the Sanctuary dream, the body and womb of a woman, and a rebirth ritual. It seemed like an awful lot of hassle to have gone through just to set up some kind of occult trap to ensnare us. It just didn't make sense. All I could say was that there seemed to be more to this whole Black Alchemist affair than even Bernard had imagined, despite what he had said that evening.

In the midst of the rising cloud of incense out in the back

Inside the brown bottle were two pieces of white blotting paper covered in blood-like stains.

garden, I broke the seal on the brown medicine bottle and asked the four archangels — the archaic forces governing each of the four elements — to carry away the negativity it contained.

Bernard's guide had been correct. It did contain two pieces of paper, blotting paper to be more precise. On each of these was a crude star-like pattern in what looked very much like fresh blood; but was, on closer scrutiny, only red ink.

With the ritual complete, I closed down the proceedings, cleared up the mess and went to bed.

Eleven
St Anne's Castle

Thursday, 29th May, 1986. For once, we tried a different pub. It was the turn of St Anne's Castle, in Great Leighs, opposite the Essex showground, some miles north of Chelmsford on the A131 Braintree road.

I had already written one article on this late medieval pub, which had once been a monastic hospice for travelling pilgrims on their way to and from such shrines as the tomb of St Thomas a' Beckett at Canterbury and the chapel and holy well of Our Lady of Walsingham, in Norfolk.

The pub was also haunted by several alleged ghosts. Only the previous summer I had appeared on BBC Television's regional news programme, *Reporting London,* exorcising the so-called witch of St Anne's Castle. She was attached to probably the most important aspect of the site — the ancient markstone, known as the Witch's Stone, which could be seen on the grass verge in front of the pub's car park.

An interesting story surrounded the Witch's Stone, for it had originally been positioned at a crossroads called Scrap Faggots Green, a few miles away to the south-east. However, during the Second World War, when the Americans had built the nearby Boreham airfield, they had found that their wide vehicles had been unable to negotiate the narrow Essex lanes, so had them widened. When it came to removing the Witch's Stone, the local folk had protested, saying that it marked the grave of a witch who, if disturbed, would wreak terror on the local community.

The US officials had chosen to ignore this idle superstition and, upon dislodging the Witch's Stone, the terrified villagers' worst fears had been confirmed when charred bones and ash were discovered beneath it.

A cloud of ill-omen had then befallen the village of Great Leighs as strange paranormal activity and bad luck began to plague the peaceful rural community. Animals mysteriously died or disappeared, and the church bells rang of their own accord. The witch, it seemed, was on the loose once more.

The plight of the village was answered by top ghost hunter Harry Price who listened sympathetically to the problem and diagnosed a solution — the witch's remains were to be re-interred in a local churchyard with a full Christian burial service. It did the trick, although for reasons which have never been made clear, the stone found its way to the car park of St Anne's Castle, where it had remained to that day. The locals often accredited the strange occurrences inside the pub to the proximity of the Witch's Stone; which also went for wanders from time to time.

Only the previous month, the stone had unexpectedly vanished one night, only to be discovered the following morning in a field not far from its former home on Scrap Faggots Green. Yet mystery still surrounded its disappearance; and it was for this reason that Bernard and I were at St Anne's Castle that evening. I suspected foul play and wanted Bernard to psychometrise the stone to find out exactly who had carried it off, and for what purpose.

However, we decided to leave this task until Bernard had familiarised himself with the place. Maybe after a drink or two, he would even be able to tell me something about the early history of the building and its resident ghosts.

As we sat in the corner of the bar, supping beer, I broached the question of whether he was picking anything up about the pub, fully expecting him to say yes.

'No,' he announced, with an almost uninterested glance around at its original Tudor wooden beams and period walls. 'Not a thing.'

Oh well, that was a good start to the evening! Nothing at all? Not even a feeling of something? Anything?

He thought before he answered this time. 'No. Nothing. No

feelings at all.'

I sighed quietly to myself in frustration. Perhaps we should turn to more topical matters — such as the Black Alchemist, for instance.

Nodding in acceptance, Bernard reached into his jacket pocket and slid out a bunch of folded A4 sheets of lined paper.

It was a four page commentary on the recent incidents surrounding and culminating in the Shenfield Common sketch the previous week. The inevitable question was then asked — had he picked up any further information since then?

Again he nodded, as a knowing smile began to emerge upon his face. 'On Saturday night I decided to sit down in the dining room and just let my mind wander. I drew the *Monas* symbol on a clean sheet of paper and waited. I wasn't sure what would happen; or whether I was doing the right thing.'

And what happened? I lit a cigarette to await his answer.

He responded by producing a further sheet of lined paper. On the top was the *Monas* symbol and below were a series of written statements, yet not in Bernard's usual careful handwriting. They were quickly scrawled responses to his concentration. I read them quietly out aloud:

> **Embodies all dark powers of universe. Think of this symbol. You will absorb all the powers and transform. Will give power over all creatures and areas of land. The point is the centre of all things.**[1]

They appeared to be statements concerning the darker virtues of the *Monas Hieroglyphica.* Each had come to him gradually, over a period of nearly half an hour, following which he had written: 'Nothing more coming.' Yet then, in a large, clearly automatic script his pen had suddenly scrawled: 'If the circle closes a message will come', after which, he had commented in his own hand: 'I was wrong. Don't know who gave this.'

It was relatively interesting material, although it did not appear to further our understanding of the Black Alchemist affair. So had he received any more since Saturday night?

'Just vague stuff really. Nothing positive,' he responded,

turning his nose up at its possible significance, even before he had said a word. 'I don't know. A stinking, fleshy heart about, somewhere.'

His words took me by surprise. A stinking, fleshy heart? Buried somewhere by the Black Alchemist?

'I don't get any more. I'm not sure,' Bernard added, fumbling with his words. 'That's it, I'm afraid.'

I was intrigued, and although I could see that Bernard now wanted to move on to a different subject, I tried in vain to steer him back to his statement.

But he would not have it.

I waited for an hour, then tried again to persuade him to concentrate his thoughts on the image of this stinking, fleshy heart to see if he could, perhaps, get any more.

'You're pushing me,' he said, jokingly, as he collected up our glasses and stood up to make his way across to the bar. 'Same again?'

Yes, I nodded, and yes I was pushing him; gently. Unless I did, then that would be that and the mystery of the stinking, fleshy heart would be lost forever. And what if it was human? And we found it . . . I'm afraid I had to know more.

He returned from the bar with two full pint glasses and placed them on to the old wooden bench-like table. 'Well,' he began, as he sat back down. 'Again, it's only vague stuff, but I get a connection between this heart and St Mary. Something to do with wombs, birth and blood.'

He lit a cigarette and remained silent for a moment to compose his thoughts. 'There is also an involvement with the planetary influence of Mercury and something to do with this circle closing, "a message will come" business I picked up on Saturday night,' he continued, from behind a thin mask of rising smoke.

Now we were getting somewhere. My pen recorded his key words on the notepad.

'I now pick up the words "squeeze the circle strong enough, the heart stops and rebirth will follow". And a feeling of something coming up, rising out of something, after which a change will then take place.' He stopped to scan his mind for any further floating messages. 'No, that's it. I don't get any more.'

It did not make a lot of sense. Perhaps it was some sort of dark ritual the Black Alchemist was carrying out at that time down his way somewhere, which was not necessarily directed at us. If not, then it was, maybe, a portent of future events. Whatever the answer, it implied that BA was not averse to using flesh and blood — something we had suspected ever since I had realised that he was using the Zosimos system of alchemy to fulfil his own alchemical transmutation.

What about the reference to St Mary? It might be a church dedication, I suggested, possibly even Ide Hill church. Perhaps he was going to strike there again. On the other hand, it could be a reference to the Virgin Mary as a divinity of the Christian faith; or to another Mary.

Finishing our drinks, Bernard was anxious to leave, so I suggested that we repair to the car park and take a look at the Witch's Stone.

Moving out into the cold air, the psychic knelt down and placed the palm of his hand firmly upon the flat surface of the polished sandstone boulder; originally a glacial erratic deposited locally at the end of the last Ice Age before being highjacked for religious purposes by our pre-Christian ancestors.

He shook his head. 'No, it was kids,' he revealed, rising to a standing position. 'A game, a lark. Carted off and thrown away. No occult or sinister implications.'

Never mind. Some you win, some you don't, I concluded, philosophically, as we got into our respective cars and started up their engines.

Winding down the window on the passenger's side, he said: 'Thomas Jennings. I think you'll find that the old hermitage on the spot was owned by a man named Thomas Jennings. Check it out.' The window went up as Bernard's car started to reverse out of the parking space.

Thomas Jennings. No, I had never heard of him.

Months soon passed by and no more was heard from the Black Alchemist. Yet the whole extraordinary affair to date was becoming more and more widely known among the magical, paranormal and questing circles in which I moved.

By the end of August 1986 I had begun to put together the chapters for a booklet entitled *The Black Alchemist,* which I hoped to have on the streets by the end of October.

The first ever Psychic Questing Conference — organised by my colleague Caroline Wise — was to take place in London on Saturday, 1st November, and I intended lecturing on the Black Alchemist affair for the very first time that day.

I wanted desperately for the booklet to be published by that date, so worked flat out from August onwards in an attempt to get the finished artwork to the printers on time.

Twelve
The Ring of Darkness

Monday, 6th October, 1986. The incessant telephone rang again and the junior clerk picked up the receiver and engaged the caller in casual conversation. At the same moment, one of the company directors spoke from behind his wooden desk before standing up and moving out of the small office.

Bernard stared into nowhere. Something troubled him. His visionary eyes saw, not the hanging net curtains covering the small office's metal-framed window, but a scene much further away; not in Essex at all, but in Kent, or Sussex. He was not sure which.

The telephone receiver went down with a thud as the junior clerk muttered words of frustration to a non-existent audience. He too then walked out of the room.

Fields. Bernard could see fields, and trees. In fact, woods, and a stream nearby. It was a pleasant green area; and yet, for some reason, one with a bad feeling. Why was he seeing this?

A shout for coffee from an adjoining room was greeted with no particular enthusiasm by the elderly director who had returned to the office to collect a completed order form he had forgotten. Picking it up from his desk, he momentarily stopped to read its contents.

Bernard could still see the fields, but now his eyes had zoomed in on four figures in black cowled robes standing in a circle. Each held a long, black wooden baton horizontally up against their stomachs which pointed towards a fifth figure, dressed in a red cowled robe, who stood motionless in the centre of the circle. Their floppy hoods concealed their identities, and their sex.

Chatter from the doorway was followed by the appearance of a cup of coffee on Bernard's desk. He forced a polite 'thank you.'

The central figure in red felt familiar and, upon realising his identity, he wanted to disown the uninvited vision. But then came movement. The four figures in black began to side-step around in an anti-clockwise direction until they had made one complete revolution.

It was the Black Alchemist. The figure in red was undoubtedly the Black Alchemist. Now the Red Alchemist?! No, it was not a joke. What was he up to now? A distinct impression told him that their adversary was conducting a powerful occult ritual and on the move again. What was more, he felt that the ritual was actually taking place as he was viewing it.

At that moment, Bernard's fellow director called out his name and the vision ceased like a television screen suddenly going blank. Yet the disconcerting memory of the clairvoyant scene remained in his now agitated mind.

Glancing up at the wall clock, he noted the time. It was 10.40 am.

I woke that morning to the sound of my father telling me to get up, following a meaningless dream which was still fresh in my mind. It concerned my finished manuscript for *The Black Alchemist*. Something had happened to make me change its contents and this had inevitably led to a delay in its publication.

It was one of those frustrating dreams which had almost certainly been influenced by the innumerable evenings I had spent correcting and re-correcting the text. It may also have had something to do with the fact that, in the past couple of days, two separate people, Caroline Wise and my new girlfriend, Gilly Street, had both strongly felt that BA was on the move again, and would soon return to Essex; a statement neither had ever made before.

Following on from her impression, Gilly had decided to give

me a Tarot card reading to find out whether she was correct. This reading had taken place the previous afternoon and the results had been intriguing, to say the least. The cards had indicated that I would soon be forced into a major confrontation with the Black Alchemist, during which I would come face-to-face with death itself. And yet, whatever the circumstances of this incident, I would come through it safely and, in the process, would learn a great deal about the true nature of our adversary. However, at the end of the day, I would be no nearer to establishing his identity.

In many ways, I actually wanted him to make further moves in our direction in the eventual hope that he would make a few serious errors of judgement which would allow me to close in on his Eastbourne home.

Bernard had not wanted to know about the Black Alchemist affair for some months. He had not attempted to pick up any further psychic information on the subject, and just hoped that we had seen the back of him.

All I wanted was to expose the Black Alchemist. Yet before this could be achieved, either with or without Bernard's help, I needed to publish the booklet, which was now ready for the printers. Until then, I could do little more than wait.

Bernard felt unsettled for the rest of his day at work. Something was certainly in the air. The Black Alchemist was up to mischief again, and the feelings were not good. Luckily, he had arranged to see Andy that evening, so perhaps they could try and sort out what was going on then.

Around 6.30 pm he left his home and drove across to Wickford. Andy had hired a small hall in Basildon so that he could show him an audio-visual slide presentation he had put together on his recent trip to the secluded Greek Orthodox monasteries at the foot of Mount Athos, in North East Greece. He had arranged to pick up Andy around seven, although the illuminated car clock indicated that he would be late.

Turning off at the Rettendon Turnpike roundabout on the

A130, he joined the Runwell Road which would take him into Wickford. Yet the further he travelled along this road, the more he began to feel agitated and unable to concentrate on his driving. He quickly found himself cruising along at well over the 50 mph speed limit.

Suddenly, in front of him on the road was a stationary car, its flashing orange light indicating that it was about to turn right. He slammed on his brakes and the car slid to a halt just inches from the bumper of the other vehicle.

He was now in a fluster. The car had twisted diagonally as it had skidded to a stop. So, for a moment or two, he decided to turn on his hazard warning lights and just let the car in front make its turn. Still slightly shaken, he waited for what seemed like an eternity before being allowed to carry on his journey.

A short distance further along the same road, he again found himself driving at well over the legal speed limit. Taking his foot off the accelerator, he just could not understand his unusual actions.

Yet then, as the car entered the village of Runwell, Bernard caught sight of an ugly scene through the windscreen — dozens of plucked chickens lay scattered across the road, squashed to a pulp by passing cars. They had undoubtedly fallen off the back of a lorry and, as he drove over the spot, the revolting stench made him retch. It was a peculiar and coincidental incident which did not help his growing state of agitation.

The road then curved to the left and in front he now saw another stationary vehicle waiting to turn right into a side road. Stamping on the brake pedal yet again, the car skidded to an abrupt halt in good time; but this was the final straw. His heart palpitated and his hands shook uncontrollably.

He waited for the oncoming traffic to pass so that the car in front could make its turn.

Glancing to his left, he acknowledged the presence of the dark, silhouetted tower of Runwell church, partially hidden among the shadows cast by the surrounding treeline. He shuddered at its close proximity for, although it had been one of the central sites in Andy's book *The Running Well Mystery,* it was a place he had never felt inclined to visit. In his mind, it

As Bernard passed St Mary's, Runwell — pictured — he realised that a black magic ritual was actually in progress within the darkened churchyard.

had always exuded an unwelcoming, oppressive atmosphere which was probably linked to the local belief that the churchyard was still used by practitioners of the black arts.

Yet as Bernard stared suspiciously at the unnerving legendary structure, still in a highly agitated state, a new, overpowering and sickly clairvoyant image now greeted him. The church appeared to be engulfed by a dense, swirling cloud of dark energies which circled upwards before streaming off towards the direction of the Rettendon Turnpike.

With this disturbing image came the distinct impression that the black swirling cloud was the resultant effect of a dark ritual carried out in the churchyard only shortly beforehand. What was more, he felt that whoever was responsible for this foul act was *still* in the vicinity. Only one car stood in the layby in front of the church, a beige Ford Escort Mk III, its lights off. No one seemed to be inside its darkened interior, although his mind insisted that it was connected to the ritual in the churchyard. In fact, as he began to move away, past the Escort, something wanted to tell him that this car's owner was the Black Alchemist.

Bernard's car pulled up outside my parents' house around 7.20 pm and, as I opened the passenger door of his Ford Orion, he asked me to sit down for a moment or two, as he had something to say.

'Some very strange things have been going on today and I feel something heavy is in progress, and I don't like it one little bit,' he said, lighting a cigarette.

Briefly, I mentioned the impressions that Caroline and Gilly had received over the weekend, and yet forgot to tell him about the Tarot card reading the previous afternoon. So what was happening then?

He told me. So BA was on the move again; and this time in force.

The church of St Mary at Runwell, and a local holy well situated a couple of miles to the north-west, known as the

Running Well, were the main focal points of my book *The Running Well Mystery,* which had been published in 1983 and had featured the mysteries and legends of the parish.

'I suggest we give the slide show a miss and head straight for the church instead,' he suggested.

Twice we drove past the church to see if we could spot any movement within its darkened churchyard. We saw none, although I jotted down the registration number of a Suzuki-style jeep, with its lights on, standing in the layby next to the church; just in case. There was no sign, however, of the beige Escort Mk III seen earlier by Bernard. That had now gone.

Further along the Runwell Road, I saw, and smelt, the putrid chicken carcasses still scattered across the road.

Church End Lane, the side road which faced on to the fourteenth century stone tower of St Mary's, seemed an appropriate place to park the car, just out of sight of the churchyard. So, after conducting a simple protection ritual, I picked up a torch and left the car. I had also come prepared for psychic trouble as stuffed into my leather biker's jacket was a psychically-charged cross, given to me by a Greek Orthodox monk on Mount Athos, and a ritual wand, one of the last vestiges of my ritual magic days during the late 1970s. These could, if necessary, help me to bind, hold, dissipate or generate psychic forces. Bernard had more realistic thoughts in mind when he picked up a penknife and silently slipped it into his coat pocket.

Moving swiftly into the churchyard, he hesitantly approached the north wall and gently touched its uneven ragstone surface. 'Somebody else has done the same,' he announced, patting the wall before moving away.

By this I assumed he meant the Black Alchemist.

'Is there a porch around the back of the church?' he asked, looking up at the stone tower.

I reminded him that the porch he was referring to had been the focal point of the many legends and folktales attached to the church and outlined in my book.

We strolled towards it.

'Ah, a porch,' he said, almost as if he had not expected it to still be there. 'Something's been going on in there. I see dark energies emanating from somewhere within it.'

Once more, I insisted on caution and suggested that he did not go any further for the time being.

He nodded towards the wooden structure. 'There's something in the porch. He's put something in there.'

Where then?

Concentrating again, yet taking care not to attune to its energies for too long, he gave his answer: 'Right-hand side. In the corner, closest to us, on the ground.'

Quickly, I entered into the porch and shone the torchlight down between the wooden bench and the red-tiled floor. Two piles of roughly-stacked roof tiles stood haphazardly next to the wall — but to their right, in the corner, among the cobwebs and dirt, was a now familiar sight — a dark grey length of stone inscribed with familiar-looking magical symbols.

Announcing the discovery, Bernard ignored my earlier words and came across to the porch to look on silently as I visualised golden energies flowing through the wand and into the stone. This would hopefully nullify and dissipate its psychic charge.

Moving in closer, he reached out with his right hand and started to deliberately attune to the stone. 'Something else,' he strained, forcing his hand into one of the two untidy stacks of roof tiles, as if feeling for something. But it was too much for him. Pulling away sharply, he stumbled backwards, almost losing his balance. 'He's left something. Look there. A message. In the roof tiles.'

With this, he vanished out of sight, leaving me to search for this 'message.' Lifting the first few tiles I soon found the root of his agony — a sealed black envelope, thick with contents, on which was Sellotaped a white strip of paper bearing — in small black type — the name: 'Andrew Brian Collins'.

My heart sank. *What the hell did it contain?*

Collecting up both the envelope and the inscribed stone, I

ran off to find Bernard. Catching up with him, we made a quick exit from the churchyard and retired back to the car.

He was complaining of a slight headache and a nauseous feeling inside his stomach, but otherwise he seemed to be in control. Looking at the sealed black envelope, illuminated by the car's interior light above me, I decided not to open it until we knew a bit more about what was going on.

'I don't think you should open it at all,' he joked.

Perhaps that wasn't such a bad idea. Yet one thing was for sure — the Black Alchemist was now in possession of my full name. In which case, he also knew of my association with Runwell church and, presumably, the legends which centred upon its south porch. So, had he managed to get hold of a copy of my book? It looked that way.

'I also think he knows that there's someone else working with you,' he added, glancing out of the window at a couple of passers-by. 'However, I don't get the feeling that he has *my* name or address.'

This was probably due to the fact that I had deliberately tried to keep Bernard's identity out of the limelight, so to speak. But to me the overwhelming fear was that if the Black Alchemist knew of my past interest in Runwell church, then he also knew of my association with the Running Well. It was an important local site of great peace and serenity, enjoyed by many visitors, and with a history that stretched back over two thousand years. I just hoped that he had not desecrated this site with his warped black magic rituals.

Bernard suggested that we get out of the immediate influence of the church and then stop for a while to see if he could pick up any further psychic clues. So, moving the car just a few hundred yards up the lane, he brought it to a halt in a side road. Here we rested for a few minutes by opening a bottle of wine we had intended to have at the slide show.

Emptying his wine glass, Bernard began to concentrate his mind on the church once more. We needed to know how effective our removal of the inscribed stone had been and what exactly we were to do next.

A minute or so passed before he spoke: 'Right, I still see this black swirling cloud around the church. Removing the stone has not stopped it. I can see it sweeping off in a north-easterly direction, like a wall of black mist. It's vapourous, very strong and appears to follow a curved path across the countryside.'

Suddenly, he went quiet for a few moments. 'Who's "Talbot"?' he enquired, quite out of the blue. 'It's a name connected in some way, I think.'

Talbot. I thought for a moment. The name John Talbot was, I knew, carved into the wood on the front of the north porch. It was the signature of its fourteenth century carpenter, or so some scholars believed. Was this name, therefore, connected with the church?

He shook his head. 'No, all I get is that "Talbot" is dead, and nothing else.'

For a few minutes more we just sat in silence waiting for something to happen. I then noticed that Bernard was once again in a state of deep concentration.

'You must go,' he whispered, breaking the long silence and coming out of his meditative state. 'Right, I'm being told by a female spirit entity that we have to go somewhere. She's on our side; a site guardian I should think, larger than life and bluey-white in colour. She's pointing towards a spot by trees; high up. There's a church there. She says the Black Alchemist has been there.'

A spot high up, with trees and a church. Could I identify it? I thought for a moment.

'I know where it is,' Bernard exclaimed, a smile beginning to build upon his face. 'It's Rettendon church.'

Rettendon. Yes, of course. A village a couple of miles to the north-east of Runwell. Its church was on a high spot surrounded by trees.

'It appears to be the next point on the perimeter of this huge "ring of darkness." Yes, that's what it is — part of a huge ring of energies curving across the landscape.' There was a further pause before he spoke again. 'That's it,' he said to himself. 'That's why I picked up such bad feelings on the Runwell Road, between the Rettendon Turnpike and Wickford, on my journey over here. It must have begun as I had unknowingly passed through the perimeter of the Ring of Darkness on its curved course between Runwell church and Rettendon church.'

I didn't quite understand what he was getting at. It seemed as if he was suggesting that the churches at Runwell and Rettendon were just two points on a great arc, or even a ring, of dark energies set up by the Black Alchemist. If so, then where did it go to after Rettendon? And what was its function, or purpose?

There seemed little doubt that our next destination was the church of All Saints, Rettendon, one of the most prominent churches in South East Essex.

'The blue lady says she will meet us there. So I suppose we should go there now.'

Thirteen
The Blue Lady

Bernard switched off the headlights as the car coasted to a halt in the trackway outside the church of All Saints, Rettendon. For a few minutes we just sat there wondering what to do next.

'Do you get anything?' he asked, hoping that I would be able to either confirm or add to the earlier information he had picked up about the site.

I said no.

He sighed to show some concern. 'Well, I've got a pain in my stomach and I feel as if I'm being pulled towards the church for some reason.'

Further minutes passed before he spoke again. 'I'm being shown an aerial view of the church as if I've been lifted off the ground to treetop level,' he announced, in a low, yet descriptive voice. 'I can see a black, swirling cloud of energies — like the one present at Runwell — enclosing the church and curving away as a black wall-like form towards a north-westerly direction.' He stopped for a minute to gather his thoughts together.

'The strongest emanations appear to be coming from a spot at the opposite end of the church. Somewhere below the tower, I think.'

Completely out of sight of the approach road; just like at Runwell, out of sight of the main road, I thought to myself.

'And I can still see the blue lady,' Bernard confirmed. 'She's now standing by the west end and pointing towards the ground. She's weak now, drained of her entire energy form for some reason.'

There was a pause before he continued. 'She's still pointing

In the darkness within Rettendon churchyard — pictured — Bernard encountered the radiant blue lady, who revealed the whereabouts of the concealed artefact left by the Black Alchemist.

. . . there's a stone . . . a white stone on the ground, near a door, about a foot across. Something about putting the sword in the stone.'

As the pauses between his sentences became longer and longer, I feared he was losing consciousness, so begged him to stop for a while. I was afraid that he was being engulfed within the powerful Ring of Darkness; and that could, I knew, lead to either possession or a complete energy drain, not to mention the usual ill-effects of attuning to the Black Alchemist's activities.

But he opened his eyes and broke his concentration without any sign of discomfort. 'Don't worry, I'm alright,' he stated, quite casually.

Soon afterwards we left the car and made our way up the gravel path towards the darkened church. The staggering view of the surrounding countryside quite overwhelmed Bernard. I pointed out the glittering lights of the Thames Estuary and the North Downs of Kent; it was a magnificent vantage point. I suggested that it had been for this reason that the church had been sited on the spot in the first place.

Reaching the western end of the church, I stood by the great wooden door below the tower and looked around for a concealment place. So, had something been buried?

'There's a white stone. That's all I'm getting.'

A white stone. I shone the torchlight across the grass. Almost immediately it picked out a smooth white slab of marble set horizontally into the earth next to a wooden seat. It was obviously a chunk off an old grave slab, and yet somehow it appeared to be exactly what we were looking for.

Seeing the white stone slab, Bernard cautiously reached out with his hand and attempted to attune to it. Instantly, and without warning, he began to violently retch as he slowly moved his fingers closer and closer to the offending stone.

But then he quickly withdrew his hand and stepped backwards. 'Down the side,' he choked, despite the obvious ill-effects. Forcing himself back to the spot, he touched the grass at the side of the stone. 'It's down there. Take it out.'

I shone the torchlight into the grass and soon found the source of his torment as a slim piece of slate, shaped into a spearhead, inscribed with familiar-looking magical symbols, suddenly revealed itself.

It had been jammed between the edge of the stone and the soft grass-covered earth. As Bernard moved away from the vicinity, I used the ritual wand to mentally conduct a powerful cleansing visualisation in the hope that it would destroy the charged energies held within the stone. Picking it up, I slid it into my jacket pocket before catching up with Bernard who was already making his way back to the car.

Something bothered me as we sat silently waiting for further psychic clues. We had now found not one but two inscribed stones that evening. It looked very much as if the Black

Alchemist was using them as fixing markers to change, hold and channel the inherent energies present at each of the sites he had selected for his apparent Ring of Darkness ritual. The first of these had been located together with an envelope addressed to me. So, if he had meant us to find these two items then he had also meant us to find the stone buried in Rettenden churchyard.

But there was more. The Ring of Darkness was almost predictable. I quickly sketched a rough map of the local landscape and drew a great circle incorporating the churches of Runwell and Rettendon. It did not take much working out to realise that the circle also included the hilltop church of Downham, a few miles north-west of Wickford; an intriguing assumption, since this church, like those at Runwell and Rettendon, had featured within a rather speculative theory I had put forward in *The Running Well Mystery*.

It suggested that many of the churches, hills and ancient sites around Runwell and Wickford had originally been sited to conform with an ancient groundplan based upon a mystical symbol, known as the Runwell Cross, featured within the various legends associated with the area.

The Black Alchemist's Ring of Darkness did not correspond exactly with my own circular layout of sites, yet the concept was the same — a circular arrangement of ancient sites based upon a central axis point. And the centre point of the Ring of Darkness looked like being . . . No, I would not even think it until I was sure. But I had to — it was the Running Well — the most sacred site in the area, and a place very dear to my heart. For the moment though, I decided to keep all this to myself as I did not want to unintentionally influence Bernard's psychic messages in any way.

'We're not finished at this site,' Bernard unexpectedly announced, breaking the silence in the car. 'I'm being pulled back towards the churchyard for some reason, and I've got to go.'

I told him to be careful as it could be a trap.

'I don't think so,' he said, opening the car door. 'I'm going out there anyway.'

Leaving the safety of the vehicle's warm interior, he made his way up the gravel path again and began cutting across the wet grass towards some unknown destination. I followed close behind, pen and paper ready in my hand.

The tireless psychic came to a halt in front of an unidentified grave in the middle of the churchyard. Here he stood, silent and motionless, in a world of his own. As I looked on, he slowly raised his arms into the air.

'Her name is Cecilia,' he began, without any follow up explanation.

It was a reference, I realised, to the identity of the blue lady. So, who was Cecilia? The spirit of the person buried in the grave he was standing over?

There was still no explanation as he began to mumble something which I could not hear properly. Approaching him, I listened carefully. He appeared to be in a light trance.

Words in a low monotone voice issued from his mouth in the form of short statements. They included: 'Church down lane . . . very near water . . . nothing left . . . linked with mind; but left no mark . . . church on hill . . . we go there . . . we find and take . . . we will destroy.'

His words were, I realised, responses to commands being given to him by Cecilia. I recognised the church on the hill. It was Downham. So I was right. Downham *was* one of the sites on the Ring of Darkness. However, I could not identify the other church down a lane, close to water.

Dropping his arms, Bernard snapped out of his trance state and confirmed that he had just been speaking to the blue lady. 'She called me to her and I found her standing by the grave in full clairvoyant form. I'm not sure who she is. She raised her arms into the air, so I thought I should do the same. She told me her name was Cecilia and that, aside from Runwell and Rettendon, BA has been to another church situated at the end of a long unmade track.' He began to pace about to keep warm.

'However, for some reason he only attuned to this church. He didn't leave a stone or anything — just a mental instruction of some sort.'

So where was this church? Lighting a Marlboro, I waited for his reply.

He shrugged his shoulders and shook his head. 'It's down a long lane and near a large expanse of water. That's all she said. The Hanningfield reservoir, I presume.'

Yes, that was my conclusion. The huge man-made reservoir at South Hanningfield, a few miles to the north-west of Rettendon.

'She also told me that BA has apparently visited another church — on a hill — where he *did* leave another artefact of some sort.'

Downham, I told Bernard. Perhaps the other church down the lane was the one at South Hanningfield. However, I had never been there so knew nothing at all about the site. Had he been there before?

He twisted around, only having caught the last part of my question. 'Er, no. No, I haven't. Anyway, if he's not left anything there, then there's no point in finding it. Is there?'

Okay, so it was straight to Downham church.

Passing swiftly along the quiet, narrow lanes of South Hanningfield, on our way to Downham, Bernard suddenly became agitated.

'I don't like this at all,' he said, in a concerned tone for the umpteenth time that evening. 'I just feel as if something not very nice is looming over the horizon, and we are walking, or driving, straight into it.'

What did he mean?

'I don't know. The one thing I do get though, is that whoever's defiling these sites is still in the area and close by at this very time.'

It was a disconcerting thought.

'I now see a horrible sight,' he announced, as the car continued on through the dark lanes. 'I see a body hanging by its neck from a noose strung over a tree. I'm not sure what it means, but I hope it's not a portent of any sort.' He forced a little laugh to try and lighten the heavy atmosphere.

I said nothing, just looked out at the passing hedgerow.

'Now I see the whole landscape engulfed by a mass of enormous flames. Above this is a vision of a huge flaming sword.'

I did not understand and the clairvoyant picture was quickly forgotten.

'Hold on,' Bernard said, re-opening the conversation and momentarily slowing down the car. 'I reckon that BA has been along this very road only a short while ago.' He shuddered at the thought.

We carried on. A minute or so later a small lane came into view on the right-hand side. A sign announced its name — Church Lane. On impulse we decided to take the turning. It was an unmade track which, after only a few hundred yards, came to an abrupt end in front of a double gate.

The headlights picked out a painted wooden signpost which

As Bernard and the author found their way to South Hanningfield church barred by the entrance to Bifrons, they realised why the Black Alchemist had not left an artefact at this site.

indicated that the gateway marked the entrance into a private estate called Bifrons. Another sign prohibited cars beyond that point.

It all appeared to make some sort of sense. Beyond Bifrons was quite obviously a church — the one mentioned by Cecilia as being down 'a long lane' — which could only be reached on foot by walking through the private estate. If so, then it was this church that formed the next point in the Black Alchemist's Ring of Darkness. It looked as if he too had travelled down this unmade track, expecting to find access to the church. Instead, he had realised that the only way he could reach it was to proceed on foot through the Bifrons estate which he had apparently decided against doing, even under the cover of darkness. In consequence, he had merely carried out some form of visualisation ritual to fix the church as the third point in his Ring of Darkness, before continuing on to Downham.

Bernard agreed. 'I get no feelings to do anything here. So I assume we carry on ourselves.'

Further along the country lane I noticed a sign pointing the way to St Peter's church, South Hanningfield. It was seemingly a separate route to the church situated behind the Bifrons estate.

So South Hanningfield church did form the third point on the Black Alchemist's Ring of Darkness.

We moved on towards Downham.

Minutes later, on the left-hand verge, a piece of red cloth was picked out by the car's headlights. It had obviously been discarded by some careless motorist or passer-by, but, for some reason, its image instantly registered in both our minds. Bernard jammed on the brakes and brought the car to a halt in the middle of the narrow lane. Yet we did not go back to pick it up, neither did we feel it was part of the quest; but it did mean something.

It was an omen of some sort.

'Like a red rag to a bull,' I said out aloud, as I tried to reason our actions. Then I knew. This whole journey was like a red rag to a bull. The Black Alchemist had set up the Ring of Darkness ritual for one specific purpose — to play us at our own game — psychic questing: following up psychic messages to discover hidden artefacts and long lost secrets of the past. We were acting like charging bulls, both of us.

Now his intentions were clear. The Black Alchemist actually wanted us to find each and every one of his hidden artefacts; and knew that this was exactly what we would do. The sealed black envelope found in Runwell churchyard was addressed to me, so, if he knew that we would find this, then he also knew that we would continue the quest and find the rest of the artefacts used to form his Ring of Darkness. So what would happen next? Was he luring us into a ritual trap somewhere? At the Running Well perhaps?

Bernard looked unsettled. 'I think you're right. He *has* been up to the well. Let's just hope he's not waiting for us there.'

Ten minutes later the car rolled to a halt in the layby next to the hilltop church of St Margaret's, Downham — the fourth and final point in the Ring of Darkness, and just two miles north-west of my home town of Wickford.

Climbing out of the car, we made our way over to the churchyard and entered the wooden lychgate. Here I took Bernard through a strong protection visualisation before we stepped into the stillness of the darkened churchyard. Swiftly, we made our way across the dew-laden grass to the secluded east end of the Christian edifice.

'Here,' Bernard announced, indicating the area below the east wall. 'He's done something around here. I can feel it.'

He ran his hand across the stonework and, about half way along, dropped it down towards the ground. Psychically, he then attempted to attune directly to the concealed artefact by placing the palm of his hand close to the earth. He moved it around, then came back to a certain spot in the grass, very close to the base of the stone wall. 'Down there,' he announced,

As night fell upon Downham church — pictured — Bernard was knocked unconscious as the author discovered the final artefact left as part of the Black Alchemist's Ring of Darkness ritual.

pointing with his hand.

Kneeling down, I parted the strands of wet grass and, in a small ready-made hole, I found our fourth artefact of the evening — another inscribed piece of shale.

The psychic stepped backwards with the inevitable ill-effects of attuning to objects used in black magic rituals, as I quickly carried out a simple visualisation ritual to dissipate and destroy the psychic charge contained within the stone. With the ritual complete, I pulled out the artefact and slipped it into my pocket, although not before I had noticed one of its crudely-inscribed images. It was the outline of a long snake or serpent, inside which were two matchstick men and the word: 'Soon'!

I was satisfied at our swift recovery of the inscribed stone without any real problems. Next stop would be the Running Well itself. It had to be. Yet whatever the real meaning and purpose of this whole affair, no one could say it was not a fantastic story. But who would believe it? Not many, I decided.

Smiling, I stood up straight and looked around for Bernard. Where was he? I could neither see, nor hear him. Perhaps he had gone back to the car? Yes, that was the answer. Leaving the spot, I walked briskly back into the more open and illuminated part of the churchyard.

Over by the lychgate, I glanced towards his Orion. It was empty. So where was he? My fears began to increase by the second. That was all I needed: Bernard's sudden, unaccountable disappearance. He had to be around somewhere.

Running through the churchyard, I shouted out his name once, twice, three times. There was no response at all. I frowned in annoyance. He could not have gone far, I said to myself, as my stomach began to churn wildly.

Walking back towards the eastern end of the church, I called out his name again.

A low murmur came in response. I shouted again to pinpoint its direction. Another faint sound emanated from an unseen source among the dark shadows cast by the overhanging hedgerow on the northern edge of the churchyard.

Running frantically in the direction of the strange sounds, the torchlight illuminated Bernard in an almost unconscious state, lying curled up on the ground. By the tortuous expression on his face I realised that he was fighting some inner conflict to rid his mind of an uninvited intruder.

In desperation I tried to carry out a powerful banishment ritual over his body using the wand. But it had no effect whatsoever, so I had to think again. What could I do next?

I knew. Placing my hands on his shoulders, I pushed my own vital energy into his body using visualisation. This would hopefully give him enough inner strength to overcome whatever was inside him. But it did not appear to be working.

I tried another banishment ritual. This time it seemed to have some sort of effect, as he gradually began to push himself up off the ground and on to his feet. But still he appeared to be in a state of mental torment; stumbling about aimlessly, until his hand reached out and grabbed hold of a gravestone which he used to support himself as he mumbled something about 'being hit' and wanting to 'earth' himself.

Constantly I talked to him in the hope that he would soon snap out of his tormented state. Yet then, and only then, he started to recover slightly and seemed a little more steady on his feet.

It was time to get out.

Lifting him up, I helped him out of the churchyard.

Inside the old lychgate, he slumped on to the wooden bench. I could see he was still very weak, both physically and mentally. So, in the hope of getting him to regain some of his lost vital energy, I led him through another simple visualisation exercise.

It took several painstaking minutes before he fully recovered, and as I waited for him to speak, he took out and lit a cigarette.

So, what had happened out there?

He pulled the cigarette from his mouth and actually began to look as if life was returning to him. 'Well, it began after we'd found the stone,' he replied. 'Its retrieval drained me of my own energies and I started to feel sick and weak. I also felt as if my protective shield was fast disappearing.'

He drew deep on his cigarette before continuing. 'I tried to get away, but then I saw and felt something hit me at great speed. I don't know what it was. All I saw was like a concentration of darkness, shaped into a ball. It just came at me and entered my stomach, after which I just hit the ground, and that was it.' He shook his head in frustration. 'The next thing I remember was you shouting behind me.'

He trod out his cigarette. 'I got up and just knew I had to earth whatever was inside me. That's why I grabbed the gravestone. Using my mind, I pushed it into the earth and things seemed to get better after that.'

Yes, Graham Phillips always used to say that it was possible to earth negative energies by mentally pushing them into a stone heavily rooted to the ground — like a standing stone or a gravestone, for instance. So it made sense. Yet I needed to know whether my banishment ritual had worked.

'Yes, I think so. It certainly helped,' he admitted. 'But I felt the need to earth the force in some way.'

Accepting his word, we walked across to the car.

Bernard was reaching a point of absolute physical and mental exhaustion. I could see it in his eyes. There was no way that he could continue on the quest to the Running Well unless he fully regained his strength. He was the driver, so if anything else tried to get at him, then it could result in the car running off the road.

We also needed to know exactly what was going on at the well and how to combat it *before* we got there. To this end Bernard really needed to make contact with his spirit guide, the Elizabethan alchemist, and he would be unable to do so unless he was in a fit state of mind. No, we needed to rest for a while.

Further along the road into Wickford was a pleasant pub called The Downham Arms. I suggested that we retire there for a while. We could have a quiet drink, suss out the situation and open the sealed black envelope to see what that contained.

Without much thought, Bernard agreed.

Fourteen
The Downham Arms

It is not often that a young man strolls conspicuously into a pub dressed in a leather biker's jacket and holding a wooden crucifix over a sealed black envelope. Upon realising this, I rapidly tried to secrete the cross and envelope about my person whilst ordering the drinks!

Sitting down opposite Bernard, I pulled out the sealed black envelope and stared at it apprehensively, dreading what it might contain. Still, I had decided that it was the correct time and place to reveal its contents so, with some slight hesitation, I used Bernard's penknife to slit open its lip. Peeking inside, I saw it contained various different bits and pieces. Firstly, there was a large orangy-red crystal of some sort. I could also make out a couple of pieces of paper, and another black envelope, sealed and folded in two. Lastly, I could see some folded sheets of paper, which looked as if they were pages taken from a book.

The crystal bounced on to the table as I slowly tilted the envelope. Quite understandably, Bernard refused to touch it! It was about half an inch square and was made of a translucent substance of very little weight. Leaving it on the table, in between the stained beer mats and an ashtray, I slipped out the folded sheets of paper. Immediately, I realised what they were — *two pages torn from my book The Running Well Mystery* — pages 31 to 34, to be more precise.

Involuntarily, I gulped at the sight.

Various words and sentences had been deliberately underlined or lined through with a red fibre-tipped pen, as if to emphasise their importance or irrelevance. Their subject matter seemed connected with our current predicament, since they featured one of the most memorable of all the folktales associated with the Running Well — the story of the Prioress' Ring. It concerned a magical, talismanic ring of office which legend claimed had once belonged to a medieval prioress of the small convent which had apparently been situated close to the well. The essence of the legend was that the great topaz stone set into the ring had been used by the prioress as a kind of crystal ball, or scrying stone, to keep a watchful eye on the activities of the young novices.

Yet it was the way in which the magical ring had been endowed with its talismanic powers that had intrigued me at the time of writing the book. For it was said that the prioress had fasted for nine days and nine nights and then, on the final night, the Virgin Mary had entered into the convent through an open window, upon a shaft of moonlight, which had then slowly moved across a table until it touched and engulfed the topaz ring.

The Running Well Mystery had shown that this curious tale appeared to embody a much older tradition — that of aligning ancient sites around the Runwell area towards prominent solar and lunar risings and settings at certain specific dates of the year.

The Prioress' Ring legend had also been used in the book as evidence for my belief that the various sacred places around the Runwell landscape, most significantly the Running Well itself, had, in the past, been associated with a strong female, lunar form of religious devotion. Not only this, but that on a psychic, intuitive level, these sites *still* possessed and exuded subtle energies which were predominantly lunar in influence and quality.

The words underlined were, in order:

> **. . . denied the balm of sleep for nine . . . nights . . . Rested a ring of noble dignity . . . gold . . . topaz . . . black . . . secret words . . . talisman . . . watch and ward . . . ring . . . talisman . . . which could, henceforth, be used to keep an ever-watchful eye . . . various mystical overtones . . . denied the balm of sleep . . . nine . . . powers . . . moon . . .**

> **ring . . . alchemy . . . setting sun on a specific date in the year . . . energies . . . dormant natural forces . . . power centres . . . altars in the east . . . giving light, life (with the word 'light' crossed through) . . . pure gold . . . practices of age-old cultures . . . bringing life . . . ring . . . ring . . . gold ring . . . topaz . . . 1514 (AD) . . . talismanic qualities . . . Where was the ring now? . . . three giant hounds 'dun coloured with eyes a-fire, foam dripping jaws and savage teeth that gnashed.'**

Some of the underlined words and sentences did not appear to be relevant to the situation, but the rest clearly were. In a sense, the whole exercise could be interpreted as a kind of cryptic message to me, provided that you read between the lines, so to speak.

Leaving the torn out pages for a moment, I turned my attentions to the remaining contents of the black envelope. Tipping it upside down, three small pieces of paper fell on to the table. They were all cuttings from, what was undoubtedly *The Radio Times.* On the first was the word 'you', and on the second were the words 'who looks after'. The third showed the front cover of a recently published book entitled *The Power of the Mind,* put together from articles which had originally appeared in *The Unexplained,* a news-stand magazine on paranormal mysteries. The cutting had obviously been taken from an advertisement in *The Radio Times* for some sort of 'mysteries' book club.

So, when placed together, the message read: 'You who looks after power of the mind'.

The Radio Times used to make the message was a recent issue, as on the back of one of the cuttings were snippets of a programme guide mentioning the 1986 Liberal/SDP Alliance party's annual conference held at Eastbourne, in Sussex, which had ended only ten days before. Even though Bernard had previously picked up that the Black Alchemist lived in Eastbourne, I decided that this had to be a bizarre coincidence, and little else.

With the cuttings still scattered across the varnished table top, alongside the orangy-red crystal and the torn out pages, I pulled out the envelope's final item — the other black envelope folded in two. Shaking it, I realised it contained some loose fragments, so hesitantly slit it open. They turned out to be further pieces of the same orangy-red crystalline substance found in the first envelope. With them were two more cuttings from *The Radio Times*. One said 'say goodbye', and the other was another book cover from the same 'mysteries' book club advertisement. Its title: *Life after Death!*

I positioned the final two cuttings on the end of the first three and read out the completed message: 'You who looks after the power of the mind say goodbye. Life after death'! It was a death threat! Well, that was the way it looked at least.

The macabre jigsaw was beginning to take shape. It seemed as if the Black Alchemist had somehow managed to link my name with the interference of his dark rituals, probably through a contact in the occult field, or perhaps through psychic means. He had then managed to obtain a copy of *The Running Well Mystery* — which, incidently, had been out of print for three years — and, upon reading it, had realised its association with the various ancient and religious sites around my home town of Wickford, in Essex. He had then familiarised himself with their history, their legends and their apparent psychic influence and power, in readiness for some kind of warped ritual.

His intended plan was to apparently eliminate not just me, but Bernard as well, whose name he did not appear to possess. In an attempt to achieve this aim, he had set up a great circle of dark energies, the Ring of Darkness, by conducting a powerful occult ceremony focused upon four local churches set in a circle around the area's mystical epicentre, the Running Well. At each of these sites — except the church at South Hanningfield — he had sealed his intentions by leaving one of his inscribed stones as fixing markers or beacons. These, he knew, Bernard and I would eventually find and remove in the correct sequence, with the final site being the Running Well itself.

In consequence, we had to assume that he had set up some

kind of ritual trap at the well which we were to have blindly stumbled into and been caught within its influence. Whether he intended eliminating us by psychic attack, or by sawn-off shotgun, we did not like to think; yet Bernard's impression that the man was still in the area did not help to calm our nerves.

However, there appeared to be more to the Black Alchemist's plan than purely this. The statements and words underlined within the torn-out pages spoke of 'denying the balm of sleep for nine nights', which suggested that the ritual trap was scheduled to come to a head nine nights after its conception. This gave a date of Wednesday, 15th October. So, by this date, it seemed that if the Black Alchemist had his way, then both Bernard and I would be experiencing life after death!

I tried to make a joke of the whole thing, but Bernard was not laughing. He quite rightly felt that this was a very serious matter. The Black Alchemist was not only an adept occultist and a dangerous psychic, he was also an imbalanced, yet devious psychopath who was ready to do us real harm.

At Bernard's suggestion, I changed the mood of conversation to the clairvoyant images he had received earlier that day showing the four figures in black cowled robes carrying out a ritual around a fifth character in a red cowled robe, thought to have been the Black Alchemist himself. Each of the four had held a long black baton up against their stomachs and had side-stepped their way around the central figure until they had completed one entire revolution.

The four figures in black had, I felt, represented the four church marker points on the Ring of Darkness. In which case, the central figure in red had therefore represented the Running Well; a fact which probably bore some link with the orangy-red crystals found in the sealed envelopes. Maybe the Black Alchemist had been trying to use the crystals to forge a psychic link with me, in the same way that the Prioress' Ring had been used to keep a watchful eye on the activities of the young novices of the convent.

Shifting the subject of conversation again, I brought up the name 'Talbot' that Bernard had picked up shortly after the discovery of the inscribed stone and sealed black envelope in

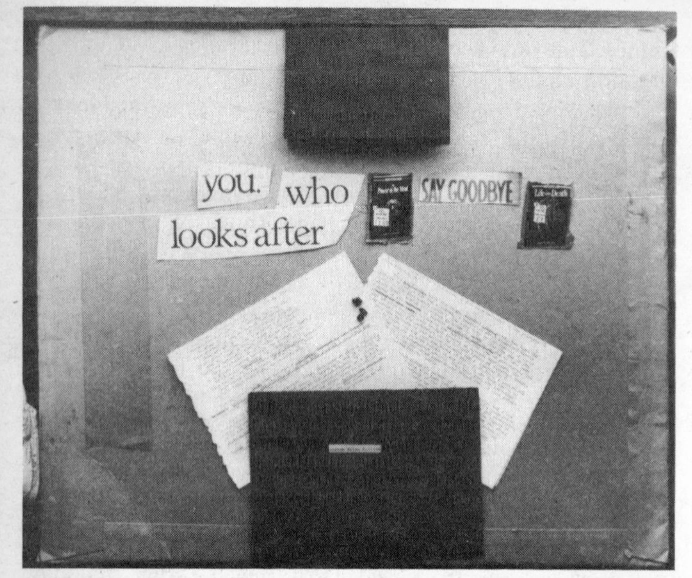

When the black envelope was opened, it was found to contain a death threat from the Black Alchemist, giving Bernard and the author just nine nights to live.

Runwell churchyard. Talbot, or John Talbot, to give him his full name, was, I realised at last, the true identity of Dr John Dee's close friend and accomplice, Edward Kelly. He had been Dee's psychic partner, or scryer, as they were known, who, for many years, had regularly communicated with the spirit world on behalf of the Elizabethan magus. I also dimly recalled that the pair had used a crystal ball and a circular scrying mirror, made of a dark volcanic glass known as obsidian. Kelly had also been an alchemist and was, by all accounts, a bit of a rogue; a fact which had often led scholars to doubt the authenticity of his psychic work with Dee.

So, did Bernard feel that the name 'Talbot' was a reference to Dee's sidekick, Edward Kelly?

As usual, Bernard shrugged his shoulders with a smile. 'I

don't know. Maybe. I haven't come across either name before.'

I left the subject. What we needed was a directive of some sort from higher sources. We had to know what to expect when we arrived at the Running Well, otherwise we could both find ourselves in serious trouble either on a physical or on a psychic level. Bernard needed to try and communicate with his spirit guide, the Elizabethan alchemist. Perhaps he would be able to tell us what was going on at the well.

'Okay, but I don't suppose I will get much,' he insisted, finishing off his drink and placing down the empty glass. 'However, I'm not doing anything in here. Let's go out into the car. It'll be quieter in there.'

As the first few noisy revellers spilled out of the pub's double doors and ambled noisily back towards their cars, Bernard sat silently contemplating the presence of his sixteenth century spirit guide. Glancing at the car clock, I noticed the time. It was now 10.15 pm.

Waiting for some sort of response, I passed the time staring out at the half full car park, yet then the sound of a pen scribbling on paper announced the guide's presence as Bernard began a bout of automatic writing.

A minute or so later, his hand ceased writing and the notepad was passed across to me. Switching on the torch, I focused my eyes on the scribbled sentences:

> **(He, BA) Is practising the (magical) art and carry(ing) to extreme psychic level. Sees water as Mercury. Is using the crystal as Dee on table of many colours. Talbot killed himself. Jumped from window. No contact is possible with him. The table is on many seals as Dee. Uses the Elder of URIEL. Knows of involvement with Glaston. Tries to contact many of the departed souls of the art. Table of many colours stands on seals. Draws the energies. Mind power is very strong. Knows much of ancient laws and Rosicrucian**

Treatise.
Energy flow at well now very dark.

It was interesting information, although it did not really tell us what was going on at the well, or what we had to do when we got there.

Still, it was now quite clear that the earlier mention of a man named 'Talbot' *had been* a reference to Dee's sidekick, Edward Kelly. I vaguely recalled reading about him killing himself whilst trying to escape out of the window of a prison. I knew too that Dee and Kelly had used magical seals to call upon the denizens of the spirit world. These had been written in a strange script known as the Enochian or Angelic alphabet, which had originally been conveyed to the pair during their psychic communications. Among the most important contacts they had made was with a supernatural entity named Uriel, the archangel who presided over the elemental power of Earth.

So, BA not only believed he was in mental empathy with Dee, he also used the Elizabethan magus' Enochian system to call upon the same denizens of the spirit world, including the archangel Uriel.

The reference in the text to a 'table of many colours', standing on seals, meant nothing to either of us. But why shouldn't Dee and Kelly have used a table of this description on which to stand their crystal ball or shew-stone used for the psychic communications.

Other than this, the automatic script was not enough. We needed more specific information from the spirit guide.

Bernard accepted this and so, once more, sat with his pen poised over a clean page in his notepad.

The car clock showed that the time was now 10.30 pm.

The pen in the psychic's hand began to scribble once again. After it had come to an abrupt halt, he handed the notebook back to me.

At least we had an answer. I switched on the torch and read the message:

To undo the Mercuric black flow (at the well) you must,

***must* use the opposite force for a short duration. You must use gold and the heavenly body.**

This time, although the communication was short, it told me precisely what we needed to do when we arrived at the well.

The Running Well, as I had pointed out in *The Running Well Mystery,* was predominantly associated with the power, influence and worship of the moon which, in Western mystical tradition, was represented by a female deity. So-called lunar sites included nearly all sacred and mystical places connected with water, such as springs, holy wells, waterfalls and lakes. Each one exuded subtle energies strongly female and lunar in nature, which a good psychic would see and experience as silvery-blue in colour, and slow and graceful in movement. Such sites would usually be associated with a female deity or guardian figure who would be seen by a perceptive psychic like Bernard.

Other types of site, such as standing stones, stone circles, dolmens, mounds and holy hills, were usually attributed to the moon's equal and opposite force — the sun. Such places were spoken of as male and solar in aspect and usually possessed a purpose, tradition and psychic influence associated with the sun and solar worship. They were usually presided over by male deities and spirit guardians. A good psychic would see these solar energies as either gold or orangy-yellow in colour, and very fast and radiant in movement.

Bearing all this in mind, it appeared as if the Black Alchemist had deliberately invoked, harnessed, then changed the Running Well's inherent lunar energies to give him the necessary psychic power and influence he needed to conduct his dark ritual. By doing so, he had apparently disharmonised and blackened the well's entire energy flow. Therefore, if Bernard and I had reached the well and nonchalantly attuned to the site's inherent lunar energies, we would have instantly fallen within the grip of the Black Alchemist's ritual trap.

The message seemed clear. We were to flood the site with its equal and opposite force — golden solar energy which could, I knew, be manufactured in the human body and sent out into the landscape by means of mental visualisation. An accurate psychic would actually be able to see these energies pouring out of a person's aura. This Bernard had witnessed during May the previous year when I had poured golden-coloured light from my body into Burlough Castle in an attempt to restore Ogmor's lost strength.

One of the most powerful forms of psychic 'solar' energy could be seen, or visualised, as a kind of burning, reddy-gold fire. In mystical terms, this 'divine fire' was controlled by Michael, the archangel who governed the elemental force of Fire. This energy was usually visualised by psychics and occultists in association with a great flaming sword of power; precisely the image Bernard had clairvoyantly seen earlier that evening as we had passed through the country lanes of South Hanningfield.

The Fire of Michael, as it was known, could be used for many purposes. It could be drawn around a place or a person to protect them from malevolent forces; it could be used to ritually purify or cleanse an animate or inanimate object or a site, and it could be used to completely destroy thought forms, place memories or localised energy fields associated with an object or a site.

It therefore seemed as if the best way to destroy BA's ritual trap, apparently waiting for us at the Running Well, was to invoke and draw down the Fire of Michael to burn and purify the site. However, I knew only too well that it would also destroy at least some of the thought forms, place memories and energy fields created over a period of perhaps two thousand or more years of religious and mystical devotion at the well. But it appeared to be the only way. The sacred site had already been desecrated and darkened to a state almost beyond repair, and it looked as if it was to be our business to sort out this mess.

Fifteen
The Blackened Well

In the darkness, Bernard's beige Ford Orion rolled to a halt outside the disused wooden barn next to Poplars Farm, on the border between the parishes of Runwell and East Hanningfield. A metal-hinged gate and a short walk across a sloping meadow was all that separated us from whatever lay ahead at the Running Well.

No cars were around, so it looked as if we might be alone after all. I thought of calling at Poplars Farm to see whether the occupiers had seen any other cars that evening. However, I resisted the temptation, as I did not feel they would appreciate answering the door to a leather-jacketed young man asking curious questions at eleven o'clock at night.

'I feel the best thing we can do is to try and attune to the well from here,' Bernard suggested, winding down his window to let out the cigarette smoke.

Agreeing, I sat with pen poised to paper as Bernard closed his eyes and began to concentrate his mind on our predicament.

Soon his mind picked out a clear vision. 'I see Cecilia by the side of the well.' There was a short pause. 'Is there a body buried at the well? I've said that before, haven't I?'

He had. Exactly one year to the day before on his only other visit to the site. On that occasion he had picked up the memory of a teenage girl who had often withdrawn to the calm serenity of the well to stare into its crystal-clear waters to gain glimpses of future events by the light of the full moon. The local people had regarded her as a witch and, one evening, as she had stood by the water's edge, she had been set upon, beaten to death and hurriedly buried very near to the well. Bernard had even given her full name and the date she had died.

'I see BA at the well,' he continued, breaking my train of thought. 'He's definitely been down there. I see him stirring the water in an anti-clockwise direction with a long, black stick . . . dark swirling energies pour out of the well. He's now quartering the water's surface . . . It will make each of the four church marker points stronger . . . I feel that somebody wants to get rid of us here at the well itself . . . There's a feeling of death; and fire for some reason . . . "A body will be found with a rope around its neck. A body will be found in a fire'."

His voice was becoming lower and more monotone — the first signs of a potentially dangerous trance-like condition. I had to stop him, so I shouted out his name.

'Don't worry,' he responded, opening his eyes. 'I'm okay. Those were the words BA said as he stood at the well: "A body will be found with a rope around its neck. A body will be found in a fire'."

It was a disturbing thought. I remembered the image Bernard had seen as we had travelled along the lanes of South Hanningfield — the body hanging by its neck from a noose strung over a tree. He wanted one of us to hang ourselves and the other to die in a fire. The thought sent a deathly chill down my spine. We had been correct, *the contents of the sealed black envelope did add up to a death threat.*

'Cecilia appears to be wearing a simple form of blue and white nun's habit,' he explained, quite unexpectedly. 'I think she was a nun at one time.'

Of course. One of the nun's of the medieval convent that had supposedly tended the well up until the time of King Henry VIII's Dissolution of the Monasteries. Many psychics who had visited the site had spoken of seeing ghostly nuns by the well.

Leaving the car, we climbed over the padlocked metal gate and began the stroll across the wet meadow towards the copse of mature trees that marked the position of the well. Being one of the high spots of South East Essex, the orange and white lights of Runwell, Wickford and beyond to the Thames Estuary and the North Downs of Kent, could be seen laid out across the countryside below us to the south-east. For a moment, we stopped and admired the scenic view before continuing on our way.

The Running Well was situated in a deep earthen hollow concealed completely within a tree-lined, triangular piece of land between three fields. Entering into the thick undergrowth, a beautiful site greeted the visitor. A large concrete platform, complete with steps down into the well, complemented the large, half moon-shaped expanse of water some eight feet square. The clear water originated from a spring positioned at the base of the well which, it was said, had never been known to fail.

Yet it was not the virtues of the well that we were there to admire on this occasion. Other more pressing matters filled our minds as we both simultaneously came to a halt some twenty or so yards from the treeline.

Something stood between us and the well. A black amorphous form shimmered above the ground within the wide gateway in the hedgerow directly in front of us.

'Do you see that?' he asked.

So he could see it as well. I knew what I could see; but what about him?

'A dark human-like shape between the gap.'

The same.

It was almost certainly a thought form set up by the Black Alchemist to guard the gateway through which he knew we would have to pass if we wanted to reach the well. If this was so, then he had obviously not bargained on the fact that *both* of us would see it.

Bernard seconded my evaluation. 'I feel that the idea was for us to have inadvertently come into contact with that thing. This would then have acted like a trigger mechanism which would have set off whatever lay in store for us in the well hollow itself.'

We could go no further. The whole site would have to be consumed by the Fire of Michael from that very spot. So, as we raised our arms, I called upon the archangel to deliver his divine fire to the Running Well by reaching down and touching the site with his flaming sword. In my mind's eye, I pictured a huge pillar of fire slowly descending out of the sky on to the group of trees surrounding the holy well. Suddenly, the waters burst into flames — as if they were petrol being ignited — which consumed, first the surrounding trees, then the entire undergrowth and earthen banks within the well hollow until the whole site was a mass of fierce psychic fire. As the flames rose above treetop level, they began to encircle the site as a cloud of reddy-gold light which gradually spiralled up into the air like a miniature tornado.

Bernard could see the whole light display with his eyes firmly open, as if the site *really was on fire. And to him it was real.* The visualisation ritual was working.

When the fire died away, I opened my eyes and asked Bernard how the sight now looked on a psychic level. At that moment, I swear I saw a tiny ball of white light flash past me, coming from the direction of the well.

'I've been seeing them for some minutes now,' he coolly announced. 'Tiny balls of bluey-white light flitting about in every direction, very close to the ground. The well's energies are in a complete frenzy, I can tell you.'

The Fire of Michael had obviously worked. It had destroyed

As Bernard and the author approached the Running Well, which lay behind the treeline, a dark amorphous form was seen suspended between the gap in the hedgerow to the right of the picture.

the Black Alchemist's ritual trap and the thought form that had guarded the gateway between the two fields; for that had now gone.

We continued through the gap and turned left to walk the final few yards up to the well. Peering through the undergrowth, I shone the torchlight on to the water's surface. Stuck upright in the mud by the edge of the concrete platform was a long black stick, cut from a tree, the bottom six inches of which were still wet. It had been deliberately placed there and, unless it happened to be a bizarre coincidence, then there seemed little doubt that this was the stick that the Black Alchemist had used to stir the well only shortly beforehand.

Stepping down on to the platform, we used the torchlight to explore every conceivable hiding place for any further evidence of our adversary's presence at the well.

'I feel he spent some time here,' Bernard revealed, staring into the shimmering water. 'Other than that, I don't get anything. The energies here really are all over the place.'

Our visualisation ritual had completely destroyed not only the Black Alchemist's own ritual, but also the site's place memories, including the very memory of his presence at the well. The only answer would be for us to move out into the field, away from the site's immediate psychic influence, where the Fire of Michael had not destroyed any of the localised energy matrix. Maybe the memory of the Black Alchemist's visit to the well would still be available there.

Agreeing, Bernard moved back out into the open as I followed close behind. After a distance of some twenty yards we stopped and turned back to face the well.

The psychic concentrated once again. 'I now see someone at the well. An energy form there. It *was* definitely today. He came across the fields, not from where we are parked.'

This was an interesting statement as it implied that the Black Alchemist had walked across the fields from Runwell to the Running Well in the pitch darkness. It was a difficult enough task during the daytime, and surely, near impossible at night. Still, if that was what Bernard felt, then I would have to accept his word.

Bernard could still picture the Black Alchemist at the well: 'He stands . . . near the water's edge . . . says words: "Mercury" something . . . "in that silvery flow" . . . "Look there" . . . a change in the water . . . more words: "Two shall end as my sword . . ." Something about a sword . . . I see him put something into the water.'

That was it. Opening his eyes, he looked at me and smiled as we both said in unison: 'It's in the water!'

Rushing back across to the well hollow, I got on to my hands and knees, took off my leather jacket, rolled up the sleeves of my jumper and put my hand into the icy-cold water. Carefully, my fingers explored the top of the first underwater step, some nine inches below the surface. I had a good idea what I was looking for as I touched the rotting leaves, little stones and slimy algae. First, I found only an old horseshoe, left there as a votive offering by some past visitor to the site. But then I touched it — a length of stone, similar in size and shape to those usually planted by the Black Alchemist.

Pulling it out of the water, I shone the torchlight on to the new find. Yes, this was definitely what we were after — a shaped stone, some four inches in length and an inch in width. It had been painted black, although it bore none of the usual stylised magical symbols found on the stone spearheads. In their place were two orangy-red crystals, each about one half an inch in diameter, which had been glued — with something like Evostick — into hollowed out sockets positioned side-by-side on one of the stone's edges. They were the same as the crystals found in the black envelopes, although upon touching one with my finger, it immediately fragmented and left a strong amber-coloured stain across my hand. They were obviously soluble chemical crystals and not rock crystals as I had first suspected.

What if the chemical was poisonous? The thought crossed my mind, so I popped the crystal fragments into my jacket pocket and decided not to eat anything until I had washed my hands, just in case.

It was not difficult to work out that the two orangy-red crystals, each gradually melting into the sacred well water,

Within the Running Well the author discovered the black-painted stone with the two orangy-red crystals glued into its edge.

in some way represented Bernard and I. Of that I was pretty sure.

Pulling up outside my parents' home around 11.45pm, I gathered together my bits and pieces and told Bernard I would ring him the next day.

Yet, as I went to get out, he turned to me with a concerned expression on his face. 'Do you know, I get the feeling that, not only is the Black Alchemist still in the area, he is trying to see what we are up to at this moment using a crystal ball or shew-stone, like Dee.'

He fidgeted, as if the impression disturbed him, before continuing on: 'I see a crystal ball on a table and he is staring into it.'

Where was he staying?

'I don't know. A guest house or a hotel, I suppose.'

He revved the engine as I climbed out of the passenger seat.

'He's trying to follow our movements, I think.'

They were unnerving words which, if true, meant that he could strike again that very night. Somewhat concerned, I said goodnight to the psychic.

Did he know that Bernard had just dropped me off and that I was now back home? I hoped not.

As Bernard's car disappeared out of sight, I retired into the house and searched around for an old shoebox I had somewhere. Within it, I placed the black envelope, with its macabre contents, and the four retrieved stones found that evening, before finding space for it in the garden shed. There was no way that I was going to sleep with that lot in the house, not for a few days at least!

Afterwards, I strolled back into the front garden and stood gazing down the road at the various cars parked along St Davids Way. The air was still and quite mild for that time of year.

I needed to think; to put into perspective the events of that evening. It all seemed absurd. Bernard and I were supposedly under the threat of death from a psychopathic black magician who had given us just nine nights to live.

I told myself this wasn't really happening; but, of course, it was. If the Black Alchemist had his way then Bernard and I would be dead by Wednesday, 15th October. So how were we to react? Should I believe the threat at face value, or was it all just a crazy idea that the shadowy figure did not intend to carry through? Could there be any other, more mundane solutions to this whole affair?

Perhaps we had over-reacted. No, that was a stupid thought. We had discovered four more psychically-charged stones, a sealed black envelope addressed to me, and a stick, still wet, seemingly used by the Black Alchemist to stir the water at the well. None of these were imagination.

More urgent thoughts now entered my mind. If he wanted to kill us, then why had he not done so before? Okay, so he did not appear to possess Bernard's name and address, but he certainly knew mine. Surely it would have been far easier for him to have blown my head off with a sawn-off shotgun instead of setting up a black magic curse with a slow burning, nine night fuse.

The two orangy-red crystals were obviously meant to have gradually dissolved within the well's crystal-clear spring water. So, had he anticipated our discovery of this stone? I thought not. It appeared as if the plan was for us to have stumbled into the psychic trap by attuning to the well's inherent lunar energies. But it had not worked, so, was the man stupid? Or did he not realise the extent of Bernard's acute psychic ability?

One nagging question did demand an immediate answer: why should the Black Alchemist want the pair of us dead? However warped and disturbed the man was, surely he would not be foolish enough to want us dead simply because we had interfered with his alchemical transmutation. No, there had to be more to it than that. Perhaps he believed that we knew more about his clandestine activities than we actually did. Maybe there were other, more sinister reasons for his actions.

All I could say for sure was that the next eight days would be the most intense, yet intriguing of my life.

Moving back into the bungalow, I made sure that the back door was locked before retiring into my bedroom. Placing Bernard's penknife on the bedside table, I stared up at my bookshelves. I was looking for something which might contain relevant information on the life of Dr John Dee and his sidekick, Edward Kelly.

One book, *Alchemy: Ancient and Modern,* written by H. Stanley Redgrove (EP Publishing Ltd., Wakefield, Yorkshire, 1973), told how Kelly had died from a fall incurred whilst attempting to escape from a prison. Apparently, the Emperor Rudolph of Poland had imprisoned Kelly on condition that he would only be released if he either produced a substantial quantity of alchemical gold, or revealed the transmutation secret of alchemy. He was, however, released in 1593, but died two years later, following a second imprisonment under the same emperor.

Too tired to peruse the bookshelves for any further confirmatory material on the lives of the Elizabethan occultist and his sidekick, I decided to call it a day and try to get some sleep.

Sixteen
Nine Nights to Live

Tuesday, 7th October, 1986. On several occasions during the night I awoke from chaotic dreams and nightmares concerning the Black Alchemist. With these came an irritating stress headache which I could not shake off.

Tense stress pains across the brow of my head still persisted when I finally got up around 7.30 am. Tired, drained and exhausted, I went off to work. Yet, however much I tried, I could not concentrate properly. Every time I attempted to listen to the advertising and journalistic needs of the shopkeepers around Leigh-on-Sea, I found my mind wandering back to the mystifying events of the previous evening.

Finally giving up around late morning, I returned to the office and tried to find out where I could check out the composition of the orangy-red crystals. News editor, Jonathan Guy, suggested I take them to his old school, Belfairs High School. One of the chemistry teachers would take a look at them, he was sure.

At lunchtime I left the crystals and the folded up black envelope with a Mr Paul Lark, one of the science teachers at Belfairs. It would take a couple of days, he said, so asked me to return for the results on Thursday morning.

I telephoned Bernard around 7.30 pm that evening to find out how his day had gone.

'Headachey,' he had answered, in a subdued manner. 'I feel

drained and exhausted. I'm going to lay low for a while. Regain my physical and mental strength.'

Any new psychic information?

'No. I shan't be attuning to anything. I'm shutting off my mind completely. I don't need the hassle. I'll give you a ring if anything happens.'

Replacing the receiver, I decided it was time to take a closer look at the various inscribed stones discovered the previous evening.

Retrieving the shoebox from the shed, I carried it into the house and placed it on the floor next to my writing desk and took out the first stone for study. Switching on the adjustable table lamp, a bright glow illuminated the inscribed stone discovered in Runwell churchyard. It was a length of unfashioned grey shale, some five inches long. Along one of its three faces were, in order, an inscribed number 2; a symbol which looked as if it was a question mark, and a large matchstick man with its head severed from its body. I put it away.

Next, I took out the thin length of slate removed from the side of the marble slab below the tower of Rettendon church. It had been fashioned to resemble either a crude spearhead or a sword tip, and was, like the Runwell stone, five inches in length and around one inch in width.

Studying it closely, I realised something almost instantly, but brought out the Lullington spearhead just to make sure of my thoughts. Yes, I was right, the symbols on one side of the Rettendon stone were identical to those inscribed on the

The inscribed stone found in Runwell churchyard showed a matchstick man with its head severed from its body.

The series of symbols on one side of the Rettendon stone were found to be identical to those inscribed on the Lullington spearhead.

spearhead found in Lullington churchyard eighteen months before. Yet those on this new spearhead were far clearer and more accurately inscribed than those of the Lullington stone.

And this time around some of the symbols appeared to be more familiar. For instance, there were three distinctive words written in a kind of joined-up script. Before, these had looked totally unfamiliar, a factor which had led Nigel Pennick to consider them to be characters from a Bardic or Druidic alphabet. Not so any more, they now looked like words composed of Greek characters; so I would have to get them checked out at some point. However, their presence on both the Lullington and Rettendon spearheads certainly lent weight to our belief that the Black Alchemist was using Graeco-Egyptian alchemy and magic from the time of Zosimos of Panopolis, who lived in Egypt during the fourth century AD.

Other symbols also appeared to make some sort of sense at last. Like the eleventh character in from the left. It was, perhaps, the astrological symbol used to represent the zodiacal influence of Leo. And the eighth character in, that looked like a Greek epsilon, the letter E in the English alphabet. The first two characters in the sequence were familiar as well; they seemed to be the letters C and H, locked together to form some sort of personal monogram. A thought passed through my mind: were they the initials of the Black Alchemist?

I was making progress. However, the rest of the symbols still remained a mystery. They did not belong to any magical alphabet I had ever come across before in my travels.

On the other side of the Rettendon spearhead was a further series of symbolic images. Nearest the tip, reading downwards,

The inscribed slate spearhead found in Rettendon churchyard depicted, on one side, the ritual trap set up at the Running Well.

was a large number 1 in the same style as the number 2 on the Runwell stone. Below this was a large equilateral triangle, point downwards, with an anti-clockwise heliacal spiral radiating out from its centre until it broke free of the triangle and trailed off as a line down towards the base of the stone. At the tail of this line was the mystical symbol used to represent the planetary influence of Mercury. This had been diagonally quartered through its arms with zig-zagging lines.

An interpretation of this arrangement of symbols appeared easy enough. The triangle, I felt sure, represented two things. Firstly, it was the alchemical symbol for the element of Water, and secondly, it symbolised the small triangular piece of land in which the Running Well was situated. The Mercury symbol, and the anti-clockwise spiral, represented the Mercurial energy flow and the Ring of Darkness with its epicentre at the Running Well. The zig-zagging cross through the Mercury symbol showed how by fixing the ritual at the four marker churches, the ritual trap had been strengthened.

What the number 1 meant, I could not say. Perhaps it indicated that Rettendon was the first of the four churches he had visited in the Ring of Darkness ritual. Yet, if this was so, and the four churches had been set up by the Black Alchemist in an anti-clockwise direction, then it would have made

Runwell church the fourth of the four marker points. However, the number of that stone was 2, so the theory did not make sense.[1]

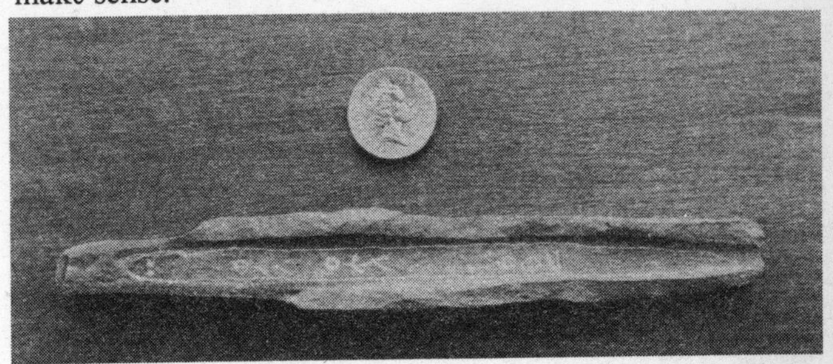

Within the body of a serpent inscribed on the stone found in Downham churchyard was the word 'soon'; a reference, it seemed, to the intended fruition of the death threat.

Putting away the Rettendon spearhead, I pulled out the inscribed stone retrieved from the ground beneath the east wall of Downham church. It measured nearly seven inches in length and was made out of a naturally-shaped piece of grey shale. One of its faces was rounded, whilst the other side contained a natural channel which looked as if it may have once contained a fossil of some sort; possibly a piece of petrified wood.

In the hollowed-out face was, as I had already noted, a scratched outline of a long serpent or snake with two eyes. Inside its body were two small matchstick men which, I presumed, represented Bernard and I. Below these was the word 'Soon'! The message seemed clear: it would not be long before the two of us had been ensnared in the Black Alchemist's ritual trap, set up and waiting for us at the Running Well.

On the other, rounded face of the stone were six of the usual Black Alchemist-style symbols scratched into a narrow flat surface.

Last up was the black-painted stone, with its two orangy-red crystals glued into gouged out sockets, retrieved from the Running Well.

It had no inscribed symbols. However, scraping away some of the black gloss paint on its surface, I had a mild surprise. This one was not made of shale. Showing through was a greeny-grey rock which I recognised as greensand, a sedimentary rock commonly found in the southern counties of England.

Forgetting the inscribed stones for a moment, I spent the next few hours with a pen held over my diary, trying to write up the events of the previous evening. But it was impossible. I just was not in the correct mood. A stress headache still dominated my left temple and I felt very tired.

The diary would have to wait until another day. For the moment, all I wanted to do was go to sleep.

Wednesday, 8th October. The day was a little more productive workwise, but uneventful in other ways.

At home that evening I continued the diary. And then the telephone rang. It was Bernard. Since he hardly ever telephoned, something had obviously happened.

'I've got to ask you for permission to be at the Running Well during the evening of Tuesday, 14th October,' he revealed, almost light-heartedly.

That was the last of the nine nights before the Black Alchemist's death threat deadline. Of course he could be at the well that evening. By why ask me?

'I'll explain,' he started. 'Yesterday I said I would not attempt to attune to the BA problem until I had fully regained my strength. However, I woke up this morning with a very clear psychic impression. I have been told that, on the final night before the deadline, soon after sunset, I should be at the well ready for some kind of confrontation.'

Confrontation? What sort of confrontation?

'It was not made clear. All I get is that we can expect trouble, and for this reason we should be suitably prepared on both levels.'

So, it was all going to kick off the following Tuesday

evening. Anything might happen. Psychic battles. Car loads of hoods turning up with sawn-off shotguns. Anything. Perhaps I should enlist the help of a few bodyguards?

'I don't know,' he laughed. 'I really don't. All the message stated was that before I could go up there I had to ask the chosen guardian and protector of the Running Well for permission to be there. So that's you, isn't it?'

Me? Possibly. Psychic guardians of sacred sites were a prominent feature in questing lore which claimed that each ancient or mystical site possessed a spirit guardian, as well as a human guardian. Such characters, it was said, were chosen by the spirit guardian and would have to possess certain qualities. They should be associated with the site, and should live and work very close to the land. Obviously, due to the extensive restoration work and research I had carried out at the well over the years, Bernard had presumed that I was the physical guardian of the site; which would not have amused the owner of the estate. Anyway, if I *was* the site guardian, then he could willingly have permission to be at the well.

'I get the feeling that I will have to sit within a circle of protection inside the well hollow and attune to the surrounding area on a psychic level,' he explained. 'You, I think, will have to keep a watch over the area in readiness for any possible interference on a physical level. Which I hope there won't be.'

How long would all this take?

'No idea. Some hours, I should think.'

I would look forward to it!

'I also believe that I now know a little more about the ritual BA carried out at the well,' he added. 'It involved the coming together of two different types of energy, both associated with the influence of Mercury, for some reason. One of these seems to be male, whilst the other appears to be female. The resultant effect was some kind of Mercurial force which manifested at the well as a humanoid thought form.'

The process did not sound familiar. Was it connected with alchemy?

'Yes, I think so. I was also told that this Mercuric entity was the thought form manifestation we encountered in the gap between the hedgerow.'

It made sense. Thought forms could undoubtedly be created through magic rituals. Perhaps the Black Alchemist had used this particular formula to manifest the entity to complete his plans at the well. By coming into contact with the thought form we were obviously meant to have triggered off some kind of ritual ensnarement which could have had very nasty consequences. Well, for Bernard at least.

Replacing the receiver, I pulled out my current 'bible' of alchemical knowledge: *The Arts of the Alchemists,* by C.A.Burland (Wiedenfeld and Nicolson, London, 1967), and flicked through its index for any references to alchemical Mercury.

To me, alchemy was a very complex and confusing science. Yet despite this, I did manage to discover one reference to the process Bernard had described. It seemed to concern a stage in the alchemical transmutation where a liquid solution, which included a base metal such as lead, was mixed with a deposit of liquid mercury. If the desired result of the act was achieved, then the mixture separated out into two substances, one a white liquid, which the alchemists referred to as Athoeter, or the Mercurial water, and the other, a deep red tincture. These substances were also known as the White and Red Mercuries which, the alchemists believed, corresponded respectively to the force of Luna (ie. the moon), the divine mother, and Sol (the sun), the divine father.

When eventually brought back together, these two substances allegedly formed a mixture described as a deep amber-gold liquid, known as the Philosopher's Gold. This new substance was considered to be a potent elixir, or life retainer, and an essential catalyst used in the ultimate stages of the alchemical transmutation. It was also the magical liquid used to form an alchemical entity or spirit known as the Mercurius; seemingly some kind of thought form used during the alchemical operation.

There was much more, but it got a bit complicated after that, even with at least three readings! However, the formation of the deep amber liquid, the so-called Philosopher's Gold, using the White and Red Mercuries, along with its use to breathe life into the Mercurius spirit, all appeared to make sense of Bernard's impressions.

The Philosopher's Gold reminded me of the amber-coloured stain left on my hand after I had touched the orangy-red crystals set into the stone pulled out of the Running Well. Quite obviously, the two crystals were meant to have gradually dissolved into the pure spring water to form an amber-coloured liquid. Was it possible, therefore, that the Black Alchemist had symbolically viewed the well water and the site's own inherent, female lunar energies as the White Mercury, the force of Luna, the divine mother? If so, then had he symbolically added to this, the Red Mercury, the force of Sol, the divine father, in the form of the orangy-red crystals, so that he could change the well water into the amber-coloured Philosopher's Gold? Then, once this had been accomplished, had he then used the waters' new psychic influence to breathe life into his own Mercurius; the dark thought form we had encountered in the gap by the well? It seemed so.

Yet, in comparison with the rest of Bernard's telephone conversation, the intricacies of the Black Alchemist's ritual at the Running Well seemed insignificant. The direct confrontation with him which, from the outset, had appeared inevitable at some stage, now looked more likely than ever before. In just six days Bernard and I could come face-to-face with our ultimate adversary for the very first time. But would the man dare to venture back into our territory in the knowledge that we could be waiting for him? Bernard thought it possible. If he really did intend to eliminate us by stringing one of us up and burning the other, then this could only really be achieved by physical means.

Seventeen
Back to School

Thursday, 9th October, 1986. A lady teacher, marking an untidy pile of school exercise books, got up to make me a cup of coffee, as I waited patiently in the staff room at Belfairs High School to see Mr Paul Lark. He had asked me to return just before the 10.30 break for the results of the crystal analysis.

Minutes later, the continuous drone of the school bell indicated breaktime and Mr Lark appeared in the doorway.

He greeted me with a polite smile.

'Oh, er, would you come this way, Andy,' he said, politely beckoning me into the corridor.

I followed. With kids scurrying in every direction, I was led up a staircase to the relative tranquility of a chemistry laboratory. Clear memories of my own schooldays, carrying out childish pranks and dangerous experiments behind the teacher's back, came flooding back.

'It's not a dangerous substance,' the teacher began, handing me back the folded black envelope and a small glass bottle containing the remaining crystals. 'They are Ammonium Dichlorate; which is strange in itself as, to my knowledge, it can only be obtained in a powdered form from industrial laboratories. These crystals must have been grown from a super-saturated solution.'

Like the Copper Sulphate crystals I used to grow in large flat bowls up in the shed. But what would such crystals be used for?

'Pyrotechnics mainly,' he explained. 'Ammonium Dichlorate is an active ingredient of indoor fireworks. Have you heard of a firework called Snake in the Grass?

I hadn't.

'When heated, the powder ignites and burns violently, giving off an irritating dust which leaves a film of black ash wherever it falls.' He moved away. 'We have a simple experiment we show the classes to demonstrate its pyrotechnic properties. Would you like to see it?'

I said I would as Mr Lark filled a beaten metal crucible with powdered Ammonium Dichlorate and placed it on a stand over a bunsen burner. Within seconds of lighting the hissing jet of gas, the powder ignited with a ferocious flame which quickly reduced the entire contents of the bowl to a mass of grey ash, and left a bellowing cloud of dust particles wafting about in the air.

'You see what I mean about the irritating dust,' he exclaimed, running his fingers across the thin, dark film now beginning to cover the bench top, before continuing to expound upon the properties of the chemical in question.

Yet my mind was on the Black Alchemist. Why had he chosen to put Ammonium Dichlorate crystals inside the sealed black envelopes? I felt I now understood why he had used these orangy-red crystals at the well, but why had he used them as a psychic link between him and us? Why had he not used real rock crystals of a similar colour, such as garnet or topaz, for instance? Perhaps they were too expensive. And what connection, if any, was there between Ammonium Dichlorate and alchemy? I had to ask the teacher.

'Alchemy,' he repeated, with some curiosity. 'I don't know anything about alchemy, but we can look it up.'

He disappeared out of sight into a store room and returned with an encyclopedia of chemicals. He searched through its alphabetical listing for Ammonium Dichlorate and, upon finding it, read the entry out aloud.

There was no mention of alchemy. All I could conclude was that the Black Alchemist had used this crystalline substance as some sort of substitute for the so-called Red Mercury. Other than this, its purpose would have to remain a complete mystery.

Caroline Wise, Alan Cleaver, and another friend, John Merron, came down from London that evening to hear about the latest developments in the Black Alchemist affair. Having picked me up from my parents' home, I suggested that we drive out to The Downham Arms; the pub where, only three days before, Bernard and I had sat and opened the sealed black envelope.

Here, amid the crowds of local youths and a noisy jukebox, I told them the whole story; the Ring of Darkness, the discovery of the inscribed stones and the contents of the sealed black envelope. An hour later, with the story brought up to date, I bought a round of drinks and waited for their comments.

All three were numbed and disturbed by the quest's implications and anxious questions were posed to make sure that Bernard and I knew exactly what we were doing.

Satisfied with my answers, the conversation moved on to other aspects of the quest, including the involvement of the Elizabethan magus, Dr John Dee, and his psychic sidekick, Edward Kelly. According to Bernard's psychic material, received in the car park of that very pub, Dee had supposedly placed his crystal ball, or dark-glassed scrying mirror, on a special table on which were magical seals and designs of many colours. However, so far I had been unable to trace whether any such table had ever existed.

Almost in unison, my three companions smiled and announced that such a table *had* definitely existed.

'There's even a picture of it in a booklet which I'm sure you must have,' Caroline cried out, almost as if she could not believe my ignorance in the matter. 'You were sent a review copy of Mog's *Strange Oxford,* weren't you?'

Yes, I was. Mog was Chris Morgan, the booklet's editor, although I could not recall seeing any references to a table which had once belonged to Dee. Still, it could easily be checked when I got home later that night. For the moment though, I looked a little foolish with everyone present knowing about this blessed table, except for me.

'So, what will you do on Tuesday evening,' Caroline asked, swallowing another gulp of Pils lager. It was a question she knew was forbidden.

By that time I had already decided not to reveal to anyone what Bernard and I would be up to that night. The reasoning behind this possibly foolhardy move was to ensure that if anyone did turn up at the well whilst we were there, then it was not because our intentions had been leaked to the wrong people.

The three accepted my silence on the matter.

Flicking through my copy of *Strange Oxford,* I quickly found the reference to Dee's so-called Holy Table. There was an old woodcut of the table top, and a brief resume of its description, purpose and history. It had been included in the booklet because a marble copy of Dee's wooden original — which no longer existed — could be seen in Oxford's science museum. The drawing of the Holy Table — the only one to have been preserved — had been lifted from a 1659 edition of Dee's spiritual diaries, edited by a man named Meric Casaubon.[1]

Although the reference in *Strange Oxford* was only brief, I soon discovered a little more about the Holy Table in a book entitled *The Heptarchia Mystica of John Dee,* edited by an old friend of mine named Robert Turner.[2]

A great deal of the book was devoted to Dee's Holy Table, including the procedure for setting it up for use in psychic communications. It described how the table's legs would be placed upon four magical seals made of wax, protected by wooden frames. A larger version of these seals — which were known as *Sigillum Æmeth* — would then be positioned on the centre of the table, surrounded by seven tablets of pure tin. The whole thing would then be draped in red silk cloth, shot with green, which would hang loosely over the sides of the table with a tassle at each corner. The crystal, or scrying mirror, would then be placed within a golden frame on the top of the red silk cloth, exactly over the position of the central *Sigillum Æmeth.*

As to the precise colour scheme of Dee's Holy Table, no one rightly knew. However, it did contain at least three distinctive colours — red, green and yellow — which might well be described as the 'many colours' referred to in Bernard's psychic message received in the car park of The Downham Arms.

Eighteen
Return to the Well

Tuesday, 14th October, 1986. Soon after seven o'clock a tap on the frosted glass of the kitchen door signalled Bernard's arrival. As he stood talking to my parents, I quickly gathered together a whole range of magical paraphernalia, including incense, essential oils, a sword and religious icons. Within minutes the pair of us were on our way to the Running Well; this time in my blue Ford Sierra.

Passing through the streets of Wickford, I brought Bernard up to date on the latest developments. Throughout the morning I had spoken to fellow questing sympathisers up and down the country, asking them all to bring Bernard and I to mind from 7.30 pm onwards that evening. I wanted them to each light a candle and periodically visualise white light travelling from them to us in the hope that it would give us a little added psychic strength and protection during our intended confrontation.

I had also visited the Running Well that afternoon. I wanted to see it in the daylight just to make sure that nothing was out of place and no beige Escort Mk IIIs were hanging around the area. However, everything was as we had left it the previous week, except for the long stick apparently used by the Black Alchemist to stir the water during his ritual there. That was found floating in the well, so I just fished it out and stuck it upright into the mud at the side of the well.

'Kids probably,' Bernard concluded, as the car passed along Wickford High Street.

I agreed. What about him? Had he picked up any further psychic material?

'No, not a thing,' he said with a sigh. 'Even at this eleventh hour. And it hasn't been for lack of trying, either. I've been trying to attune to the situation all day, but on each occasion the airwaves have been silent. It's really peculiar, almost like some sort of radio blackout before a major military confrontation.'

So he still had no idea what we were to do or what we might expect to find when we reached the well?

'No. We shall just have to wait and see what happens.'

A dreamy, low-lying mist had hung like a white shroud over the flat Essex landscape for most of the day, but this had now disintegrated to leave a dull overcast sky. The prospect of rain was inevitable.

Several minutes later the car turned into the private road which led down to Poplars Farm. Passing this on the right, we continued on the extra 100 or so yards and came to a halt on the concrete foundations of an old cowshed used by visitors to the well as a makeshift car park. No other vehicles were around, so it looked as if we were on our own.

Before we left the sanctity of the car, I emphasised the need to carry out our normal protection ritual. For once we had climbed over that metal gate and entered the field, we would be within the influence of the well's energies and therefore vulnerable to any psychic attack.

'If you want,' Bernard responded, almost amused by my suggestion.

But it *had* to be done, as there was no way I wanted any repeat performances of the nasty scenes I had witnessed at Lullington and Downham.

He accepted this, and with the ritual complete, I locked up the car and joined Bernard who was already climbing over the gate.

Strolling across the meadow, trying to follow the footpath through the wet grass, a drop of rain on my forehead made me glance up at the dark, overcast sky. I hoped it would keep off, for a while at least. Further on, I stared hesitantly towards the gap in the hedgerow where, only the previous week, the black amorphous thought form had awaited our arrival. There was nothing there now. In fact, the whole atmosphere around the well appeared to be one more of calmness than oppression.

However, psychic impressions were not my concern that evening. I would leave that to Bernard. My job was physical protection and surveillance, I reminded myself, as I began to carefully scan every dark corner, distant field and silhouetted treeline for any sign of movement.

Reaching the well, Bernard shone the torchlight through the undergrowth into the hollow. No one was present so, with some slight apprehension, we pushed through the nettles and brambles and edged our way down the steps on to the square concrete platform. The stick still stood upright in the soft mud by the side of the well. No one had been there since my visit that afternoon.

Quickly, we set up a psychic circle of protection using crystals and a further visualisation ritual. An incense associated with the element of Water was then placed into an earthenware bowl and ignited on top of a small round charcoal block. This would clear the air of any unwanted psychic influences, or so it was believed in questing lore. Following this, two green candles — green being the colour which Bernard had deemed appropriate for the occasion — were then lit and positioned in candle holders, one each side of the incense burner.

With the circle complete, I left the psychic in the hollow, his notepad on a clipboard poised and ready in one hand, and a cigarette in the other. Emerging out of the undergrowth, I wandered off and sat beneath a large tree next to the gap between the two fields. From here I could keep a vigilant watch over the surrounding landscape without any obstruction to my view.

It started to rain. The sound of the droplets of water splattering down upon the leaves was broken only by the occasional rumble of a passing aircraft or a distant train. Once in a while I caught the distinctive aroma of the burning incense and, here and there, the smell of cigarette smoke wafting up from the well hollow.

Bernard flashed the torchlight on to his watch face and wrote down the time: 8.20 pm. He lit another cigarette in the false belief that it would keep him warm.

Nothing positive, but certain intuitive feelings were beginning to creep into his soul. He decided to record them, just in case:

> **Feeling a bit cold and wary of anything. Will have to write and scribble and hope to decode later. Strange energies here. Keep feeling a presence. Shivery. Letting mind drift by staring at the well.**

Then he saw, in his mind's eye, a curious and complicated symbol being carved on to a magical talisman of some sort. He sketched what he could see. It disappeared and was replaced by a second symbol. Yet before he was given the chance to draw it in any detail, it too vanished from his mind. He looked at his crude sketches and tried to make sense of them. No, he had not seen either symbol before, he decided.

An impression now explained what was going on. Their adversary was, it seemed, sitting down somewhere, carrying out a meditational ritual and drawing these symbols at that very moment. He focused his mind to get further clairvoyant pictures. It was a wood. Yes, that was it. The Black Alchemist was sitting in a wood. However, he did not feel close for some reason. Yet then came another, more disconcerting impression which he felt compelled to crystallise on paper:

> **Picking up very bad force. I hope it's what was left by BA (at the well the previous week) and not his close presence. Feeling frozen to the spot. Held in some 'field' of energy. Can't move!**

At that moment their minds became linked as one, allowing Bernard to involuntarily scribble down his adversary's very thoughts:

Rage comes as a beam, trampling the stone to dust, squeezing the forces into a first matter. Re-fix with mind. Add blood. The one shall spread beyond the places of my knowledge settling and growing amongst the roots, the woods, the trees and the streams. Place beneath the stones. Impregnate. Let it grow. Let it form. The master shall form. All white methods wrong. All teachings of the stone are despicable. I re-write.

As the scrawled automatic writing became almost uncontrollable, it suddenly changed from English into a strange foreign script which, at the same time, Bernard's clairvoyant eyes could see being engraved on to the edge of a snake or serpent curled into a circle, biting its own tail.[1]

Yet after only a dozen or so of these distinct foreign characters, he began to feel nauseated and frozen to the spot, so decided to promptly break off the communication and visualise the protective circle around the well. On his tongue he placed a few drops of a herbal essence known as the Rescue Remedy. It had been given to him earlier by Andy who said it could be used to prevent unwanted psychic energies from entering into the body. And it appeared to be working. Gradually, he started to return to his normal self again.

A few minutes passed as he tried to recover his lost strength. Linking in mind with the Black Alchemist had not been a clever thing to do, but somehow he had got away with it. But where was this wood he could see him in? It did not feel close; not even in the county. A smirk formed on Bernard's face. So the Black Alchemist had bottled out of returning to confront them face-to-face. It pleased him. Yet then, without warning, his train of thought was suddenly broken as he realised that he was no longer alone in the well hollow. Had Andy returned?

Turning around, an extraordinary sight startled him into an instant state of fear. A shimmering blue apparition; a radiant lady, dressed in a blue and white cowled nun's habit, now stood on the earthen bank behind the well, not twenty feet away.

It looked like the Virgin Mary. Perhaps it *was* the Virgin

Mary! Should he kneel? No, it was someone else. As he concentrated on her motionless, phosphorescent image, he scanned her form for a name. Cecilia. Yes, it was the blue lady whom he had first encountered in Rettendon churchyard the previous week. She had returned to aid them in their confrontation. He was sure of that.

Bernard just continued to stare, wondering how to react. Yet the glowing apparition merely remained still and silent, gazing serenely into his eyes. He felt scared, yet almost as if she sensed his fear, he began to experience a sensation of warmth, well-being and comfort emanating from her aura. It eased his mind.

Then natural inquisitiveness intervened. He wanted to know more about the nature of this strange, but beautiful blue lady. Who exactly was she?

An answer returned in the form of a gentle, melodic, yet authoritative female voice. 'My life was as a prioress to the shrine that served this holy place. Upon my death I chose to become an eternal guardian spirit of these sacred waters.'

Bernard glanced quickly at the calm surface of the water and understood her words. He did not write them down.

'My body was laid to rest in the church of Our Lady at Runwell, but I requested that my relics be gathered together and brought to this place. They did this for me and reburied them here.'[2]

With her soft words now came the awareness of a specific spot within the well hollow. He looked towards a certain tree and *knew* that somewhere beneath its roots her relics had been re-interred and still remained to that day.

Then, Bernard's eyes espied two huge hounds, like overgrown labradors, clambering down the bank into the well hollow to the left of where the blue lady was standing. They were heading in his direction. But were they psychic, or were they real? He became frightened.

Without further word, Cecilia glanced towards the sandy-coloured hounds and put out her right hand as if commanding them to halt. This they did, before vanishing on the spot.

Following this unexpected intrusion, the blue lady began to fade, although not before Bernard decided that her style of dress dated her life on earth to either the twelfth or thirteenth century AD. He also now knew why she had appeared to him. In some peculiar way, she was there to protect them from the full force of the Black Alchemist. It had been her site that he had defiled the previous week; and now that she had regained her full strength, she intended protecting those who had saved the well from this desecration.

The psychic felt grateful and, with the comforting knowledge that her presence was still around somewhere, he mentally thanked her for her help. More confident now, he decided to use the torchlight to examine even the darkest corners of the well hollow.

Interesting, but unconnected psychic images and impressions wafted in and out of his mind, like snatched reviews of the well's long-forgotten past.

He watched intrigued as a human hand reached out of the depths of the well's crystal clear water, before fading away.

A group of giggling young nuns came into view, huddled together, staring innocently into the starry surface of the well, engaged in a little forbidden amusement. They too soon vanished.

Then, an infinitely more sinister vision — the sight and sound of a teenage girl being set upon, clubbed to death and hurriedly buried by a group of frenzied, but frightened villagers who thought she was a witch. It was the body of the young girl he had twice before thought was buried near the well. To his utter relief, his psychic faculty quickly curtailed the imagery of this ugly scene.

Bernard now felt a little safer within the magical circle of protection, so began to visualise a green mist of energy spiralling upwards from the well and growing in power like a glowing tornado of psychic energy. This he then pictured spreading out like a widening ripple which touched, surrounded and engulfed the entire landscape within the Black Alchemist's Ring of Darkness, smothering the four unfortunate churches chosen for his black ritual. This, he felt, would help to restore and harmonise the subtle energy fields disturbed and damaged by their adversary's activities the previous week.

Even more confident of the situation, and feeling that he now had the Black Alchemist on the run, Bernard attempted to send out a few psychic thunderbolts in his direction, a sense of silliness having taken control of his actions. In his mind's eye he viewed green fireballs of light reaching BA, still sitting within the wood. As soon as he had done this, the overwhelming presence of his own spirit guide was felt close by and he was warned not to use unnecessary retaliation.

Then came another disconcerting incident. Bernard received the strong impression that a pair of dismembered hands were reaching towards his neck from directly behind him. Thankfully though, they were, he felt, beyond the circle of protection. Yet their presence was too strong to ignore. Even so, he could not bring himself to turn around to see what was going on. Eventually the sensation faded, leaving him at a loss to understand what had happened, aside from the feeling that it had been an unsuccessful attempt by something to break through the circle of protection.

Once again, a gentle air of calmness returned to the darkened setting. The tall flames on the two green candles, standing at the water's edge, still flickered about in the slight draught passing through the well hollow. However, the rising smoke from the earthenware incense burner had now ceased.

The stillness was then interrupted once more as Bernard again felt the growing presence of his own spirit guide, the Elizabethan alchemist. It seemed he wished to convey a message of some sort. The compulsion to write became an irritation in his right hand. So, putting pen to paper, his hand leapt into an unstoppable bout of scrawled, almost illegible automatic writing:

> **. . . I used my lifetime to perfect the Art. Many they called me a *soulfleur.*[3] The way is the way of the ancients. An abusing of the four grades of heat and the sacred laws of the Art. I tell you that no interest is shown in the teaching of the final stone with its accompanying knowledge of the mystics of old.**
>
> **It is found in the country, in the town, in all things created**

by God. Yet it is despised by all. Rich and poor handle it, but not one prizes it. Next to the soul it is the most precious thing upon earth and has the power to pull down kings and princes. It is cast away and rejected by all.[4] From black to white to red. Numerous varied are the steps along the path. Some say 7, some 12, some 20. Some even more. The (Philosopher's) stone is one, the medicine one, the vessel one. One the operation and one the method. *The great magistery,* I say.

The laws of the Art are capable of great variance, but the most successful of the works and those who formulated those reasonings were only interested in finding their own Red stone/God by overcoming the terrors and trials of the mind. The dedication was carried to the finality of what you will understand as Kether[5] or the highest unknowable in an attempt to bring into manifestation the final truth.

All works are hidden with many riddles because the trials are of a highly personal nature and so cannot be followed word by word. It is possible to stay with calcination, the black dark side of the dualist's treatise, to raise the mind through the 10 rooms,[6] the 32 steps[7] to reach the inner heights is possible on both sides. But on the dark (side) the end result will always be the same, the death of the practicer of this Art.

It may well be that this is the final step of the years of dwell with the serpent and toad. In your knowledge Neshama, Yecidah, Chia, Ain Soph.[8] A black crucifixion and resurrection of the anti-lord preparing the palace for the coronation.

It is hid within the 3 principles of *archeius* and *balsamum elementorium externum.* There is a continuation of the base within many trees within woods. *Caput corvi* and the *corpus invisible.*[9]

You must understand I can only give the reasoning from what I know of this. There is nothing of the righteous soul here (in the Black Alchemist), only the growing power of the *black magistery exorcista.* He works on chaos of the Earth, chaos of the Water, chaos of the Air, chaos of the Fire and

Magia Metaphysica, **the art of occult secrets. He also uses *pentacula* the signs on virgin paper, metals or stones inscribed with many sigils which are the conductors of arcane forces in the universe.**

In order to end the rising chaos you must use the strict Laws of the Teachings of your Lord. Use what methods you have well learnt. Use circles of your holy waters for your protection. Do not use evil vengeance (as you did earlier). You can use your method of colours incorporating elixir the essence of anything. *Graeca magia* art of making things appear which really were not in any existence. You should interpret *majus noster,* the lodestone to your aid of purification . . . Study the Cabala and make use.'

The pen stopped scribbling. His hand ached intensely. Anyway, there was no way he could have gone on without a break. He smiled as he realised the amount of time it would take to decipher this lot. Dozens of specialist books would be required to translate the entire message. Yet then, as if in response to this very thought, the Elizabethan alchemist returned to compel Bernard's hand to write again: 'You think of manuscripts?'

What happened next both amused and astounded him, for his hand began to set down the titles of several ancient manuscripts apparently concerning the alchemical and magical arts:

Abul Quesim al Iraq.
Aurora Aufore Artis.
Pretiosa Margarita Novella de Thesaro
ac Pretios simino.
Hermetic Musuesum.
Nei Pen of Ko Hung.
Amphitheatrum Sapientia Aterna
Viridorium Chymicum
Monas Hi(e)roglyphica

Only two of the titles made any sense to him: Henricus

Khunrath's 1609 work *Amphitheatrum Sapientia Aterna,* or *Amphitheatre of Eternal Wisdom,* and Dee's 1564 work *Monas Hieroglyphica.*[10]

Pacing about, he lit another cigarette and awaited Andy's imminent return. So what would happen next? It was becoming an intriguing evening, full of psychic surprises. But what about the Black Alchemist? What had happened to him? His intuition told him that BA would make no further moves that evening. Yet he still retained the impression that he was sitting quietly in a wood somewhere; in Kent. Kent? It came to him at that moment.

But then, yet another psychic interruption. Beyond the well hollow, in the field on its northern side, he overheard the sound of male voices, talking together and moving towards him. They were not speaking English. He listened. Was it Latin? He was not sure. A gut feeling informed him that they were a group of six Roman soldiers, an officer and five others, who were passing close to the edge of the well hollow. He could neither see them, nor understand their conversation. All he knew was that they were an inconsequential memory of an event which had taken place at that very spot nearly two thousand years beforehand.

Then came another presence, moving nearer and nearer. Footsteps sounded beyond the south side of the hollow. It did not feel hostile. He waited and hoped he knew what was going on.

Andy's face appeared through a corridor of overhanging branches, rising nettles and tall ferns, a smirk upon his face.

I had given it 45 minutes before calling it a day and returning to the well hollow to see how Bernard had been getting on. I found him standing on the platform, seemingly in good health, his notepad and clipboard in one hand, and a cigarette in the other.

So, what had happened?

'Pages of scribble,' was his reply, holding up the clipboard as proof of his statement.

And the Black Alchemist?

'Not here. Elsewhere. In some woods, I think, in Kent.' He looked at me as if I was going to object.

I did feel slightly disappointed. I was almost looking forward to some sort of confrontation in a strange sort of way. So what exactly *had* happened?

He told me.

Looking with the torchlight at the pages of automatic writing from the Elizabethan alchemist, I tried to quickly read them. It didn't seem to make much sense at all.

'I haven't bothered to look at it,' Bernard admitted, pacing about on the spot. 'It didn't seem to make much sense to me either.'

Where exactly was the Black Alchemist? Had he any ideas of the location of this wood in Kent?

He shook his head. 'I just don't know.' Then he stood still for a moment and stared into thin air. 'I now get two place-names — Monksdown and Mereworth. Where are they? They're woods, I think. Both in Kent somewhere. I reckon that's where he's been tonight.'

The names meant nothing to me. However, they could easily be checked in the road atlas I had in the car.

Several more minutes passed as I stood in the well hollow waiting to see if Bernard would come out with any further information.

Breaking the long silence, he cleared his throat. 'No, no more. Let's go.'

Accepting his word, I closed down the circle of protection and left the well hollow with Bernard close behind.

For a moment, he stopped and stared out into the field below the well.

What was it?

He shook his head and turned away. 'A white horse galloping around the meadow. Quite large.'

I looked at the darkened field, devoid of any visible or audible life. Yet I knew what he could see. It was the spirit of one of the other guardian figures of the well, a Romano-British mare goddess often seen by psychics visiting the well.

'Really?' he responded, as he walked away.

I soon found Mereworth in the road atlas. It was a Kent village a few miles north-east of Tonbridge. Just above it was a large wooded area known as Mereworth Woods. However, there was no mention of anywhere nearby called 'Monksdown.'

'I'm now picking up somewhere else, some more woods connected with the Black Alchemist's activities,' he revealed, flicking ash from his cigarette out of the side window of the Sierra, as we sat in the darkness by Poplars Farm.

'They're at a place in Sussex called Clapham,' he stated, with some slight hesitation. 'I see woods, with a very bad feeling attached to them. Something's been going on there; ritual, I think. I also see a church, reached down a long, winding road. Not a nice place at all.' He shook his shoulders as a shiver ran down his spine.

Clapham Wood. Near Worthing, in West Sussex. I knew the name from my days as a UFO investigator. Back in the mid 1970s I had travelled down to nearby Angmering to investigate various UFO sightings, some of which had been reported in the vicinity of the woods at Clapham.

Vague memories reminded me that Clapham Wood had also played host to a series of extraordinary paranormal mysteries around that time. These had included dogs mysteriously disappearing or going mad; strange footprints being found, and visitors to the woods feeling unaccountable presences and atmospheres. There was also something about a horse vanishing into thin air, if I remembered rightly.

Yet, despite all these stories, I could recall none which had mentioned anything about black magic or witchcraft taking place in the woods.

'I shouldn't bother to waste your time checking it out,' Bernard interrupted, having heard enough. 'It's only vague stuff, and I don't think its got anything directly to do with what's been going on up here tonight.'

I accepted his word. It would take me long enough to check out the psychic material relating to the well itself. Vague impressions concerning a weird wood in West Sussex would have to wait.

Nineteen
Aftermath

Thursday, 16th October, 1986. Alone in the *Leigh Times* office processing copy around six o'clock that night, the telephone rang out.

The polite female voice at the end of the line announced that she was ringing from Tonbridge library, in Kent.

'Are you the gentleman who requested information on a wood in this area called "Monksdown"?' she enquired, obviously having lost the name she had been given.

Indeed, I was that gentleman. I had rung the library the previous day to see what they could discover, not having been able to trace Monksdown on an Ordnance Survey map of the area.

'Well, I'm afraid the library has only been able to find one such wood of that name,' she continued, feeling that they may have let me down.

Grabbing some paper and a pen, I pulled up a chair and sat down.

'And it's not called "Monksdown" either, it's Monkdown Woods, to be more precise.'

That would do. Where was it?

'It's a wooded area on the top of a hill about three miles north-east of Maidstone and eight miles east-north-east of Mereworth. Apparently, in medieval times it was known as Munkuca Dun.' She spelt it out. 'Or Monks Hill. It would seem to have been the property of nearby Boxley Abbey, according to J.K. Wallenburg's book *The Place-names of Kent,* published at Uppsala, in 1934.'

It was almost certainly the second location Bernard had

picked up in association with the Black Alchemist whilst within the well hollow two days before. He could be excused for calling it Monksdown, instead of Monkdown, I decided!

Thanking the lady for her invaluable help, I replaced the receiver and returned to my work. But I was itching to tell Bernard the news so, an hour or so later, I just had to ring him.

After dialling the number he came on the line and sounded pleased. 'I've found Monksdown.'

So had I.

'I was searching through a Kent Ordnance Survey map earlier on and found it clearly marked. I was going to ring you this evening.'

It had not been on the map I'd glanced at. However, I soon realised that I had been looking at the wrong one!

Moving on to other topics, I asked him the most obvious question.

'No, I haven't picked up a thing since the other night. I told you, I'm putting the whole affair out of my mind.'

Accepting his words, I mentioned some of the reactions to the results of our Running Well confrontation.

At 7.30 pm that night, white candles had been lit by individuals across the country. In London, one entire mysteries class had broken off their lecture to concentrate on our fate at the appointed hour. Many psychics had picked up images which they felt were connected with the confrontation. None of them made a lot of sense though, except, perhaps, for one particular statement which kept cropping up. They had all felt that the Black Alchemist was in a wood at the time of the confrontation. However, because no one knew where exactly Bernard and I had been positioned, they naturally assumed that we were there with him!

Some psychics felt they saw a huge psychic battle waging between the forces of light and the powers of darkness; with final victory going to the former, of course. Naturally, this battle had featured Bernard, myself, the Black Alchemist and a whole host of spectral beings and awesome supernatural forces.

'We must have missed out on that,' Bernard said, a note of

Gilly Street at the Running Well following the discovery of the Black Alchemist's ritual stone within its waters.

humour in his voice. 'Perhaps it happened up on the astral planes.'

I laughed with him.

The late day at work had left me tired. In fact, I had been constantly tired and had suffered headaches ever since the Black Alchemist had set up his Ring of Darkness ritual. Despite this, I sat down that evening and attempted, for the second night running, to try and write up the events of the past couple of days.

It was hard going and I felt my eyes wanted to close. But I pressed on with the knowledge that I could give up and go to bed at any time I wished.

Reaching across the paper-covered desk top, I pulled across the sheets containing the Elizabethan alchemist's lengthy automatic script scribbled down during the Running Well confrontation. If Mereworth Woods and Monkdown Woods both existed, then what was I to make of this? Would it prove to be just as accurate in content? Already I had read and dissected the script dozens of times in the hope that it would eventually make some sort of sense. I could not read Latin, and did not possess a Latin-English dictionary, so the meaning of the various Latin words and terms still eluded me. All I could say with certainty was that Bernard's spirit guide had been trying to tell us how to combat the future activities of the Black Alchemist. Unfortunately though, the message had been conveyed in a style suitable only to another Elizabethan alchemist. It was of little use to me at all.

And how was I to interpret the automatic script for *The Black Alchemist* book? I pondered long over this question before deciding to leave any interpretations to the reader. They could then draw their own conclusions from its contents, or simply skip over it and get on to more exciting matters. Otherwise, it would have taken literally dozens of pages to have done it any justice at all.

Putting down the pages of scribbled script, I pulled out and lit a Marlboro.

For a short while I continued trying to set down an account of the confrontation at the well. But something kept nagging at the back of my mind. Something about the automatic script. Something it said rang bells for some reason.

Stubbing out the cigarette, I again pulled across the bunch of pages containing the automatic script and the various notes Bernard had made whilst in the well hollow. I began to read through them for the umpteenth time. The Elizabethan alchemist had suggested: 'It may well be that this (ie. the Black Alchemist's work) is the final step of the years of dwell with the serpent and toad . . . A black crucifixion and resurrection of the Anti-Lord, preparing the palace for the coronation.'

I thought long about these enigmatic statements and then ran back through the automatic writing Bernard had scribbled down as his mind had linked as one with the very thoughts of the Black Alchemist.

The one shall spread beyond the places of my knowledge

settling and growing amongst the roots, the woods, the trees and the streams . . . Impregnate. Let it grow. Let it form. The master shall form . . .

The master shall form? What master? Maybe the Black Alchemist believed he was preparing the way for the coming of . . . No, this was getting silly.

Pushing the papers to one side, I looked back towards the lined sheet of A4 paper in front of me, picked up my pen, recalled the memory of the Running Well confrontation and continued to write.

Twenty
Danbury

It was late; well past midnight. At first he saw nothing; only darkness. But then came a sense of motion; and light, raining in from the full moon outside, illuminating rigid features all around. Bernard's squinting eyes identified rows of pews on either side.

He was in the central aisle of a church.

Involuntarily, his fixed gaze moved closer and closer towards the high altar. And then a peculiar sight: crouching mythical beasts, grotesquely carved in wood, sitting upon the end of each pew; awesome, repulsive and yet somehow warm and familiar. In pairs, they approached and passed by, each one maintaining their own unique frozen stance.

He carried on.

The building appeared quiet and empty, and yet also somehow overwhelmingly imbalanced, oppressive and *wrong*. He disliked what he sensed and wanted to leave. But he could not. There was no choice.

The raised neo-Gothic pulpit moved out of sight to the left, while to the right, the menacing stare of the wooden lectern eagle appeared and disappeared without incident. He moved on.

Then he was revolted.

For there upon the tiled floor, above the stone steps which led through the choir, lay the prostrate corpse of a black-robed clergyman sprawled across a crudely-chalked inverted pentagram enclosed within a circle. Sticky, crimson rivulets of thick, congealing blood still oozed from horrifying wounds and seeped into the dusty gaps between the ceramic floor tiles.

Something was missing.

Slowly his eyes followed the line of the body, along the erratic trails of blood stains, across the altar rail, and on to the wooden-fronted high altar.

A dreadful nausea welled up inside his stomach and he retched at what he saw.

Upon the once-white altar draping stood the holy man's almost unrecognisable head; its mouth agape and its thick, grey hair matted with viscid blood.

And worst of all, he knew the church, and the culprit.

It was, he realised, just a scare-mongering dream. A vision. A warning. A portent? He hoped not. Yet Bernard knew that the Black Alchemist was now nearer than ever before; and it concerned him greatly.

The soft lunar light spotlighted the psychic as he twisted and turned in his sweat until the movement finally broke his sleep.

His head pounded and ached with acute pain and, for a moment, he desperately fought to keep his eyes from closing again. There was no way that he wished to return to the disgusting nightmare. Yet as he began to fully wake up, he accepted it was over. He could now rest in peace.

But no way could he forget or ignore what he'd seen. He knew the church. It was Danbury — the church of St John-the-Baptist, just over the road from The Griffin pub. It was here that over the past two and a half years they had researched the village's medieval mysteries for Andy's book *The Knights of Danbury,* published in 1984.

The Griffin was still his choice for their regular get-togethers to discuss on-going and future research projects. Danbury was his manor; his domain; in the same way that Andy was very much associated with the Running Well area.

Surely the Black Alchemist would not strike there.

Tuesday, 21st October. Danbury would be his next target, I pointed out as we sat supping beer within the confines of The Griffin.

'Ah, well, I've already had a dream about that,' Bernard admitted, having not mentioned it earlier when asked whether he had picked up any further information since the Running Well confrontation. 'Last week. Thursday or Friday night, I think. After you rang me about Monkdown Woods.'

That was Thursday, 16th October; the night of the full moon.

Bernard revealed the details of his dream concerning the prostrate body of the black-robed priest lying in the choir area of Danbury church.

It sounded revolting.

'He knows about Danbury,' Bernard said, a slightly worried expression having formed upon his face. 'And I'm not sure what to do.'

It was inevitable. Shenfield, Runwell and now Danbury. He was obviously warning Bernard, in the form of a dream, that he knew about Danbury and could strike there with a vengeance if he so desired. Whether he would or not, was another matter.

Anyway, if the Black Alchemist did ever turn up at the church then Bernard would know about it.

'How would I know?' he asked, intrigued.

Because he was very much attuned to the hilltop site and had, in the past, known when people were up to mystical mischief inside the church.

It had happened before, in March 1985, when two French students had visited the church. They had carried out a simple form of occult ritual during which they had concealed a folded parchment, containing magical symbols, beneath the head of one of the two medieval wooden knight effigies in the north aisle. Working in his garden, Bernard had picked up that something untoward was taking place in the church and had gone up there on impulse.

Inside the church, an oppressive atmosphere had hung in the air and upon asking the site's guardian, thirteenth century local lord of the manor, William de St Clere, what was going on, he was told to 'remove the parchment.' With this had come the mental image of one of the recessed, wooden knight effigies and the feeling that he should look beneath its head. Here he had discovered the concealed parchment.

Further psychic prying had revealed the names of the two students and the fact that they were studying psychology and lived in Paris. I had put the feelers out among my French contacts and had eventually tracked them down. However, I was advised to: 'Stay away from them as they are into heavy stuff.'

'I know all that,' Bernard interjected, lifting his glass from the table. 'But if someone like the Black Alchemist carries out a major ritual in the churchyard then it will seriously affect me. It'll be like someone playing about inside my own head.'

I had an idea. Why didn't he create a kind of energy barrier around the church. He could achieve this, quite simply, by planting a ring of tiny crystals around its exterior walls, with the purpose of the ritual in mind. This would then act as a psychic alarm system which would let him know when anyone with dubious occult intentions entered within the ring of crystals, whether it be on a physical or on a psychic level.

'If I feel the need to do so, then I will,' he responded, obviously trying not to tempt any sort of future conflicts with undesirable characters.

He should do it, just in case.

'Only if I think it necessary,' he said, emphasising the point. 'I'll let you know if I do.'

Tuesday, 11th November. Bernard appeared in the doorway of The Griffin and joined me in the corner, by the old Tudor fireplace.

It had been three weeks since I had last seen him, and I was eager to know whether anything further had happened since the Danbury church nightmare the previous month.

'I was moved to set up the crystals around the church on Sunday,' he announced. 'I came up here and laid a circle of small green crystals.'

What had made him want to do this?

He grimaced and shrugged. 'Just got the feeling to do it.'

And why green crystals?

'Green is the colour relating to balance, harmony, I suppose. I don't know really. It just felt right.'

Any new psychic material?

Bernard said: 'No,' but then thought about his answer before throwing in a passing statement. 'The only thing I can add to the dream is that the Black Alchemist carries a swordstick.'

A swordstick? Like those carried by well-to-do gentlemen in Victorian times?

'Yes, that's what I mean,' he confirmed. 'But I don't think he necessarily uses it for physical protection. He uses it as a ritualistic tool to invoke and banish supernatural forces.'

Now, this *was* a peculiar statement. Never before had I come across an occultist who used a swordstick for ritualistic purposes. Occultists usually used swords, daggers, staffs and wands to wield magical forces; not swordsticks. In fact, I don't think I had ever come across anyone who even owned such a thing.

Yet then, as I thought about the idea, it began to dawn on me just how useful a swordstick would be on both a physical and an occult level for someone like the Black Alchemist. He could openly walk around with it in the most conspicuous public places and no one — save perhaps a keen-eyed policeman — would ever know what was concealed within his walking stick. And, unlike a proper broadsword, a swordstick would be ideal for ritualistic purposes in circumstances where other people were likely to disturb his magical activities at any time; like in a church, or a churchyard perhaps? He could slip out the sword blade to invoke and banish magical forces, or merely leave it inside the walking stick and use the weapon as a ritualistic wand or staff. It was easy, and very clever.

I wanted one! If the Black Alchemist had one then I would have to have one as well! Visions of scouring local antiques shops filled my mind. At least I would have a good time trying to find one as browsing around antiques shops was a regular pastime of mine.

Tuesday, 18th November. A small, white Honda hatchback came to a halt on the gravel-surfaced track at the side of the green in front of Danbury church.

The driver's door slowly opened and a young, muscular-looking man with short, military-style hair and a moustache, stepped out and peered about suspiciously. Slamming it closed, he strolled across to the churchyard and was lost from view behind the corner buttress, close to the west door.

Left inside the car was a fair-haired woman, in her thirties, who sat holding a small child in her arms. It was Carole Smith's birthday, so her husband Ken had decided to hire a car for the day so that he could take her and their small son Beren to see some of the few remaining ancient sites around Essex. Beren was now asleep so, as she had been to Danbury church on several occasions before, she let Ken venture inside on his own.

Carole was an astrologer and a psychic who, for some years, had worked with Andy Collins and his locally-based Earthquest group visiting different sites around the country and picking up psychic information with remarkable accuracy. Indeed, some of her most revealing material had been featured in Andy's book *The Running Well Mystery*. She had also picked up information on Danbury church, although it was unlikely that she would get anything that day, just sitting out in the car waiting for Ken to return.

For several minutes she waited in silence with little else to do but stare at the church's exterior walls, with its weathered Gothic window tracery and its tall conical-shaped spire.

Then, quite unexpectedly, she received a disconcerting, but vivid vision of the church's interior. It was as she remembered it, however, there was an additional feature which had not been drawn from her memory. She could see, walking down the central aisle in slow procession, a group of some ten to twelve figures in black cowled robes.

Danbury church, where Bernard's disgusting nightmare and Carole's extraordinary vision implied the Black Alchemist would strike next.

As the curious clairvoyant image started to fade, she knew it was a bad omen, a portent of something ugly that was soon to take place inside that very church. And, for some reason, she believed it had something to do with the Black Alchemist.

'I think the Black Alchemist intends striking at Danbury next,' Carole said, concluding her story of the vision she had received that afternoon.

Holding the receiver, I thought before I spoke. She was not aware of Bernard's dream concerning the church and did not know that we had also concluded that Danbury would be the Black Alchemist's next target. Yet it could have been a calculated guess on the part of her imagination. It would not have been that hard to work out that Danbury would inevitably follow the Running Well as the site of a future confrontation with our adversary.

On the other hand, her vision was too coincidental to be ignored. Even so, after telling Carole about Bernard's dream and his planting of the ring of crystals around the church's exterior, I partially dismissed her psychic material. Perhaps her acute psychic ability had merely picked up the thought of expectancy created, not by the Black Alchemist, but by Bernard himself when he had planted the crystals earlier that month.

Carole reluctantly agreed.

I gave the same explanation to Bernard upon speaking to him later that evening

Thursday, 27th November. Getting up and making a pot of tea, I tried to recall the dream I had experienced during the night.

This swordstick business was obviously getting to me, as I was even dreaming about them now. I remembered a group of people, I did not know who they were, who had presented me with a swordstick as a magical tool which I was to use to combat the powers of the Black Alchemist.

I could recall receiving it in my hands and sliding out its slim blade to reveal an inscription of fine decoration peppered out with a sharp point. But that was all I could remember.

Although it had been an unusually vivid dream, I dismissed it as a flight of fancy on my part. It was a product of my imagination, generated by my sudden interest in swordsticks. Despite this, it made me more determined to find one, even though I had already combed virtually every antiques shop in the Southend area without so much as a rumour of a swordstick for sale.

Still, I would continue the search.

Twenty one
The Mystic's Gift

Sunday, 30th November, 1986. There was something nagging at the back of Bernard's mind as he got up that morning. An impulse. An urge to go somewhere, meet someone, find something, although what exactly he did not know.

The feeling intensified as the morning grew older, and with this now came the distinct impression of an area in Essex; and an event taking place that very day.

Without either believing or disbelieving his feelings, he consulted a comprehensive local newspaper to see what that had to say. Finger-flicking the pages, he first passed, but then returned to the page he was looking for — the coming events section. Scanning the different display adverts, he found it — and yes, it was that day — an antiques and collectors' fair not far from the Essex village of Margaretting.

He wanted to go. But what would he find if he went? A relevant book on heraldry. Yes, that was the answer. For the past year he had been researching and painting the heraldic devices of all past and present members of the Order of the Garter, from its commencement in the fourteenth century right through to the present day. Not an easy task by anyone's standards.

Yet to achieve this aim, he needed books. Old, rare, out-of-print and second-hand books which were often difficult to obtain; and it was in this respect that his acute psychic faculty had come in handy. As on at least three occasions he had received similar distinct impulses to go to either specific second-hand bookshops or, indeed, to antiques and collectors' fairs, like the one taking place that day. Once there he had been intuitively drawn to rare books on heraldry relevant to his research at that particular point of time. Such an ability was, he believed, one of the few 'perks' of being an accurate psychic.

So he would go, and should he be wrong and there was no book to be found at the fair, then it would still be a good excuse to get out of the house for a few hours before dinner.

Having locked the car, Bernard walked across the car park to the entrance foyer and queued behind a couple waiting to pay their admission fee. Seconds later he was through the pay desk and within the hall itself.

Before him stalls selling every kind of antique and collectable item filled the entire hall, wall to wall. The air was alive with the muted conversation of stallholders, dealers and visitors buying, selling, bartering and admiring. Yet the large hall was by no means full. There was still ample room to wander from table to table without hindrance.

Bernard strolled about not quite noticing anything other than the occasional pile of dusty books occupying some corner of a stall dedicated to other, more valuable items. One by one, he turned them over, pushed them about or lifted up their covers to search for an author or a title. None appeared to be relevant to his work. However, something should leap out at him eventually, he told himself.

For twenty minutes he wandered about studying more or less every stall in the hall. But there was nothing there which interested him. Growing a little disappointed, he began to accept that, on this occasion, his psychic ability may have let him down. His earlier feelings were probably just his own imagination giving him an excuse to get out of the house for a while.

Having given up, Bernard wandered aimlessly and without interest along the rows of stalls stacked with curious objets d'art of every shape and colour.

Glimpses of faces and snippets of conversation broke through his senses as he ambled about, not really knowing what to do next.

'I can come down to twenty two. No less, I'm afraid,' a male face with receding grey hair and a moustache responded to a lady close by.

'No, these are repro. Those over there are original Deco,' a pretty girl with shoulder-length black hair said from behind another stall.

He did not glance to see what they were talking about. It did not seem to mean anything to him. He was lost in his own frustration. *Why had he been led to this place?* There had to be something here somewhere, he began to conclude. Images blurred into moving and stationary forms, and distinct conversation now became just a background murmur. He was losing orientation and perspective. Something was happening.

'Yes sir. Can I help you?' said the clearly Asian-accented voice.

Bernard stared up at the intrusion. A smiling Indian youth in his late teens, or early twenties, dressed in an old, out-of-fashion man's casual shirt, with a frayed collar, stood behind a stall waiting for a reply.

In front of the boy was an assortment of Indian and oriental curios and antiques, mostly either of brass or wood. Geometrically-patterned plates stood behind brass incense burners, cheap jewellery and crudely-cast statues of Hindu deities.

Bernard shook his head, but found his eyes scanning the stall for anything of interest. They caught sight of an antique brass cobra, standing some three inches in height, nestling among the collection of statuettes. He picked it up. It was a little worn and, turning it around in one hand, he saw that on the snake's head was a small Hindu deity who appeared to be dancing. He recognised the cobra's erect stance as the same as a pair of much larger cobra candle holders that Andy used for meditation. So how much was it?

The young Indian took hold of the item and surveyed it for a moment. 'Two pound,' he announced, a note of certainty in his voice.

Nodding in acceptance, Bernard produced two one pound

coins and handed them over.

The Indian carefully wrapped the brass snake and returned it to him. For a few seconds he paused, but then spoke in a clear, but hesitant voice: 'You are in conflict with the one who reverses the wheel. Is this true?'

The question caught Bernard off guard. Looking up at the youth, he realised that he was merely conveying the question on behalf of an elderly Indian gentleman sitting down behind the stall, who was also now looking up and waiting for a reply.

He tried to take in the situation before even contemplating an answer to the curious question. The old man looked strange. He wore a long white robe which contrasted sharply with his deep brown wrinkled skin, his piercing jet black eyes, and his long grey hair and beard. In his right hand he was rhythmically turning over a string of orange worry beads; an act he almost appeared to be doing involuntarily. It seemed that whilst he had been studying the brass cobra, the old man, who, he assumed, could not speak English, had asked the youth to put the question to him and now the pair eagerly awaited an answer.

What did they mean? 'You are in conflict with the one who reverses the wheel.' Bernard decided that the statement had to be a reference to the Black Alchemist and his warped alchemical and magical activities. Could he not be described as 'reversing the wheel' by causing the harmonious forces at ancient sites to fall into a state of chaotic disarray through his dark rituals? It was the only explanation so, in reply, he said, simply: 'Yes.'

Accepting his word, the old man beckoned for the youth to lend him an ear again. More words were spoken and, nodding, the boy returned to Bernard. 'There is one who seeks to unblock the dam. Is this true?'

He thought carefully before answering. One who seeks to *unblock* the dam. That had to be Andy. Yes, Andy. He was undoubtedly attempting to repair the psychic damage caused by the Black Alchemist. It was a reference to him so, once again, he said, simply: 'Yes.'

The reply was acknowledged by the old man who again

beckoned the boy down to his level. Further words were exchanged and once more the youth stood up straight and looked towards Bernard. 'Is he the one where the two rivers meet?'

Where the two rivers meet. That was a tricky one. Andy lived with his parents in Wickford, but was he anywhere near the meeting place of two rivers? He was nowhere near the Thames. But what about the River Crouch and the River Blackwater? He couldn't think. It did not appear to be an answer.

He thought again. Was it then, perhaps not a reference to real rivers, but rivers of psychic energy, opposing magical currents of energy, one positive and the other negative; one black and the other white.

Andy often trod a narrow path between what some might consider as black and white magic. One week he would be in prayer with Orthodox monks in a secluded Greek monastery; whilst the next he would be wielding powerful and dangerous occult forces under the cover of darkness, combating fire with fire, so to speak. This was the answer the Indians were looking for, so he agreed and once again waited for their response.

The old man, still turning over the worry beads in his hand, then spoke again via the youth, a more serious expression on their faces this time. 'The one you seek is like the coiled serpent.'

It was, he felt, another reference to the Black Alchemist's cunning activities, so he agreed once more.

More conversation between the old man and the youth produced another strange statement: 'The one will stand in front of many dangers.'

'Oh', he responded, assuming this to be another reference to Andy.

'My grandfather asks if you will accept a gift?' A sort of smile appeared on the face of the old man and the youth as if Bernard's presence had finally been given a vote of confidence.

'Yes, but what for?' he replied, wondering what was going on.

More words passed between the grandfather and the

grandson before the youth cleared his throat and spoke again: 'But it will not be yours. You will not keep it.'

Bernard saw that, with this statement, the old man had now raised up his hands in a gesture which said: need I say more? You will know who it is for.

He did. It was to be given to Andy.

At that point the young Indian turned around and picked up a long, thin package wrapped in brown paper, which he handed to Bernard. It was over four feet long, pole-like and quite weighty.

Instantly, he began to feel his hands tingle, almost as if he had just grabbed hold of a live wire. What was this 'gift'? It seemed to be exuding an intense energy field of some sort, so much so that he almost dropped it.

Still the conversation between the grandfather and the grandson continued. The boy looked up at Bernard. 'It will protect you and give protection of the seven.'

Protection of the seven? He did not understand. Seven what? And protection from what? The Black Alchemist? Was he to just take it?

'Yes,' the grandson responded.

Did he want any money?

The boy shook his head, and the old man merely lifted up his string of worry beads with a smile, as if to gesture goodbye.

It was time to leave. Bernard moved away from the stall still holding the gift out at arms' length, as if he should not get too close to it. Without stopping, he walked away from the hustle and bustle of the fair and stepped out into the solitude of the gravel-floored car park.

Once inside the car, the wrapping paper was carefully removed from around the gift. It was a long walking stick in varnished, black wood with chiselled grooves grouped in rings and lines running down its shaft, and a metal cap protecting its tip. Around the bottom half of the handle was an inch wide brass ring set into the wood, and nudging up to this was, what looked like, an inset bone piece with a recurring floral pattern. Screwed into the cap was the face of a lion in brass.

It looked very much like a standard design in oriental

walking sticks, had it not been for one seemingly unique feature. Scratched into the wood were strange mystical-looking symbols composed of zig-zags, circles and lines. He partially recognised their symbolism, but decided to leave their interpretation to Andy for when he saw him at The Griffin the following evening.

More extraordinary than the walking stick's physical appearance was the bright aura of light which surrounded the shaft and extended beyond each end by at least a couple of inches. But that was not all. Moving down from the handle towards the tip was a pulsating spiral of rainbow-coloured energy which — about midway along the shaft — altered into individual coloured rings of light which slowly advanced towards the tip, before reforming back into a spiral and extinguishing completely just beyond the metal cap. At any one time, no less than five of these detached rings of light could be observed moving down the central axis of the walking stick.

It was an amazing sight, yet one which Bernard knew would only be seen by another psychic.

And its purpose was becoming apparent as well. It was a rod of magical power, a highly-charged ritual tool, imbued with supernatural energies by someone — possibly the old man, maybe someone else — for a specific purpose. If this was so, then it was to be used by Andy to invoke, banish and channel psychic energies for magical purposes. What was more, it would be able to protect them from the rising might of the Black Alchemist.

Twenty two
William's Warning

Monday, 1st December, 1986. '. . . and so I wrapped it back up and left it in the boot of the car,' Bernard said, concluding his story. 'Which is where it's been since yesterday.' He picked up his drink and awaited my response.

I sighed in utter disbelief. I had listened to a few unreal episodes from the psychic's remarkable life before, but this one took the biscuit. I told him to go and get it.

'Right, I'll be back in a minute,' he said, getting up and walking out of The Griffin's lounge bar.

I pondered over the whole uncanny story. Who were the two Indians? The old man had almost certainly been a mystic of some sort. The description was classic. But had he known that someone was going to approach him at the fair? It seemed so, as the walking stick had already been wrapped when it was given to Bernard. Perhaps those sort of people regularly gave away 'gifts' to others who they felt some affinity with.

Bernard re-emerged whistling to himself and holding the long, wrapped package.

Excitedly, I removed the brown paper. For a few moments, I just stared at the stick in utter amazement. But then, bringing it closer, I studied the two symbols scratched into its varnished black surface.

One was a finely-carved, anti-clockwise swastika scratched into the handle. The other, a little further down, was a little more complex. It consisted of a nine-pointed, circular star with a small circle at its centre, overlaid on to which was a circle inscribed with a much thicker instrument. Cutting through both the circle and the star, was a thick, zig-zagging line, dissected diagonally by a single straight line.

They were mystical symbols alright. The swastika was a Hindu solar emblem, and also a representation of the single creative force of the universe. However, an anti-clockwise swastika very often represented the dark, hidden side of the Hindu and Buddhist religions, generally referred to as the Tantric tradition.

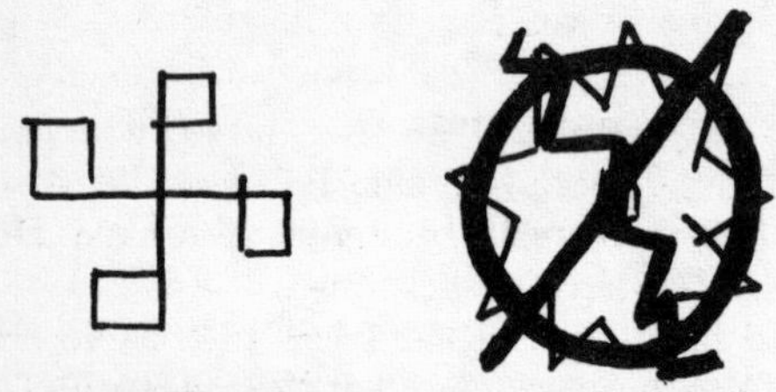

Precise actual size drawings of the two mystical symbols carved into the wood on the outside of the walking stick given to Bernard by the Indian mystic.

The nine-pointed star, with the circle in its centre, was another symbol of the creative driving force of the physical universe. The thicker circle overlaying the star, and the zig-zagging line across the star, were a little more difficult to interpret. The zig-zagging line, I felt, was a simplified image of a serpent, or a water flow, which, in universal symbolism, were both used to represent the flowing or wielding of cosmic and terrestrial energies.

As to who had inscribed the stick, I could not say. Each of the symbols appeared particularly Hindu in design, so it could be assumed that they had been put there by an Indian mystic during some kind of ritual act to charge it with psychic power.

Fiddling around with the wooden rod, I heard something rattling inside its shaft. Looking up at Bernard, I felt a sense of butterflies rise in my stomach. I knew what it was. Twisting the brass ring released the handle which I then pulled away from the rest of the stick. A long, thin blade, greased for protection, suddenly emerged.

It was a swordstick!

Bernard looked delighted and bent across the table to study the blade. Inscribed along one of its surfaces was the word 'India' between two simple decorative patterns. It had been pricked into the iron blade with a fine point and instantly it made me recall my dream the previous week about being given a swordstick by a group of people. That one also had a peppered design on its blade. Bernard knew nothing of this dream as I had dismissed it as a flight of fancy on my part. However, it now seemed as if it might have been a portent for the arrival of the real swordstick.

Yet then a curious thought spilled out as a question to Bernard: how come *he* had not realised it was a swordstick?

'I didn't really look at it that closely,' he responded, wondering the very same question himself. 'I only studied it for a short time before re-wrapping it and putting it into the boot. And that's where it's been until now.'

I accepted his word. Yet the whole story still baffled me completely. What had a Hindu swordstick to do with our confrontations with the Black Alchemist? Okay, so he had one the same . . .

'No, not the same,' Bernard interjected, to put me right. 'The one I saw him with had a more rounded cap. I don't think it had a brass ring either.'

So his one appeared to be more traditional in design. More like the sort that Victorian gentlemen had carried around. But how old was our one?

The top of the swordstick given to Bernard under somewhat bizarre circumstances, which was said to 'give protection of the seven', according to the Indian mystic.

'Don't know,' he admitted, getting up to go to the bar. 'Same again?' he asked, nodding towards my empty glass.

I placed the swordstick on the table for a moment. A tingling sensation throbbed across the palm of my hand. Whether this was the result of auto-suggestion or not, I could not say; but my hand actually felt as if it had been caned.

Bernard placed down a glass of Pils in front of me, before sitting down with his own pint of Kaliber. He very rarely drank alcohol any more.

So what was this strange sensation in my right hand? Was it me, or what?

He glanced towards the swordstick before answering. 'Well, it's as I said, some kind of rod of power. The feeling I get is that it can be used to affect subtle energy fields present in the body and out in the landscape. It can produce or change energies and create thought forms.'

He then hesitated for a moment as if composing his thoughts. 'You know, I get the distinct feeling that although the swordstick is not old in itself, it embodies an essence, or spirit, of another far older ritual wand of immense power.'

He was, I felt, saying that it was not so much what it was, but what it contained which was of importance.

'I think so,' Bernard agreed, extinguishing his cigarette in the already busy ashtray.

Shaking my head with a disbelieving smile, I twisted around and stood the swordstick up against the side of the stone Tudor fireplace. It looked a little out of place among the pokers and coal scuttles.

Turning the subject of conversation to other matters, half an hour soon passed.

Yet then, suddenly, and without warning, Bernard lunged forward in front of the fireplace and made a grab for the swordstick as if it was about to fall to the floor.

What was he up to?

Having realised that the swordstick had not moved, he returned to the comfort of his seat, somewhat embarrassed by his actions: 'It really did appear to change into a snake. Perhaps it's some kind of serpent stick.'

A serpent stick. Yes, of course. The zig-zagging symbol on the shaft seemed to suggest a connection with serpent energies. Bernard had said that the swordstick's subtle energy field consisted of a spiralling band of rainbow light, and now he claimed it had momentarily changed into a writhing snake. It was all beginning to sound a little like the accounts of the Rod of Moses that the Biblical prophet of Jehovah was able to change into a writhing snake and back again, purely by verbal command.

Snakes and serpents were — as I had already pointed out that evening — universal symbols of the movement and flow of cosmic and terrestrial energies. The rod and staff, on the other hand, were both symbols of the priest magician's ability to control the power of these serpentine energies; the reason why snakes and rods of power were often linked together.

Bearing in mind Bernard's belief that this swordstick contained an essence, or spirit, far older than its physical counterpart, was it therefore possible that it embodied some kind of ancient serpent rod used in the past to invoke, banish, alter and control magical forces? Remember, the whole Black Alchemist affair had begun with another, quite separate quest — the search for the so-called Stave of Nizar, a golden serpent rod apparently fashioned in Ancient Egypt. Perhaps we had finally found the ethereal counterpart of the Stave of Nizar?

Bernard found this amusing. 'I don't know about that,' he laughed. 'Yet it does seem strange that a quest to locate an Ancient Egyptian serpent rod should turn into a separate quest to track down a black magician working in the same area.'

Then, as if to bring the whole story full circle, we end up with a serpent rod; yet not a physical one — one embodied in an ethereal form within a swordstick given to us by an Indian mystic under somewhat absurd circumstances. Just who was going to believe all this?

'Fate moves in mysterious ways,' he exclaimed, with a smile.

I picked up the swordstick again. So if it was that powerful then what would happen if we were to take it out into Danbury churchyard and play around with it for a while? Perhaps he would be able to see its inherent energies more clearly out in the open.

Bernard looked at me in utter astonishment as he began to shake his head. 'No way. It's cold out there. It's also raining and I don't think it's the sort of thing you play around with. No, I think I'll stay here in the comfort of the bar.'

I persisted. If we were to try something out in the churchyard then I felt sure that we would get some sort of reaction from the swordstick. Seeing that Bernard had confidence in its dormant power, then, if nothing else, he would probably see or experience a change in the energy field surrounding the swordstick.

Eventually he relented. 'Alright, after we've finished our drinks then, he said, like a father who had just given his son permission to play with his latest toy.

I was jubilant. Something was sure to happen out there.

In the relative stillness of the cold, damp and darkened hilltop churchyard, the two conspicuous figures came to a halt on the gravel path next to the old horse chestnut tree, their usual spot for carrying out psychic activities. Here they readied themselves for the paranormal experiment.

Bernard stood by as I half closed my eyes and ritually rammed the magical swordstick into the soft mud at the side of the path. In my mind, I visualised golden energies pouring from me, through the swordstick and into the ground. I saw them radiate out in all directions, like the spokes of a huge wheel filling the whole of the churchyard. Mentally, I began to turn the golden wheel of energies in a clockwise direction until its spokes blurred into a swirling mass of fast-moving waves of vibrant light. This was what I could see. What about Bernard?

'The swordstick is glowing gold,' he revealed, in a quiet, decisive voice, as he began to pace about. 'Golden energies are encircling the whole churchyard.'

Good. He could actually see what I was creating through visualisation.

But Bernard was experiencing much more than that. He

stood and listened to the night. 'Can you hear anything?'

No. I continued to visualise the golden wheel of energies, pulsating and rippling around the churchyard.

'Can you hear something like a choir . . . an angelic choir coming from somewhere?' he asked, as he started to walk back towards the silhouetted image of the spired church. 'You *must* be able to hear it.'

Still I continued the visualisation. My eyes caught sight of Bernard walking into the great shadow cast by the Christian structure, still gazing skywards, as if searching for the source of his angelic choir.

For a moment, just a few, brief seconds, I forgot Bernard. Then, without warning, an almighty *BANG* sounded from the direction in which Bernard had vanished into the darkness.

I looked up. *What the hell was he doing?*

Fearing for his safety and curious to know what was going on, I quickly curtailed the visualisation and scurried across the wet grass towards the church — some 70 or so yards away from where I was standing.

Within twenty yards of the church's south wall I found Bernard. He just stood there, perfectly still and silent, staring towards the south door, some five or so yards in front of him.

Instantly, I saw the cause of his obvious concern. The great wooden door was wide open! Something was clearly amiss. In my three years of constant visits to the church I had never once known this door to be unlocked, never mind open.

What had happened?

'It opened by itself,' he announced, quite casually. 'I was listening to the choir, which sounded as if it was coming from the church, so I came over here.'

Then what happened?

'As I got closer to the church I could see a silhouetted human form standing in front of the door. When I reached this point the door just opened on its own, almost as if the lock had been blown off with an explosive!'

This night was getting silly. First the swordstick, and now the church door blasting open by itself. I shook my head. Could I take any more?

Moving up to the open door, I inspected its lock and handle for any signs of damage. There were none. However, the bolt had retracted into the lock mechanism which indicated that the door had unlocked and opened of its own accord. I suggested to Bernard that this was a sign that we were to go inside the church for some reason.

'You won't get me in there,' he protested, obviously quite troubled by the suggestion. 'What if someone comes along and finds us in there. How would we explain that?! No, I'm staying out here, thank you.'

I desperately wanted him to go inside the church. Doors don't open of their own accord without good reason. It was quite apparent that if we were to go inside, then he would probably gain a psychic message from the church's spirit guardian, William de St Clere.

Perhaps the Black Alchemist had already visited the church. Maybe we were meant to discover whatever he'd left behind. We *had* to go inside, and I told Bernard so.

Advancing into the church itself, I at last managed to coax him into moving just inside the south door.

'This is as far as I go,' he categorically stated.

Knowing that a message would now follow, and that we might not have much time, I told him to ask William to tell us exactly what was going on. He agreed, so I waited for a response.

'There's a threat, he's telling me,' Bernard revealed, referring to William's words.

A thread? What the hell had a thread to do with this?

'A *threat!*,' he corrected me.

I see. From whom?

'Visitors,' came the stern reply out of the darkness.

What . . . visitors will come?

'Yes.'

When?

'He doesn't know. But I will know when.'

I recalled the swordstick still in my right hand. Had *that* anything to do with the door opening by itself?

There was a momentary silence. 'No answer to that

question.'

So what was all this about?

Another pause. 'I know what this is about and I think it's time to leave.' Bernard shuffled in the darkness, as if about to go.

Why?

'I see the same images I saw during the nightmare. The decapitated priest. The blood stains. Everything. Come on, it's time to go.' He moved away from the door and back out into the cold December air.

Closing the heavy door, I followed him on to the path.

'I'm going home,' he exclaimed, making his way across the green.

So it seemed as if the Black Alchemist was on the move again. He and his devotees looked set to pay Danbury church a little visit; and it would not be to attend a service, either! Hopefully, however, Bernard *would* know when this was going to take place, so at least we would have a chance to suitably prepare ourselves for the next confrontation with our adversary.

For the moment though, we had a more immediate problem on our hands — such as what we were to tell the rector? Sorry, our magical serpent swordstick — which was given to Bernard by an Indian mystic — has just blasted open the south door of your church so that a medieval knight could inform us that the site was about to be attacked and desecrated by a nasty black magician from Sussex. I wasn't too sure if he would quite understand!

So what *were* we to do? As I waved goodbye to the psychic, I had an idea. What about telling the rector that we had been sitting in the pub, when Bernard — whom he knew was psychic — had suddenly received the impression to go over to the church. This we had done and, feeling that something was amiss with the south door, we had discovered that it was unlocked, so had decided to report this to him.

Yes, that was the answer. Turning around, I strolled back towards the green in front of the church, before turning right into the rectory's long driveway.

The rector's wife answered the door. 'I'm sorry but my husband's out at the moment,' she responded.

I told her the story and she accepted my word.

'Oh dear, that was probably the choirmaster. He uses the south door for choir practice on a Sunday evening.' She sighed with concern. 'I shall have to tell him about that. Perhaps he forgot to lock it when he left last night.'

Perhaps. Either that, or there was *another* explanation . . .

Twenty three
The Proclaimer

Monday, 5th January, 1987. The eleventh night. So The Griffin was still in keeping with seasonal tradition, as they had one more day in which to take down their Christmas decorations.

Sitting down in the corner of the bar, with a pint of best bitter in my hand, I awaited Bernard's arrival.

I had fully expected the Black Alchemist to force another confrontation over the Christmas period. But there had been no frantic telephone call from Bernard.

In a way, it had seemed obvious. After William's warning of imminent problems, following the discovery of the Indian swordstick, I had predicted that the Black Alchemist would make his next move within a few weeks. Probably around the winter solstice — between the 21st and 23rd December — the next significant event in the pagan calendar. If not then, I had expected trouble either on Christmas Eve, or over the new year period. Yet all these dates had passed without incident.

Only two possible dates remained: Old Christmas Eve, Monday, 5th January — that very night — or the following day, Old Christmas Day. If he did not put in an appearance on either of these dates, then I would have to accept that I'd been wrong. In which case, I would have to forget the subject of the Black Alchemist completely until something tangible really did take place.

In over a month I had only spoken to Bernard once; and that was merely to confirm our meeting planned for that evening. I knew from past experience that over the Christmas period he usually 'closed down' almost entirely on a psychic level and would not respond to anything.

Still, our meeting would at least provide us with a chance to review the psychic events of 1986, and set us in motion for a few new quests in the coming year.

Bernard strolled into the bar around 7.30 pm, a smile as usual upon his face. After exchanging coins for a pint of Kaliber, he joined me at the table and sat down. Almost immediately, he produced two folded sheets of paper which he placed on the table. 'Take a look at this lot and see what you make of it,' he suggested.

Virtually all of the scribbled psychic notes and crude sketches related to a topic new to us — the mysteries of India and Tibet. Having digested these, I read on to certain impressions he had unexpectedly received on New Year's Eve.

Under the heading: 'Scribbles about BA.' he had written:

> **Roger Bacon says two Antichrists will appear, the mystic and the Antichrist proper. There is only one way to prepare against his coming. Study the secrets of nature, the curative properties of herbs, the nature of stones.**

Intrigued, I looked up at Bernard. Did Roger Bacon, the thirteenth century English alchemist and philosopher, say these words?

'That's what I picked up,' he replied, not quite understanding my query. 'I think the message actually came from the Elizabethan alchemist.'

Roger Bacon, I pointed out, was one of the leading figures in alchemical history whose works, we already knew, the Black Alchemist had studied, as the name 'Bacon' had cropped up in psychic material at the time of the Ide Hill sketch. However, I was not aware that he had studied apocalyptic matters, so why should Bernard have picked up such statements in association with this great alchemist?

He merely shrugged his shoulders in dismissal and

swallowed another mouthful of Kaliber. 'I don't know. It was just there, so I scribbled it down.'

For a moment, I tried to contemplate the implications of his psychic notes. Christian so-called apocalyptic writings stated that the Second Coming of Christ would be preceded by the appearance of his antithesis, the so-called Antichrist. He was Satan's own prodigy who would be sent to earth in an attempt to con and mesmerise the multitudes by carrying out all sorts of miraculous deeds, seemimgly in God's name. These would include mimicking the life of Christ and performing a mock crucifixion and resurrection. Yet, in the end, Antichrist would be exposed as the incarnate aspect of the devil and destroyed just prior to the return of the real Son of God.

However, in what little I had read on the subject, I could recall no indication that there would be *two* Antichrists — one an actual person of immense mystical power, an incarnate aspect of Satan himself, and the other an ethereal being or force who would then physically manifest within this world, like the returning Jesus Christ, 'the Antichrist proper', as Bernard's automatic writing described him.

In a way though, it made sense as, in Christian tradition, St John-the-Baptist was the forerunner of Jesus Christ. He had proclaimed the Messiah's imminent appearance in this world. Perhaps Antichrist would have a similar proclaimer who would prepare the way for his master's eventual appearance on earth. This, therefore, would then represent the two Antichrists.

So did I believe any of this? The answer was no, not really, even though I was familiar with the ideals of fundamentalist Christians who undoubtedly believed that the Second Coming of Christ was just around the corner.

'I'm not sure what I believe these days,' Bernard admitted. 'However, I feel that Antichrist's name is Apollyon. He's some sort of opposing force to Apollo, the Greek sun god.'

Apollyon? This stopped me in my tracks. Was this statement psychic, or was it something he already knew?

'I'm picking this up now,' he revealed. 'The Antichrist is a seven-headed beast with ten horns who will rise up out of the sea. The Beast 666.'

Yes, that was right. In the Bible's *Book of Revelations,* written by St John-the-Divine, Antichrist was associated with a great beast who would rise up out of the sea with seven heads and ten crowns. Yet this was only one of his forms. However, I had not come across the name Apollyon before.

'The seven heads will represent the Seven Deadly Sins of mankind, his ultimate evil, and the ten crowns will represent the opposing ten commandments Antichrist will attempt to preach. Did you know that?' he asked, as if picking the information out of thin air.

He flicked ash from his cigarette into the ashtray before continuing his dialogue. 'And what do you know of the two prophets — Elijah and Enoch? They have remained incarnate on earth so that, in the final days, they will oppose and expose Antichrist. However, I feel he will kill them to show the multitudes that he is stronger.'

I knew nothing of the two prophets he spoke of, so could not confirm or deny his extraordinary statements. Never before had Bernard ever touched upon this delicate subject. In fact, it was most out of character with his normal psychic material, so why was he picking all this up now, on 5th January, 1987?

'Well, it's something to do with this Roger Bacon,' he concluded, stubbing out his cigarette and then picking up his pint of Kaliber. 'He wrote about the coming Armageddon, I feel.' He paused for a moment. 'I would also say that his name was only a pseudonym. What do you say to that?'

Very little, but it could easily be checked out. Yet I was still not satisfied with his answer to my question; so I asked it again. Why was he picking up this information now?

'It must be relevant to our future, I suppose. Things are imminent,' he announced, almost prophetically.

Imminent? How imminent? And whose future was he referring to? Ours, or the world's?

'It must relate to *our* situation in some way.'

In respect to the Black Alchemist?

'Yes, I reckon so. Don't you?'

I felt he was going to say that. At the time of our

confrontation with the Black Alchemist at the Running Well the previous October, there had been indications that BA believed he was preparing the way for the coming of Antichrist. This had been suggested again within the lengthy automatic script Bernard had received from his Elizabethan alchemist spirit guide whilst in the well hollow.

At the time, I had dismissed any possible connection between the Black Alchemist and Antichrist, purely because I had no firm belief in a literal translation of the *Book of Revelations*. It was a Christian concept which should not be taken at face value. However, I also knew only too well that if enough people believed in a certain religious concept then it could breathe life into its existence.

Yet all this was not to say that the Black Alchemist could not believe in the imminent approach of the final days. What was more, there was nothing to stop him believing that he was the Proclaimer, the one preparing the way for the coming of 'Antichrist proper', in much the same way that St John-the-Baptist had prepared the way for the coming of Jesus Christ. So was this what the man actually believed?

'Yes, I think so,' Bernard admitted.

Okay. Then another question. Was he *really* preparing the way for the coming of Antichrist?

He smiled. 'I can't answer that. Can I?'

The conversation stopped dead. The bar's normally warm and relaxed atmosphere became icy cold as a blast of freezing air passed across the table, sending the feather-light silver and green tinsel over the windows flickering to and fro. No window was open, and no one had walked in or out of the bar. It was an interesting synchronicity if nothing else, especially in view of my last question.

Bernard looked at me in amazement before twisting his head to stare intently at the flickering tinsel, a note of genuine curiosity upon his face. Shuddering, he returned his eyes to me. 'Did you feel that?' he asked.

I responded calmly, but it did not dispel his obvious concern.

'A presence has entered the room. Over there.' He nodded towards the large window below the tinsel. 'I've gone all shivery.'

Now, this *was* unusual. Bernard was not the sort of psychic who continually went around feeling and seeing presences every five minutes. In fact, I could not recall the last time he had made such a statement, so I noted the time, just in case. It was 8.09 pm.

'Now I see a dark, shimmering form in front of the window, suspended in mid air. It's just there; watching us. Be careful of your conversation.'

I just listened as I picked up my pint glass and sipped its dark brown contents. So who was it?

'Don't know. Just ignore it. It will go away; eventually.'

At home that night, I retired into my bedroom and made straight for a book I knew would help me check out many of the points Bernard had raised earlier on. It was an intriguing work I had picked up a while back entitled *Antichrist in the Middle Ages – A study of Medieval Apocalypticism, Art and Literature,* by someone named Kenneth Emmerson (Manchester University Press, Manchester, 1981).

Having scanned its index and found no references to Apollyon, I turned my attentions to finding references to the seven-headed beast that would rise out of the sea.

Bernard had been correct. Certain medieval scholars had believed that the seven heads would represent the Seven Deadly Sins, or vices, of mankind. However, I could find nothing which indicated that the beast's ten crowns symbolised the antithesis of the Ten Commandments as set down by Moses, the Biblical lawgiver.

Moving on to the two prophets, Elijah and Enoch, I found mention of these in many places within the book. They were, in fact, referred to as the two witnesses. Elijah (or Elias) and Enoch, it was said, would preach for 1,260 days — three and one half years — and, through their spiritual power, they would perform miracles and preach in an attempt to turn away the multitudes from the false ways of Antichrist to the true path

Antichrist, in his guise as Apollyon, the Beast of the Abyss, seen here killing the two witnesses, Elijah and Enoch.

of Jesus Christ. Yet then, as Bernard had suggested, they would be killed by Antichrist and their bodies would be left unburied for three and one half days, so that they could be inspected by the followers of Antichrist. However, the two witnesses would then be resurrected and allowed to join God and the saints in Heaven.

Such was the story given in the Apocalypse of St John. Indeed, the prophesied appearance of Elijah and Enoch, just prior to the coming of Antichrist, had been one of the most popular themes of medieval theological art, literature and discussion.

Next, I turned my attentions to the forms that Antichrist would supposedly take during Armageddon. Were there two forms of the Antichrist: one the mystic or Proclaimer, and the other the true Antichrist, a supernatural humanoid manifestation of the false holy spirit?

I could find no definite answer.

As Emmerson's book explained, the Apocalypse provided

theological scholars with fertile ground for those searching for symbols of Antichrist. It was filled with references to marvellous creatures rising out of the earth, the sea and the abyss. Some creatures would be multi-headed, whilst others would be composites of various animals or human-like in appearance. All would battle against the saints and were to be identified with Antichrist himself. Yet, in the final days of these times, they would each be destroyed by the returning Saviour.

Apocalyptic studies were obviously a complex and rather contradictory subject which required a lot of careful study and analysis. So I left Antichrist for a moment and went on to Roger Bacon. Bernard felt that the thirteenth century alchemist, philosopher and scientist had spoken much about the Apocalypse and the coming of Antichrist; and he had not been wrong. Glancing through the index of Emmerson's book, I saw it contained several entries for Roger Bacon, each of which I read before jotting down a few notes.

The exercise left me with a somewhat more enlightened understanding of Roger Bacon, for it appeared that in one of his works entitled *Opus Majus,* he had given a lengthy commentary on the coming of Antichrist. However, very little of it was quoted in Emmerson's book, so I could do little to either confirm or deny Bernard's statements about the man.

Turning now to other books, this time on the subject of alchemy, I discovered that the name 'Roger Bacon' was suspected to have been used as a pseudonym by other alchemical writers of a later period who had wished to remain anonymous. Therefore, it was very possible that not all the works accredited to Roger Bacon were, in fact, written by the man himself.

Now for another attempt at Apollyon. In a book entitled *A Dictionary of Angels — including the Fallen Angels,* by Gustav Davidson (The Free Press, New York, 1967), under the entries for the letter A, I found him. Apollyon, it stated, was the Greek rendering of the Hebrew title Abaddon, meaning 'destroyer,' the name given to the dark angel of the bottomless pit in *Revelations 9:11* who rises up to bring desolation to the world. He was also identified with both the angel of death and

A curious mural taken from the wall of one of the monasteries on Mount Athos, in North Eastern Greece, depicting Antichrist, as Apollyon, rising out of the Abyss to attack the two witnesses. Around the strange form are the locust-like beasts of *Revelations 9:3*, said to be the forces of Antichrist.

destruction, and the winged demon guardian of the abyss, the form of Antichrist that would allegedly put to death the two witnesses, Elijah and Enoch.

In many ways, Apollyon *was* a Greek title for Antichrist. Therefore, if he was the antithesis of Jesus Christ, the Christian solar king, then it could be reasoned that Apollyon was the opposing force to Apollo, the divine solar god of Greek mythological tradition, as Bernard had suggested.

Placing the heavy book back on the shelf, I thought carefully about the situation at hand. Here I was, studying Christian interpretations of the Biblical Apocalypse, almost as if it was an accepted series of future events. But this was certainly not the case. Although Bernard's psychic material was checking out pretty well, all it meant was that he had picked up the interpretations and writings of others who had studied the question of a coming Apocalypse, like Roger Bacon, for instance. It *did not* mean that he, or anyone else, even St John-the-Divine had got it right. No one really knew what the future would hold for us in the final days.

Final days? I didn't even believe in them. Back in the late 1970s I had listened in all seriousness to respected psychics who had firmly believed that the world was about to be plunged into an Armageddon-like situation. They had been wrong. Their predicted dates of great global catastrophes had all passed without incident, so there was no way that I was going to fall for that sort of stuff in 1987.

Annoyed at the situation, yet satisfied with my findings that night, I decided to call it a day and go to bed.

Time passed. Winter melted into spring. Spring blossomed into summer, and summer matured into autumn. The nights grew longer, the air turned colder, but still the Black Alchemist did not turn up at Danbury, or anywhere else for that matter.

Bernard and I continued to meet for a drink in the familiar surroundings of The Griffin Tavern and the subject of the Black Alchemist would inevitably crop up in conversation here and there. In answer, he would merely shake his head and say: 'No, nothing on him at all.'

As each passing month pushed the October 1986, Running Well confrontation even further back into the past, the more the Black Alchemist began to slip out of our conscious thoughts.

The hidden powers of the Indian swordstick remained dormant, and other, more productive psychic quests occupied our lives.

August 1987 saw my departure from my parents' home in Wickford to a comfortable first floor flat in Leigh-on-Sea, overlooking the Thames Estuary. It was exactly what I needed, independence and a place to write freely.

Twenty four

Night of the She-wolf

Thursday, 15th October, 1987. 8.00 pm. 'Tonight I want you all to imagine yourselves as a tree, with your body as the trunk and your arms as its branches,' the vivacious lady teacher told the small, but attentive class. 'Sense the wind blowing through its leaves. See it. Feel it. Experience it. Then write and draw whatever comes into your mind. I'll give you ten minutes.'

The class quietly opened their loose-leafed files and picked up their pens in anticipation.

Little Chesca Potter was first and foremost an artist; a painter of magical and mystical themes and subjects. Indeed, success and recognition had come to her in recent years in the form of several commissions for book covers and illustrations. However, the creative writing class, held close to her tiny North London flat, was helping to develop her writing abilities and she enjoyed the company of the other young writers.

Content, Chesca picked up her pen and mentally contemplated the evening's chosen image, which she found comparatively easy to visualise as many of her pictures were intuitively painted in a similar way.

For a few moments she closed her eyes and became a tree. Yet she had to stop and re-open them as the image disturbed her for some reason. A nauseous feeling began to well up inside her stomach, and she shivered with concern. Something was undoubtedly wrong, and it worried her.

Chesca looked around at her classmates silently engrossed in their own work and could not understand her irrational feelings. Why should visualising yourself as a tree produce such an oppressive sensation?

Perplexed, she sketched a silhouetted image of a storm-struck tree and continued the writing exercise.

Friday, 16th October. 3.00 am. Chesca had been unable to get to sleep. The disturbing feelings she had experienced whilst at the writing class the previous evening had grown with intensity as the night had advanced, and with them had come a sense of depression and hopelessness. Why, she could not say. It worried and concerned her almost to a point of desperation. And the gale-force winds had not helped to calm her nerves. They had started around eleven o'clock and had been growing with ferocity ever since that time.

She was on edge, and something else was now happening. An ugly image kept looming out of the dark depths of her inner mind — a hideous demoness with a long tongue protruding from her open mouth. Yet she recognised its form from her past studies of Hindu mythology. It was Kali, an Indian goddess of death and destruction, whose image she had wanted to paint for some while.

Chesca could almost sense her oppressive presence building within the room and it disturbed her. Yet there was more — a sudden realisation that this image was in some way connected with her experience at the writing class and, for some reason, the growing intensity of the gale-force winds.

Something was building up both within her, and outside across London. Distraught, she searched for answers. The response came as a sudden compulsion to paint a picture of the demoness — almost as if Kali was compelling her to do so. And she would not ignore it. It would take her mind off the events of the past several hours and would, in some strange way, release them from her mind.

Picking up a sharp pencil, Chesca Potter began to sketch an image of Kali, which she knew she must finish before the first light of day washed away the darkness.

3.30 am. The sound of the violent winds woke me from my slumber. The air in the room was warm, even humid. Strange for that time of year, I thought.

Laying in bed, I listened. Never had I heard anything like this before. The ferocious gusts every few seconds sounded dangerous, even frightening. Window panes banged, masonry crashed to the ground, fences gave way and tree branches snapped. And all the time the wind, roared, rumbled and hissed incessantly.

Time passed, and the gales worsened. Suddenly, a loud thumping crash sounded overhead. It was a chimney stack, I was sure. But whose was it? Mine, or somebody elses'?

Still the wind increased in ferocity. With each almighty gust more crashing sounds followed.

Something very powerful was manifesting itself. I could feel it. A hurricane, yes. But something more . . .

Slipping out of bed, I toured the first floor flat in the darkness making sure that every window was shut and secured, before moving into the black room, my place of meditation. Kneeling down, I contemplated the chaotic strength of the winds and closed my eyes.

Images appeared of an almost demonic female face, cackling with laughter. No, I could not look. Re-opening my eyes, I raised my hands up into the air and asked: 'What the hell is going on?'

4.00 am. Caroline Wise could not sleep in her second floor London flat because of the worsening hurricane winds. The dim light of the bedside lamp on the clock radio gave her the chance to block them out. She would read.

Minutes passed as the howling pitch of the terrifying gales grew louder and more violent. Continually she broke off her reading to glance cautiously at the vibrating bedroom window which looked like it was about to implode from the impact of the oncoming winds.

The room was a darkened miniature city of angular shapes and forms. Looking again towards the window, a new shape now blocked out the faint oncoming light from the nearby orange flourescent street lamps. It was human-like and advancing towards her.

Ethereal light illuminated its horrendous supernatural form. The end of the bed obscured its lower half, but she could clearly see that its torso and head were that of a wolf. A she-wolf, she felt, and it was no mere image in the mind's eye. It seemed physically present in the room and even its most minute details could be distinguished — its coarse bristles encircling a long reddy-coloured snout, even the sticky saliva around the edges of its long, jagged teeth.

She did not want to view the disgusting sight, so mentally pushed the spectral form back towards the window and the oncoming winds. It vanished, but the lingering thought of its presence nauseated and revolted her.

Somehow, she instinctively knew its nature — malevolent, female and, for some inexplicable reason, linked with the presence of the chaotic, destructive might of the hurricane.

She let minutes pass by before responding. Casting off the duvet, she slid out of bed and stumbled across to the door. Pulling it open, only darkness and a sense of calm greeted her in the hallway.

A window in the kitchen rattled in sympathy with the ebbs and flows of the gusting winds. She would have to close it. Anyway, it would give her a chance to compose herself in different surroundings.

Switching on the kitchen light, her eyes squinted as her raised hand made for the rattling pane, which she secured and then forgot.

The door behind her slid open and a female form moved into view. It was her flat-mate, twenty year old Gaynor Sunderland, bleary-eyed and in her dressing gown. Using the back of her hand to shield her eyes from the intensity of the bright light for a moment, she leaned back on the kitchen unit. 'I heard someone get up,' she said, in a low voice. 'So I thought I'd see what was going on.' Her eyes kept closing as if she was about to fall back into a sleeping state.

'I was having this horrible nightmare,' Gaynor began to reveal, not thinking that Caroline would be particularly interested. 'I was being held in a house against my will by an old woman with a wolf's head; a she-wolf of some kind. And there were two men as well. They also had wolves' heads.'

Caroline's disturbing vision returned to her instantly. Another she-wolf incident. This time in the form of a dream. Gaynor was psychic, so had she telepathically picked up the image of the she-wolf from her? Or was it something else — an intrusion into the house of a hideously malevolent force? And who was this she-wolf? They were questions which Caroline did not wish to answer.

Leaving Gaynor, she returned to her bedroom and climbed back into bed. She attempted to ignore the disgusting memory of her own supernatural intruder, and the disturbing sound of the gusting winds, by once more trying to read by the dim light of the clock radio.

For a while she just lay there listening. Yet then, over a period of no more than a few seconds, the entire input of light coming in through the window gradually extinguished as the different electricity sub stations lost their power and London was plunged into total darkness.

The time was now 4.50 am.

9.00 am. The car tyres crunched over shattered roof tiles and broken pieces of masonry as I swerved to avoid yet another fallen tree sprawled across the road, its branches twisted and fractured by the sheer weight of its heavy trunk.

The hurricane had left a trail of absolute chaos and mayhem in Leigh-on-Sea. Roofs were missing from houses, trees blocked virtually every road, fences had simply vanished and shop fascias, perspex blinds, broken glass and gates littered everywhere. The scene was like something out of an apocalyptic nightmare.

One of the casulties of the hurricane was the ancient fir tree in the churchyard of St. Clement's church, within the author's home town of Leigh-on-Sea, in South East Essex (Photograph: Brian Fenning, *Leigh Times*).

At Leigh-on-Sea, in South East Essex, the glass fronts of a great number of shops imploded with the sheer force of the hurricane. Here we see the front of Richard Wrenn Antiques, in Broadway West (Photograph: Brian Fenning, *Leigh Times*).

Further on, shopkeepers were desperately trying to collect up what was left of their stock, which now lay scattered across the road, as emergency replacement glass vans frantically tried to board up yet another disintegrated shop front. On the other side of the street people were clearing away the fragments of a collapsed brick wall which now blocked the pavement. And all around, chimney stacks were either inside roofs or scattered across people's front gardens.

It was the same story wherever I went. As I cruised about, taking in the situation, I just shook my head in disbelief.

Pulling into a side road, I searched for a parking space. On the corner, wrapped around a bent signpost, was yet another shop blind, lying next to which was an ornamented pinnacle that had fallen from the roof of a nearby bank.

No, I had never seen anything like this before.

9.30 am. Jonathan Guy, news editor for the *Leigh Times,* was the only person who had managed to reach the office before me.

'The 'phones are out,' he announced, pacing up and down the office in frustration. 'However, if you do want to use one, keep trying, as I somehow managed to get through to my father. There's a tree on his car. A fence has smashed my mum's car and the roof of their flat caved in as the chimney stack toppled down. He didn't sound in a very good mood over the 'phone!'

The telephone did work spasmodically and, obtaining a line, I seized the opportunity to ring Brian Fenning, head photographer on the paper. We needed some pictures as no one was ever going to believe this in years to come.

Brian was almost insulted by my suggestion. 'Er, before you go on any further, I've just got back actually. I've been out since first light this morning and have taken over three hundred pictures, so far,' he announced, somewhat indignantly.

'The whole of Leigh, Chalkwell and Westcliff has been completely devastated. I've never seen anything like it,' he

The roofs of houses were ripped into the air as the hurricane tore across South East Essex. This house in Chalkwell Avenue, Westcliff, was a typical example of such damage (Photograph: Brian Fenning, *Leigh Times*).

Millions of trees were torn down during the hurricane. Here we see the devastating damage discovered the following morning along Hillside Crescent, at Chalkwell, in South East Essex (Photograph: Brian Fenning, *Leigh Times*).

admitted, trying to contain his excitement. 'The houses along the cliffs have really taken a battering — roofs off, chimneys gone, windows out; and there are trees all over the place. In some roads every single tree has fallen on to the houses nearest to them. It looks really bizarre. Anyway, I keep bumping into photographers from the '*Echo,* so I suppose they'll be running a picture special in tonight's edition.'

Hopefully, we would do the same. As morbid as it might seem to some, a full pictorial account of the damage done by the hurricane would have to be made and recorded for posterity in a local paper such as ours.

Anyway, it would make a good advertising feature!

3.00 pm. John Merron, Caroline's other flat-mate, had finally managed to get to work despite being turned back by police on his first attempt to reach the heart of London.

Even though it was now early afternoon, the electricity had still not been switched back on and the telephones still appeared to be out of operation.

Caroline contemplated the absurd situation. With the roads blocked, the electricity not functioning and the telephones out of order, it seemed bizarre to think that one of the world's most technologically-advanced capitals had been brought to a complete standstill by the powers of nature. She explained this to Gaynor as they hunted around for batteries to use in an old radio they were trying to repair in the hope of reaching the outside world.

Then, as if to signal its return to life, the telephone rang out. Answering it, Caroline heard the relieved voice of her best friend, Cath, who lived nearby.

After establishing that each other's homes were still in one piece, Cath went on to a different matter.

'Caroline, something awful happened when I woke up around four this morning,' Cath revealed, in a clearly hesitant and concerned voice; which was not like her. 'As I opened my eyes I swear I saw Graham as a wolf.'

During the hurricane, falling trees careered into houses destroying roofs and cars. Here we see a house at Chalkwell, in South East Essex, that suffered the destructive might of not one, but three falling trees (Photograph: Brian Fenning, *Leigh Times*).

The houses along the cliffs at Leigh-on-Sea, in South East Essex, took the worst battering during the hurricane. Many lost roofs, chimneys, or windows, as in the house pictured (Photograph: Brian Fenning, *Leigh Times*).

Caroline had to reassure her that she was not going mad before she would continue.

'I even saw a long snout and a hairy face. It was horrible and it frightened the life out of me so much that I screamed out, waking Graham. At that moment his face returned to normal,' she explained. 'I'm not kidding you, Caroline. I bet you think I'm going round the bend. Don't you?'

She knew her friend was not lying, or mad. Even though Cath claimed not to be psychic she had conclusively shown to Caroline, during their many years of friendship, that she was more susceptible to paranormal experiences than she liked to believe. And seeing her husband as a wolf was not as outlandish as Cath obviously believed it to be.

Wolves again. Three separate experiences, and all at the height of the hurricane. It had to mean something.

Minutes later she answered the telephone to someone else who had been desperately trying to get through to the number for some hours — Marion Sunderland, Gaynor's mother, calling from her home in North Wales.

'I've been trying to get through,' she confirmed, in her distinctive Liverpool accent. 'The lines have been down all over the place. We haven't seen much of the hurricane up here, but I heard about it on breakfast television earlier on. Is everyone alright? How's Gaynor, and yourself?'

Having assured her everyone was fine, Caroline asked Marion if she had picked up any psychic messages during the night; any unusual dreams or visions?

'No love, I didn't,' Marion responded. 'Why, what did you get?'

Caroline refrained from giving the game away, and instead asked Marion if she felt anything as they spoke.

'All I get now are some words. I don't know what they mean. I get "The wolves are running."'

The wolves are running. The fourth person to pick up the wolves theme. But why wolves? Perhaps they were some sort of mystical aspect of hurricanes? It was certainly a pattern, but what did it mean?

At Leigh-on-Sea, in South East Essex, lifelines were cut off completely by the hurricane as trees blocked roads or fell on to cars (Photograph: Brian Fenning, *Leigh Times*).

4.30 pm. The *Leigh Times would* put together a pictorial special on the hurricane, so we needed to find out exactly what had taken place, both locally and over the rest of the country as a whole. We needed to know what had caused it, the full extent of the damage, and why it had not been predicted.

And, by the end of the day, this was how it looked . . .

During the early hours of that morning, England had been struck by the worst gales in living memory and the first hurricane since 1703. Tropical winds gusting up to speeds in excess of 110 mph had torn through the south-eastern counties, leaving a horrifying trail of death and destruction in their wake.

Never before had anyone seen anything quite like it on these shores. Thousands of families had been left homeless as buildings collapsed like houses of cards. Roofs had been wrenched into the air and windows exploded. Millions of people were now without heat, electricity and telephones as overhead cables and power lines had crashed to the ground. Caravans, lorries and vans had been overturned and boats in coastal regions had been scooped up and tossed on to dry land.

Hundreds of years of heritage had been destroyed in an instant of time as an estimated fifteen million trees were torn from their roots and sent crashing on to roads, railway lines, overhead cables and houses. And worst of all, as the first light of day had brought with it a harsh sense of calmness and reality, twenty people were found to have died as a direct result of the nightmarish winds.

And there were angry questions being asked by everyone. Why had a hurricane not been forecast? There had been no mention at all of any approaching gales the previous evening. The Meteorological Office at Bracknell, in Berkshire, could give no satisfactory answer. They had plotted the birth of the gales in the Bay of Biscay around noon on the 15th when a collision of hot air currents from Africa had fused with cold Arctic air from the North Atlantic to form the deepest depression ever recorded. Yet they had predicted that the

Another house along the cliffs at Leigh-on-Sea, in Essex, which had its chimney, roof and windows damaged by the force of the hurricane (Photograph: Brian Fenning, *Leigh Times*).

Even the car of the editor of the *Leigh Times* did not go undamaged by the hurricane. Left outside his house, at Chalkwell, in South East Essex, it was crushed by a falling tree (Photograph: Brian Fenning, *Leigh Times*).

imminent storms would hit northern France; not England.

They had been wrong. The hurricane was on its way, unannounced. By 9 pm, as the winds entered the English Channel, they had increased to speeds of up to 75 mph. At 1 am that morning the gales had reached the Channel Islands with winds now gusting up to 110 mph. Around 3 am, as the majority of the country lay asleep in their beds, the malevolent southerly and south-westerly winds had begun their path of destruction across the coastal counties of Dorset, Hampshire and Sussex.

For three terrifying hours, the hurricane had wrought havoc and mayhem as it gradually moved north-eastwards towards the East Anglian coast. Only with the approach of dawn, around 7 am, had the winds begun to subside and move peacefully out into the relative safety of the North Sea.

A massive clean up operation was now under way, although it would take weeks, if not months, for life to return to normal and the full extent of the hurricane's damage to be fully realised.

Twenty five
The Dark Goddess

Saturday, 24th October, 1987. 'There have been more accounts of strange dreams and visions over the night of the hurricane,' Caroline revealed, as the car began to move off from outside her South London home for our journey to Oxford to attend the second Thelemic conference being held that day. Thelema was the term used to denote the teachings and magick, with a K, practised and developed by Aleister Crowley (1875-1947), probably the country's most notorious ritual magician of the past few centuries.

'A girl named Karen from the same mystical group I belong to in London said she dreamt of wolves that night. And she came out with this without any prompting at all.'

Any more?

'Yes, Chesca Potter. At the height of the hurricane she was compelled to intuitively paint a remarkable picture of a fierce Hindu demoness called Kali,' Caroline said, staring out at the crowds of Saturday shoppers lining the streets. 'I met her last week. She felt she had to finish it before dawn, for some reason.'

Kali. A hideous Indian she-ogre, known as the goddess of death and destruction, and a name of Lilith, a Mesopotamian demoness associated with the storm and the night, among other things. Chesca was an excellent artist and illustrator who, I knew, was a very intuitive person.

'Anyway, she will be at the conference exhibiting her paintings. So you can speak to her there.'

I had also come across accounts of strange dreams and psychic incidents that had taken place at the height of the hurricane.

In Leigh-on-Sea, Carole Smith — my psychic friend who, during November 1986, had seen the image of the black-robed figures inside Danbury church — had spent the night of the hurricane listening to the terrifying intensity of the gusting winds. Apparently, around 4 am her ears had unexpectedly heard a disturbing sound — a long, piercing woman's scream which lasted for several seconds and appeared to be carried upon the wind itself.

So real was the voice, that Carole had immediately jumped out of bed and stared out of her bedroom window, believing it to be a woman in some sort of distress. Seeing no one, she had moved to the landing window. Nothing could be seen, other than a fair-sized tree being dragged along the road by the sheer force of the incredible winds. Perplexed, she had then given up and returned to bed, concluding that the female scream had perhaps been supernatural in origin.

Carole had been unaware that the shrieking sound of a high-pitched female voice carried upon the wind was a sign of Black Annis, an ancient British Dark Goddess who was seen as a hooded crone or hag; a form more commonly remembered by her Greek name of Hekate.

Elsewhere in the country, a girl named Andrea from Aylesbury, in Buckinghamshire, had spoken to me about a powerful and vivid dream she had experienced on that fateful night. Like Gaynor, she had found herself being held prisoner in a house by an old lady of hideous appearance, who she described as a 'crone.' The building, she recalled, had been sited by a crossroads which, like the appearance of the crone-like woman, was associated with the attributes and traditions of Hekate, the Greek goddess of the underworld.

The crone appeared to possess some sort of hold over Andrea, which she found unnerving. The dream had culminated in the old woman continually approaching her and opening her mouth full of ill-formed teeth to emit a foul-stinking breath which, she emphasised, had reeked of 'rotting flesh and blood'; even death itself.

Shortly afterwards, Andrea had awoken to the sound of the

The catastrophic damage left by the hurricane in the gardens at Emmetts House, a National Trust property at Ide Hill, in Kent. Oddly enough, Ide Hill — scene of an earlier Black Alchemist ritual — was one of the worst hit villages in Kent (Photograph: Mike Howarth, National Trust).

Aerial view of the extensive damage left by the sheer force of the hurricane at Emmetts House and gardens, at Ide Hill, in Kent (Photograph: Mike Howarth, National Trust).

gale-force winds which had by no means been intense in Buckinghamshire. She had eventually concluded that the bizarre and unusual dream had been linked with the physical presence of the hurricane that night.

'Oh, and Graham Phillips experienced something strange that night,' Caroline added.

Graham Phillips. The super-psychic extraordinaire, with whom I had uncovered a hidden sword and a talismanic green jewel back in 1979. He had been a friend of ours for many years.

'Apparently, on the evening prior to the hurricane, he was intuitively drawn to a deserted pool in the Midlands area. Once there, he had felt the necessity to meditate on the elemental force of Air and the imagery of The Moon card in the Tarot pack — which shows two baying hounds. He also used an association with wolves *and* the goddess Hekate.'

More wolves, and more Hekate. What was going on? Why had there been so many closely related dreams, visions and mystical experiences during the night of the hurricane? More particularly, why had so many people picked up imagery, impressions and dreams of wolves, goddesses of the night and crone or hag-like women? It had to mean something.

As the car moved out of London and on to the M4 motorway, we worked out a few answers to these enigmatic questions; and after a couple of hours of heated discussion, it looked this way . . .

In the past, the chaotic, destructive force of the hurricane winds would have been integrally associated with a female deity who, because of her various guises and names, was now collectively referred to among the mystical fraternities as the Dark Goddess. She was known by various names — such as Astarte, Agriope, Kali, Lilith and Black Annis — yet ultimately they were all variations of the same supernatural force or energy; as that was all gods and goddesses were at the end of the day — powerful, raw energy.

In the western mystical tradition, the Dark Goddess was most revered, feared and worshipped as Hekate, the Greek goddess of the underworld. Her titles included Queen of the

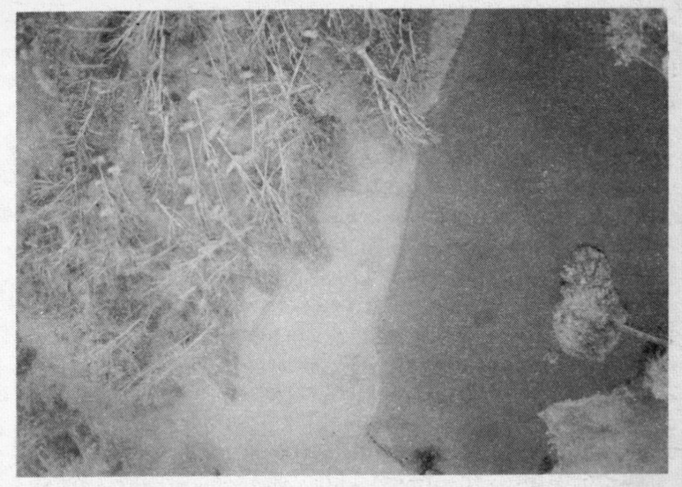

Trees were left looking like fallen matchsticks all over Essex, Kent and Sussex. Here we see an aerial view of National Trust woods at Chartwell, in Kent (Photograph: National Trust).

Night, Devourer of Corpses, Lady of Suicides and Untimely Deaths, and Mistress of Magic and Sorcery. She was also known as the Triple Goddess who presided over the three realms — sky, earth and the underworld — and possessed three bodily forms; one with the head of a frenzied canine bitch, one with the head of a maned horse and one with the head of a savage snake.

As a lunar goddess, Hekate symbolised and ruled over the dark or waning moon — even though she was often worshipped on the eve of the full moon. In this aspect, her appearance was that of a hideous crone or hag dressed in a black or grey cowled robe, and it was in this form that she took the title — Queen of the Witches.

Of particular significance to our own debate was the fact that Hekate — and the various other forms of the Dark Goddess — was at her most potent between the autumn equinox in September and the winter solstice in December. She reached her maximum power and influence at the midway point, the so-called quarter day between these two significant solar events in the yearly calendar.

This quarter day, which generally fell around the 6th or 7th November, had been known to the Celts of Northern Europe as the festival of Samhain. Over the centuries, however, this festival date became fixed to 1st November and, in the later Christian calendar, became known as All Hallows' or All Saints' Day; the eve of which was given the name Hallowe'en. In superstitious lore, All Hallows' Eve was still held to be the night when the spirits of the dead rose out of their graves to haunt the living, and a time when supernatural forces were abroad and magic, sorcery and witchcraft were rife.

During the festival of Samhain, Hekate — or her localised form — would have been appeased and worshipped with great ceremony and sacrifice, whilst her presence would have been confirmed through dreams and visions experienced by the oracles and shamans of the community.

Lastly, and most importantly, Hekate was said to ride the storms of the night with her wild hunt of *wolf-like hounds* which, along with dogs, were her favourite animals. *And she herself would often take the form of a nightmarish female wolf, and in which guise she was feared and revered by the name Lykaina – Greek for she-wolf.*

As the car sped along the M4 towards South West England, I rationally summed up the situation to Caroline. Somehow, the destructive might of the hurricane — due to the fact that it had struck unannounced, under the cover of darkness — had unleashed a secondary primeval force of equal strength. Not so much an age old supernatural deity, more a race memory of the chaotic, destructive might of the Dark Goddess, held deep within the minds of man in archetypal and symbolic form.

The result: a large number of intuitively aware people up and down the country experiencing dreams and visions involving the different guises and aspects of the Dark Goddess; and one in particular — Hekate, the hideous crone of darkness, known also as Lykaina, the she-wolf.

But had these psychic experiences been purely that —

An inscribed stone depicting the three forms of Hekate in her guise as the Triple Goddess. The one facing outwards shows her as Lykaina, the she-wolf.

archetypal and symbolic dreams and visions, or had a very real primeval force of immense magical potency been unleashed into life that night?

'It was as if Kali was compelling me to finish it. It was like an obsession,' said the petite and effervescent artist, Chesca Potter, as she held up her picture of the Hindu demoness, painted at the height of the hurricane. She stood behind a table laid out with examples of her paintings and illustrations in the Oxford guildhall during the conference's afternoon break.

'And that business at the writing class the previous evening. It was almost as if I had sensed the oncoming hurricane by attuning to the image of the tree. And yet, because I didn't understand what was going on, I just thought it was me. But I feel I experienced the impending death and destruction of the trees; which, of course, is Kali's aspect.'

I nodded in agreement. We had finally made it to the conference just before the lunchtime break due to my bad navigation. I had completely lost the junction on the M4 which should have taken us along the M25 and on to the M40 into Oxford, and had not realised my error until the road signs had indicated that we were now in Wiltshire!

I listened with great interest to Chesca's account of how she had painted her picture of Kali, before moving out into the foyer area for a cigarette. However, I had other reasons for being at the Thelemic conference that day. I wanted to try and find someone who might be able to read and interpret the apparently Greek words, and possibly even the other strange symbols, on one of the Black Alchemist's inscribed stone spearheads.

The previous year's conference had included a lecture on Graeco-Egyptian magic by a man named Terry DuQuesne. At the time, I had considered that he would have been the ideal person to look at the Black Alchemist's inscribed stones. So this year I had brought along the slate spearhead found in Rettendon churchyard exactly one year before, in October 1986. It contained precisely the same three Greek words as those on the Lullington spearhead. However, on this example, the finely-scratched symbols on its slate face were a little clearer. If these words *were* Greek, then someone would surely be able to read them. But who could I ask?

'Terry DuQuesne is here,' Caroline informed me, as we stood out of the way of the conference goers returning to their seats inside the great hall.'If anyone will know what they mean, it will be him. He is probably the country's leading expert and authority on classical and Egyptian alchemical and magical texts.'

He sounded just the job; but I could not remember what he looked like.

'I'll introduce you to him when he comes out of the hall,' she said, now sitting down on an old neo-Gothic throne chair which blended in well with the rest of the guildhall's revival decor.

We waited outside. The after effects of the beer consumed at lunchtime were now beginning to leave a dry, smoke-tinged bad taste in my mouth which would not go away. I paced around, felt thirsty and talked of other matters.

Eventually, faces appeared as the hall once more began to disgorge its audience. Young and old, long haired and short haired, punks and hippies. All passed by and began to mill around the foyer area or wander off to the small canteen. More and more people appeared. The conference was over. Caroline moved silently into the crowd and came out with a tall, stocky gentleman with short, wavy, light-coloured hair and rectangular metal-framed glasses.

'I wonder if you can help us,' she was saying to the bewildered, but intrigued man who she knew was Terry DuQuesne. 'I want you to meet my friend Andy Collins. He's been having some problems from a bloke called the Black Alchemist who keeps leaving his calling cards behind at ancient sites.'

The large man politely held out his hand for me to shake.

'Terry DuQuesne, Andy,' Caroline said, stepping out of the way with a look of accomplishment on her face.

Before he had a chance to say a word, I presented him with the Rettendon spearhead and pointed out the apparently Greek characters without giving him any real story behind its discovery.

His look changed from one of bemusement to intrigue as he held the inscribed stone closer to his face and studied its symbols. Silently moving over to a nearby table, he opened his attaché case and slipped out several sheets of personalised headed notepaper. Placing them down, he began to immediately reproduce the same three words that appeared on the inscribed stone spearhead.

It was looking good. So, were they Greek words then?

'Oh yes, they're Greek alright,' he confirmed, still studying the spearhead which he had now placed on the table next to the headed notepaper.

'Look here, at this word.' He pointed a finger towards the longest of the three words on the slate's face – Μαλιαριοσ– before reproducing it again on paper. 'M-A-L-I-A-P-I-O-S.

And this one,' he continued, scribbling down the second word — σαο. 'S-A-O. I'm not sure about the third word.' He wrote it down — Ομοη. 'It seems to be composed of the letters O-M-O-Ee.'

Maliapios, Sao and Omoee. What did they mean?

Terry took in a deep breath. 'Well, although I have not come across these particular spellings before, I have seen very similar words in Graeco-Egyptian magical papyri,' he explained. 'They are goetic barbarous names. Words of power used as chants or tonal calls to invoke and banish magical forces by priests and magicians during the first centuries after the death of Christ.'

Goetic barbarous names. I had heard the term before, but that was all.

'Goetic means, literally, "to howl." Such words were always thought by scholars to have been gibberish, just meaningless expressions,' he continued, the foyer around us now full of people. 'However, I have been studying this subject for some years and have established that a great many of these names are corruptions of Aramaic, Egyptian and Hebrew titles of gods. Look at this.' He returned to his own renderings of the three Greek words from the spearhead.

Caroline and I stood one each side of him, taking in his every word.

'Maliapios,' he pronounced. 'It is a word found in certain Graeco-Egyptian magical papyri, under the spelling "Modorio" or "Mabarroia," which appear to be corruptions of the Aramaic/Hebrew title "Lord of Luminaries" or "Lord of Hosts." Titles given to the Hebrew god. Indeed, I am working on the translation of a magical papyri containing this word at this very time. It is a Graeco-Egyptian magical formula known as the Headless One, the same ritual that Crowley used under the name the Bornless One.'

I felt I understood.

His index finger moved on to the second of the three words: Sao. He explained this one in a similar way. 'S-A-O is probably a mispelling of Iao, the Coptic and Gnostic name of the supreme being, which is itself a corruption of the Hebrew title

Sabaoth meaning, simply, "hosts." As I said, these goetic sounds are very often scrambled divine names of power.'

What about the third word? Omoee?

Terry took his attention away from the spearhead and notepaper scattered across the table. 'Unfortunately, it means nothing that I know of.' Shifting his interest to the Black Alchemist himself, he summed up his suspected image of the man: 'All I can say about the person who wrote these words is that they don't use Greek fluently. They are poorly written. However, whoever inscribed this stone is fully conversant with Graeco-Egyptian magic and could only have obtained the word Maliapios from one of a very few obscure sources.'

I wasn't entirely sure what Graeco-Egyptian magic really was. Greek-influenced Egyptian magic, I presumed.

He shook his head. 'Graeco-Egyptian magic is a combination of Egyptian, Greek, Roman, Hebrew and Gnostic Christian ritual magic which came out of Egypt between the first and fifth centuries AD. It even had its own magical alphabet and language called Coptic.

'A large percentage of the alchemical systems and ritual magic used today has its roots within Graeco-Egyptian magic. Yet so little of it has ever been translated. Anyway, I would certainly like to know a little more about this Black Alchemist.'

So would I. Collecting up the spearhead and the notepaper, I told Terry I would give him a ring and arrange to meet him at some future date.

Terry was now being coerced away from Caroline and I by a group of conference goers who appeared to want to steal his attention. 'Are you coming to the café for a cup of tea?' he asked, glancing back towards us for the last time.

We thanked him for the offer, but instead made our way out on to the balcony which overlooked the hall's foyer.

'So BA is using Graeco-Egyptian goetic barbarous names,' Caroline began, resting her arms on the top of the balustrade.

It seemed so. However, it also confirmed something which Bernard had indicated as long ago as June 1985, after his dream about the Black Alchemist's Eastbourne home. At the time he had suggested that our adversary was an academic who had access to rare books and manuscripts.

It was further confirmation, but little else, and it would certainly not take us any closer to finding him. That could only come from fresh moves, and there seemed little chance of this as well over a year had now passed without so much as a hint of his imminent return.

'Perhaps you really have seen the last of him this time,' Caroline suggested.

Perhaps. I wasn't sure.

Twenty six
The Body of Christ

Sunday, 25th October, 1987. In the ten days since the hurricane had struck the southern counties, Bernard had spent much of his spare time clearing up the damage done to his own property. He had lost a number of roof tiles, a pair of double gates and three sizeable trees from his back garden.

Having replaced the tiles and repaired the gates, he turned his attention to sawing up the uprooted trees which still littered the lawn. After lunch that afternoon, he took out the saw from the shed and started to attack a thick tree trunk.

Time passed, and as the sun's orange orb began to sink closer and closer towards the western horizon, a sudden urge began to pull at his stomach.

Something wanted him to go up to Danbury churchyard. He felt more — a connection, somehow, with fire, and heat. He was being drawn up there and, unless he went, then he would get no peace of mind.

Frowning, he put away his saw and announced to his wife that he was going up to Danbury for an hour or so.

Bringing his Orion to a halt alongside the triangular-shaped green in front of the church, Bernard was confronted by a group of some eight or more cars parked outside the entrance into the churchyard. There was obviously a service in progress and, noting the day and the hour, he realised it was a christening.

Moving into the churchyard, his thoughts returned to the

night of the hurricane as he espied a number of slates missing from the tall conical spire which stood above the medieval stone west tower. Still, if that was all the damage it had suffered then it was a blessing, he considered, as he strolled past the west door and entered the extensive graveyard section of the churchyard, set within what remained of the old Iron Age ditch and bank earthwork which crowned the hilltop site.

But then a sight saddened him greatly. The old horse chestnut tree, just to the right of the path, where he and Andy had stood to receive psychic communications on numerous occasions, lay uprooted and sawn into small cylindrical sections. It had obviously been wrenched out and thrown to the ground during the hurricane and had been cut into pieces so as not to block the path nearby.

The scene disheartened the psychic. He had always felt inexplicably drawn to that tree; *their* tree. It had exuded a warm, protective atmosphere ideal for psychic work. Light-heartedly, they had always referred to it as 'the centre of the universe,' as it had appeared to be at the very centre of the hilltop site. Now it had gone forever. Never again in his lifetime would he see another fully grown tree at that same spot.

For a few moments he stood in silent respect to the death of the tree. Then, moving in closer, Bernard became annoyed when he saw that someone — kids he presumed — had extensively burnt the area on one side of the tree stump which, although still *in situ,* was now on its side, like a plug twisted out of its socket. A thick layer of fine silver ash covered the charred stump and the ground around it. He felt that the tree had suffered in more ways than one.

Suddenly remembering his earlier impressions of fire and heat, the burnt tree stump now took on a particular significance. He mentally focused his psychic mind on the spot and immediately gained the distinct feeling that something — an artefact of some sort — lay secreted somewhere around the base of the stump. Glancing about, his eyes saw nothing. However, he felt intuitively drawn to a crack-like hole in the ground, caused as the hard earth had split and fractured when the ball-like stump had turned within its socket. It was half

All that remained of the tree in the centre of Danbury churchyard, following the October hurricane. Yet it was here that the psychic clues appeared to lead.

filled with soft earth and ash, and yet his instincts told him that something was down there.

Making sure that no one could see what he was doing, he picked up a stick and began to prod about in the hole. Realising that this was not going to solve the mystery, he tossed the stick away, got down on his hands and knees and felt about within the loose dirt. Unexpectedly, his hand caught hold of something cold, hard and irregular in shape. Withdrawing it, he picked off the encrusted earth and recognised its shape and form — it was a well-oxidised cast iron figure of Christ crucified, about six inches in length and five inches across. Quite obviously, it had once been attached to a wooden cross or plaque, but how had it got there in the earth? And who had put it there, and when? Only one point was clear, it had seemingly laid at the spot for some years and would not have been brought to the surface had it not been for the hurricane.

Flicking off more of the dry earth clogged around the metal figure, Bernard contemplated the new find and tried to open up

Within the crevice-like hole at the base of the hurricane-struck tree in Danbury churchyard, Bernard discovered the buried figure of Christ.

his mind to the situation. Only a name came — 'Chris'; or 'Christopher' which, he soon realised, was merely the word Christos, the Greek rendering of the name of Christ.

Something else told him that, although the Christ figure was psychically 'clean,' it *had* once contained a relevant memory concerning its burial. However, this had been inadvertently wiped out, or destroyed, when the fire had consumed the area around the upturned tree stump. Any feelings or energies that may have been present at the spot were now gone forever.

It was a frustrating and peculiar feeling, but there was something slightly more to it than that. Something he could not quite put his finger on. Something out of place and not quite right.

He became aware of a sudden gust of wind which swept swiftly through the churchyard, blowing an assortment of autumn-coloured leaves up into the air. As the breeze dropped, they fluttered back down to earth several yards on from their former resting place.

On the surface of the cast iron figure of Christ — found psychically by Bernard in Danbury churchyard — was evidence of oxidisation caused by fire.

His stomach ached as he turned his gaze back to the sad tree stump. A chill now ran down his spine, sending his body into a sudden shiver. Somehow the churchyard felt unfamiliar, even a little unwelcoming; a feeling he had never before experienced at Danbury. He almost believed that he was intruding, and that unseen eyes were burning into his back. But that was absurd, he told himself as he shook his head and began to walk away from the spot.

Yet now he felt angry. Looking at the rest of the churchyard, he saw that, out of the dozens of trees of all shapes and sizes, only their tree, and one other, had been torn down. Others in more vulnerable positions had been left unscathed. It was a bizarre thought, but it almost seemed as if the hurricane had been selective in its targets.

He had to leave. Wrapping up the figure of Christ in a paper tissue, Bernard slipped it into his jacket pocket and promptly left the churchyard, clearly perplexed by his attitude and feelings about the site.

Danbury churchyard was different. Something was changing and he did not like what he felt.

Twenty seven
The Foul Virgin

Tuesday, 27th October, 1987. 'No one would have found that Christ figure had the tree not fallen down in the hurricane,' Bernard emphasised, after having revealed the story behind its discovery two days beforehand.

As he disappeared off to the bar of The Griffin to order more drinks, I studied the cast iron figure very closely. Its reverse was hollow and several clods of oxidised earth still clung tight, like small orange growths. This oxidisation had not been caused naturally, it was the sort of effect achieved when a buried object was exposed to a great amount of heat. No wonder any vibrations it had contained were destroyed by the fire, which I was sure had not been caused by kids, as Bernard believed. It had almost certainly been lit to consume the branches and leaves removed from the tree shortly after its fall.

There were also two screw holes in its hollow back which indicated that the object had once been attached to a wooden cross. However, as no screws were present then it suggested that the figure had been buried on its own for some reason, either before the tree had been planted or whilst it was still in its infancy. Therefore, assuming that the tree had been around 100 years old when it was torn down, then the figure had to be a similar age, probably from around the turn of the century. But who had placed it there, and why? The logical answer was that someone, a past Danbury parishioner perhaps, had placed it at the spot as a devotional act of some kind in remembrance of someone who was buried nearby. Maybe the tree had been planted for the same reason.

We could go no further on the matter, so our conversation

inevitably switched to the subject of the hurricane itself. I felt that it had been a cleansing agent, cropping the countryside like a gardener might cut back a tree. Although the tree would look ugly for a while, it would ultimately benefit from the cropping.

Bernard disagreed. 'Look at the way it struck. It was calculated and destructive, and it hit the country under the cover of darkness. It almost appeared as if some supernatural intelligence had co-ordinated its path of terror.'

Where had I heard those words before! I explained how, during the night of the hurricane, many people had experienced strange dreams and visions concerning the Dark Goddess. I said little more than this as he did not appear to be that interested.

'Well, all I saw that night were balls of electric-blue light bobbing up and down above some distant treetops,' he said, bringing his cigarette to his mouth. 'Did you know that the hurricane reached its peak around 4 am — the darkest point in the night, and the time when the human body is at its most vulnerable.' He sat back and looked as if he knew what he was talking about. 'Did you also know that more people die around 4 am than at any other time of the day.'

No, but what had that to do with us?

Bernard frowned, stubbed out his cigarette in the ashtray and looked serious for a moment. 'Look, I know the hurricane was a natural disaster. That, no one can deny. Even so, the winds were an elemental force of immense potency which could have been tapped and utilised by those who knew what they were doing.'

Partially understanding his statements, I returned to the figure of Christ still lying on the table in front of us. There was something I had just remembered which could be relevant to its discovery. Just a day and a half after the hurricane, during the evening of Saturday, 17th October, Bernard had picked up a clear image — his first clairvoyant vision for some time — of a metal figure of Christ crucified affixed to a wooden cross. He had seen it floating above a flickering flame of light. With this had come the presence of a saint named Anne, whom he had

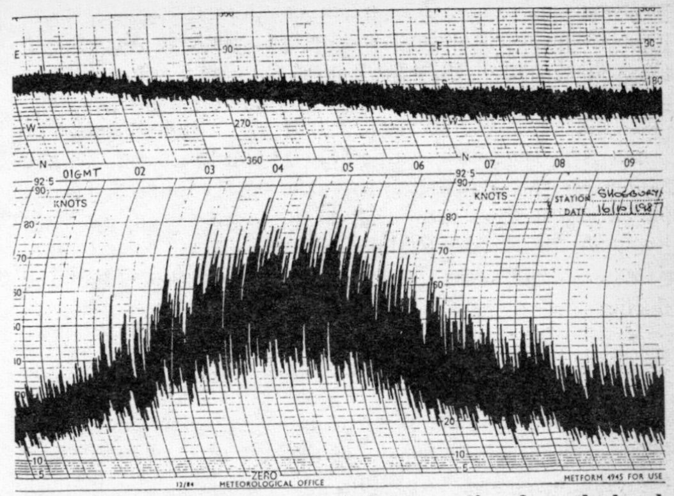

Copy of the Anemogram — or 'wind record' — from the local meteorological office at Shoeburyness, in South East Essex, showing how the hurricane reached its maximum strength between four and five o'clock on the morning of Friday, 16th October, 1987 (Reproduced by courtesy of HMSO).

felt was with the influence of the crucifix.

At the time, I had discovered that in Christian mythology St Anne was the Christianisation of the ancient British goddess Anna, Annis, or Black Annis, a form of the Dark Goddess. However, as this psychic image had entered Bernard's mind whilst we had been working on a completely separate quest, I had obviously attached it to that. Yet this vision now appeared to take on a new significance in the light of him finding the cast iron figure by the burnt tree stump. So, was this earlier clairvoyant image now relevant to the current situation?

'I had thought of it,' Bernard admitted, taking a sip from his pint of cold Kaliber. 'Although I hadn't really come to any sort of a conclusion.'

For a moment, I let the subject drop. But then I thought seriously about the matter. It was a strange coincidence. Hold on, there was no such thing as coincidence in this game. It *had* to be connected in some way. Surely he could see that?

'Well, alright. I suppose it must be linked somehow,' he concluded, forcing a grin.

Thank you. At the time, I had asked him whether he considered the crucifix to be buried somewhere, and he had said it was. We were therefore meant to have found this figure of Christ for some reason, and I intended to find out why. Bernard seemed eager to show me exactly where he had found it, so, after emptying our glasses, we left the noisy pub and ventured out into the cold autumn air.

In the darkness of the mid evening, kids heading across the green towards the small hall at the side of the church were shouting, screaming and letting off fireworks.

Fireworks. Of course, Thursday week was Guy Fawkes' Night.

Perhaps we should retire back to the warmth of the pub and return later.

'No, let's carry on,' Bernard said, as we began to pass between the groups of youths standing by the front entrance to the church.

Having forgotten to bring a torch, Bernard attempted to use his disposable lighter to illuminate the crack-like hole to the side of the upturned tree stump where, only two days before, he had unearthed the cast iron figure of Christ. In turn, we both probed the dirt and ash-filled hollow with our fingers to make sure that nothing else lay secreted. Satisfying ourselves that it was empty, I asked Bernard if he would attempt to tune into the site by holding the Christ figure and contemplating the situation.

'I won't get anything,' he quipped, as he reluctantly stood in a quiet, meditative state next to the upturned tree stump.

A minute or so passed.

Breaking his concentration, he shook his head. 'No, I get nothing. Only the same name again: "Christos".' Losing interest, he began pacing about and lit a cigarette. 'It's as I said. The fire has cancelled out any memory or message left in both the Christ figure and the ground itself.'

There was no way that I was going to let him give up *that* easily. There *had* to be more to the discovery of the Christ figure than simply this, so I asked him to go over to the other side of the path and touch a similar-sized tree which was still standing. Maybe by making contact with this one it would allow him communication with the inherent energies present in the churchyard.

Reaching out towards the tree with his right hand, a sudden strong wind unexpectedly gusted across the hilltop and hissed through the branches of the trees. I commented on this.

'I know. Not a good sign,' he admitted, light-heartedly. 'I'm not sure I like it.' Yet, calming down, he stamped out his cigarette, relaxed his mind and concentrated sensibly.

Minutes past, but then the information began to flow.

'I pick up a laying to waste of good intentions caused by both the hurricane and the fire . . . and an opposite force to what there should be; here in the churchyard.' He paused for a moment to work out his feelings.'There are odd forces abroad at the moment. Someone is working on a magical level. On the night of the storm several occult groups and individuals took advantage of the situation . . . many not even known to each other. Those forces are still about . . . I feel I ought to be careful.'

Another long pause followed before he turned his attention to the effects of the hurricane. 'The gales destroyed countless millions of trees in a very short space of time. Each of these were focal points of localised energies. These points are now, simply, no longer there, leaving gaping holes in the landscape's normally balanced and harmonious energy matrix.

'This has now forced a gross imbalance in the entire country's energy levels. I see many other points like this site. All have changed. I also see and feel uncontrollable heat coming from here and other similar places across the countryside. Yet the hurricane also seemed selective in its targets, almost as if somebody chose which sites were to be destroyed.'[1]

In complete darkness, I tried frantically to scribble down his every key word. I just let him continue without interruption.

'Things are brewing,' he proclaimed, as he released his hand from the tree and began to pace about in his unstoppable shamanic mood. 'Opposites . . . so an imbalance . . . the way now open for other darker aspects to build up . . . a state of chaotic mayhem.'

But what about the Christ figure? Why had he found that?

'The tree coming down, and the fire. It was a spoiling . . . a deliberate cancelling of good intentions left by whoever buried it. There is a strong link between the spoiling of this place and oddball.'

Oddball? I stopped writing and looked up for an explanation.

'BA.'

The Black Alchemist. What had he to do with all this?

'Working . . . that night . . . took advantage. I shall have to be on my guard,' he warned himself, as he continued to pace about looking for further psychic clues.

Then he stopped and flicked his finger at me as if he wanted to crystallise an impression. 'Write this down. A name. I will spell it. T-H-E-O-S-O-P-I-A.' He attempted to pronounce it. 'Thee-o-soap-pia. It's an opposite force. Not good. A female aspect . . . dark.'

At this he walked away from the tree and moved on to the path.

Silently, I followed close behind, my pen still held up against the notepad, awaiting his next statement. Yet, from past experience, I was beginning to realise that he was sinking deeper and deeper into his own psychic vision. I would have to watch him closely.

He continued to stroll slowly along the path and did not seem aware of my presence behind him. He was undoubtedly falling into a trance state, and it concerned me. What should I do? Shake him out of it? Or leave him? I decided to leave him, for a few minutes more at least.

'Lots of things in the air,' he calmly announced, as he

glanced into the night sky, before walking further along the path. Then he shook first his left, then his right foot.

What the hell was he up to? Something was definitely wrong.

'I now see a hag . . . name something like Pap-hot-tia.' He paused to study the clairvoyant form. 'Who winds the serpents.'

It was the manner in which he said those last chilling words that confirmed my worst fears. His mind was being overshadowed by a malevolent influence. I had seen it before. He was in a trance state and, unless he withdrew quickly, then his body would be fully taken over and possessed. Almost knowing that I was too late to save him, I pleaded with him not to go any deeper. But it was a useless exercise. He would not respond in any way.

Still following in his footsteps, I caught him uttering further, almost unintelligable words in a low menacing tone which were clearly not meant for my ears. But still I scribbled them down, or those I could make out. Words such as: 'the Dark Virgin,'

In the darkness of Danbury churchyard — pictured — Bernard encountered the demoness Paphotia as the writhing black snakes began to slither on to his feet.

'the familiar,' and 'Nelos.'

The rest became inaudible as he muttered strange gibberish in a disgusting gutteral voice.

Bernard could no longer hear the voice of his friend. He felt as if he was inside a great bubble, away from the usual dark tranquility of the churchyard. In the air around him were hundreds of wriggling, black eel-like snakes, just suspended in space. It mesmerised him for a moment or two.

On the path ahead stood a hideous form — a crone or hag-like woman, wearing a black cowled robe, its hood concealing her face.

She was just standing there, penetrating and feeling within his mind, reading his every thought.

Yet he also understood her nature. She was a product, a visible manifestation of the chaotic mayhem which had festered into existence at the height of the hurricane.

So who was she? What was her name? She was many, he realised. But then a name did come — Paphotia, Winder of the Snakes.

Why was she here in the churchyard? And what did she want from him?

No answers came from the supernatural entity. She just remained silent, facing towards him.

Looking down, he now saw that around his feet was a moving carpet of snakes, curling and writhing about. Rapidly they began to wriggle and slide on to his shoes.

Frantically, he attempted to shake them free from each foot, but still more and more slithered on to his shoes and started to twist and curl around his legs. They felt warm and dry. He began to feel sick, dizzy and . . . weak.

But the mental contact with the crone was allowing him answers, without her having said a word. *He* had sent her here — this living evil. *He* had opened up the gateway that night and *she* had walked in. The Christ figure had held her, but only for a day and a half. The fire had removed the final barrier, and now she was waiting . . . for him.

Darkness was slowly enveloping his senses and he could no longer fight it. She was taking control and he . . . was . . . losing . . . consciousness.

He would have to come out of it, and *now*. Shouting out his name, I put my hands on his shoulders and began to shake him. But he did not respond.

I told him to visualise a white cross of light forming and growing in brightness within his body. Nothing happened. Thinking again, I rapidly tried to conduct a protection visualisation using verbal commands and pushing streams of golden energy through my arms and into his body.

Still he did not respond. So, guiding him over to a nearby gravestone, I told him to try and discharge the negativity into the stone — to earth it away, whatever it was — exactly as he had done in Downham churchyard when he had experienced similar problems.

Bernard, still fighting the alien intrusion within his mind, reached out and held on to the standing cross.

At least I knew he could now hear me. A banishment ritual. Yes, that was what I would try next, using strong words of power. Moving slightly away from him I frantically tried to shout out the words: In the name of the Father, the Son, and the Father . . . It came out all wrong and had no effect whatsoever.

What could I do? Another Cabalistic cross visualisation. I asked him to visualise a great white cross of light forming and growing inside his body as I again grabbed hold of his shoulders and attempted to see streams of golden energy pouring from me to him.

Only at this point did he begin to respond by lifting his hands and touching the brow of his head. Gradually he emerged from his psychic coma and returned to the land of the living.

Slowly regaining his senses and orientation, he pulled out and lit a cigarette to calm his nerves.

I suggested that we leave the churchyard immediately and go back to The Griffin to find out what the hell was going on.

Twenty eight
The Chaotic Gateway

'Make mine a Guinness,' Bernard called, as he sat down at a table and I walked up to the bar. 'I think I need it.'

I laughed with him. It would be the first alcohol I had seen him drink in nearly a year, and who was I to argue with his reasoning? Yet, despite the distressing scene I had just witnessed out in the churchyard, he appeared to be none the worse for his encounter with Paphotia, the Winder of the Snakes.

So who was this Paphotia, and who was Theosopia? The former was quite obviously a hag-like form of the Dark Goddess similar, if not the same, as Hekate. The latter was presumably a corruption of the Greek word *theosophia,* meaning God-like wisdom.

'I keep thinking about Zosimos, for some reason,' Bernard mentioned, as he took the first sip from the creamy head of his cold pint of draught Guinness. He said nothing for a moment, but then leant forward as if about to make a profound statement. 'Let me put something to you. Did Zosimos have a sister?'

My initial silence and blank expression said it all, as I reminded him that very little historical information survived concerning the life and times of this fourth century Graeco-Egyptian alchemist.

'I think you'll find he did,' Bernard said, a note of certainty in his voice. 'She was this Theo. woman. She was like an opposite force to everything that Zosimos represented.'

Lighting up a Marlboro, I reached for my pen and notepad. He was obviously picking this up as he was saying it.

'Whereas Zosimos was of the light, so to speak. A good bloke. She symbolised his dark side. His shadow.' He sat back and glanced about at the crowded pub. 'She was a spell caster, into serpents, demonology and chaos. The Pap. woman, whatever her name was . . .'

Paphotia, I reminded him.

'Yeah, she was some form of Dark Virgin. A sort of opposite to the Virgin Mary, but looking like a hag or crone. A sort of mockery, I suppose. Theo. invoked her into visible form along with other demons,' he continued, pausing to light a cigarette.

Quickly, I scribbled down his words. Paphotia, therefore, appeared to be a localised form of a Graeco-Egyptian Dark Goddess, very much like Hekate in aspect. I pointed out that, in mythological tradition, Hekate was often accompanied by a moving carpet of writhing snakes.

But Bernard was on to other things. 'Theo. worked with a corrupt priest named . . .' he paused to search his mind for an answer. 'Nelos.'

Nelos. The name he had mumbled out in the churchyard.

'Give me your pad,' he said, pulling it in his direction and picking up a pen. For a minute or two he just sat there staring into nowhere. Then he wrote for a little.

I let him continue. There seemed to be a noisy crowd in The Griffin that night. A large group of women, probably on a hen night, stood around the bar continually bellowing out shouts and laughter. Hopefully, they were going somewhere else pretty soon.

Bernard still appeared to be miles away from the hectic background noise of piped music, noisy women and passing bodies. Nothing seemed to disturb his psychic faculty when it was fully operational.

Eventually he placed down the pen and slid the notepad back across the table. Twisting it around, I picked it up and read its contents.

Theo. was into the black side of alchemy with a virgin (Paphotia) and a priest (Nelos) who was a short, wizened old man. Water was also used. An open pond, where they would

The mass devastation left by the hurricane looked like scenes from an apocalyptic nightmare. Here we see the desolated woodland surrounding the property called Foxwold, at Brasted Chart, in Kent (Photograph: *Sevenoaks Chronicle*).

> **scatter ground-up bones of animals hoping to invoke demons from the dark.**
>
> **She was warned by Zos. but chose to ignore these warnings. She also knew that the ultimate search was not for a stone (ie. the Philosopher's Stone), but a higher force who would change the landscape to deserts, but would build her many castles in order for her to spread her word, hoping to bring forth the final chaos.**

Reading the reference to 'a higher force who would change the landscape to deserts' reminded me of the mass devastation caused by the hurricane.

'And I reckon that after her death Theo.'s soul essence joined as one with her own deity, Paphotia,' he added, breaking my train of thought. 'They became one very powerful malevolent psychic force. And I reckon that this was what I encountered out in the graveyard earlier this evening. Don't you?'

How was it that an antithesis of the pregnant Virgin Mary could be synonymous with an ageing hag or crone-like woman? It was not natural. Surely the archetypal form of a virgin, black or white, should appear youthful and maiden-like. The hag archetype usually referred to the barren woman, past the stage of menopause, who represented the dark phase of the moon and the dark autumn and winter months between September and December.

His answer was simple: 'She is a shape changer of many aspects, appearances and names, all of which have combined together over the centuries to become one primeval force. To some she *will* appear as a younger woman, a maiden, albeit a dark-aspected one. To others she will appear in her guise as the crone or hag. That was how I saw her tonight.'

For the next hour Bernard and I attempted to put into perspective everything that had taken place over the past twelve days, and this was how it looked . . .

During the night of the hurricane the chaotic, destructive might of the howling winds had unleashed an equally destructive power — a primeval psychic force of immense magnitude, collectively personified as the Dark Goddess — ruler of chaos, darkness, death, destruction and disorder. Her true name was irrelevant, as her manifestations were merely representations of a raw force or magical current, inherent within the minds of mankind, and therefore not a single deity. Different psychics would see and experience her in different ways — although her most common and easily accessible archetype was as Hekate, Greek goddess of the underworld, who had appeared in two of her forms — as the crone or hag, and as Lykaina, the she-wolf.

This chaotic psychic force was purely that — an elemental power that had desolated the countryside and dissipated only when the hurricane winds had subsided as the first light of dawn had brought with it a sense of calmness and reality.

Coastal areas suffered widespread damage during the hurricane. Here, at the Rushy Hill caravan park at Peacehaven, in Sussex, 200 caravans were smashed to pieces as their frightened owners dashed for safety (Photograph: *Brighton Argus*).

There the matter might have rested, had not certain practitioners of the black arts, including the Black Alchemist, realised the magical potency of the Dark Goddess that night and decided to seize the opportunity to contain and wield its power for their own degenerate purposes. They had known full well that any magical operation carried out at the height of the hurricane, in the name of the Dark Goddess, would be many times more potent and effective than if they had utilised the same magical force at any other time. Even the time of year had been correct, mid October, when the Dark Goddess was reaching her maximum power.

The Black Alchemist could have called upon the Dark Goddess under any one of a number of guises — Astarte, Black Annis, Lilith, Kali — yet he chose a form that he could clearly relate to within his own unique brand of Graeco-Egyptian magic. He had called upon Paphotia, apparently a Graeco-Egyptian demoness, who also seemed to be synonymous with one of her former earthly acolytes, Theosopia, the corrupt sister of Zosimos of Panopolis.

Our adversary had utilised this primeval force to affect the normally harmonious solar-orientated energy field present in Danbury churchyard, the site he had been waiting to infiltrate ever since his failure to ensnare Bernard and I at the Running Well exactly one year before, in October 1986. Indeed, the hurricane had taken place precisely a year and a day after the Running Well confrontation; a synchronicity he would not have overlooked when deciding to strike at Danbury. It was also not the first time that BA had struck under the cover of very high winds. The ritual trap set up in Shenfield Common, during May 1986, had been carried out on the same day that some of the worst gales had hit the country that year.

Either by accident, or by design, the hurricane had torn down the old horse chestnut tree in the centre of Danbury churchyard which, up until that time, had been the site's epicentre of localised energies. This left the place psychically imbalanced and with a dark wormhole or doorway where the tree had once stood.

Utilising this chaotic gateway, the Black Alchemist had forged a psychic link with the site, allowing him to manifest and crystallise his Dark Virgin, Paphotia, in readiness for his next move. However, even though the tree had been removed, one obstacle had still remained between Paphotia and her total domination of the site — a cast iron figure of Christ seemingly left at the spot as a simple devotional act by a well-meaning parishioner at the turn of the century.

As long as the warm psychic memory of the emotions attached to the Christ figure had remained in place, it would have prevented her full manifestation and stopped whatever the Black Alchemist had in mind for the site. It therefore had to be removed and — as I knew only too well from my own use of the Fire of Michael out at the Running Well the previous year — fire destroys place memories.

No one can deny that the October hurricane was a natural disaster unparalleled in this country since the Great Storm of 1703. Yet its elemental power was seen as a separate entity to some people that night. Here we see the unbelievable storm devastation to woodland near Brighton, in Sussex (Photograph: *Brighton Argus*).

So, once again, either by accident, or by design, this final psychic barrier had been removed when fire consumed the area around the upturned tree stump. The memory surrounding the figure of Christ was therefore destroyed forever. It was my reckoning that the fire had probably taken place the same day that Bernard had first received his clairvoyant image of the crucifix suspended above the flickering flame, on Saturday, 17th October, the day after the hurricane and exactly a year to the day after he had received the sickening nightmare about the decapitated priest inside Danbury church.

'Very likely,' he agreed, glancing at the crowd of noisy women who had just let out a colossal drunken roar. 'Well, whatever this Dark Goddess is, it is here now, in that churchyard. However, I don't get the impression that anyone has actually been up here as I'm sure I would have picked it up.'

Why?

'The energy field I set up around the church with green crystals is still in place, despite the hurricane.'

How could he be so sure?

'I checked it when I was up here on Sunday,' he revealed, a note of smugness in his tone.

How were we to get rid of Paphotia before the Black Alchemist had a chance to use his new found hold over the churchyard?

'Perhaps we should do something at the tree,' he suggested. 'What about closing the gateway by placing a new crucifix in the hole where the original Christ figure was found.'

Of course. Another simple act of devotion, such as laying a new crucifix, was all we needed to do. However, it would need to be done during daylight hours so that another nocturnal confrontation with Paphotia could be avoided. Naturally, the act would have to be accompanied by a simple ritual, or a prayer. It was so simple, it was ridiculous.

A time and date for the burial of the new crucifix was quickly decided. It would be buried at 4 pm the following Sunday, just before sunset, exactly one week after Bernard had unearthed the original figure of Christ.

With the arrangements agreed, our conversation turned to

Never before had anyone seen anything like the effects of the October hurricane. Here we see the damage caused as the spire of St Luke's church, at Hastings, in Sussex, crashed to the ground during the fierce winds.

other less important matters, such as the goetic barbarous names on the Lullington and Rettendon spearheads.

But then my mind went back to the idea of burying a new crucifix. If the Black Alchemist intended to utilise his chaotic gateway in Danbury churchyard, then he was not going to sit by and clairvoyantly see us closing off his link with the site without putting up some kind of fight. Indeed, if he discovered that we were going to conceal the cross on Sunday, then surely he would try something before that time.

Perhaps he would even use Paphotia's presence to ensnare Bernard by enticing him up to the churchyard on his own one night. BA might even take the bull by the horns, so to speak, and pay Danbury a visit himself. The inevitable consequences of that could result in some very nasty scenes indeed!

Bernard twisted his head as he watched a glamorous-looking woman with shoulder-length dark hair and a powerful, lingering perfume who happened to walk past the table. 'S-sorry,' he exclaimed. 'Distraction. What did you say?'

BA might pay Danbury a visit himself.

'I hoped you wouldn't suggest that,' Bernard said, with a grimace. 'I don't even want to think about the possibility. I don't need the worry.'

He had always known that, should the Black Alchemist hit Danbury, then he would have major problems on a psychic level. 'Anyway, if BA does turn up here then he will win,' he added, rather pessimistically.

I told him not to be so stupid. However, I did suggest that he refrain from going up to Danbury church on his own before Sunday for *any* reason. If he did receive an overwhelming urge to do so, then he was to telephone me immediately and I would meet him up here.

Yet then, and *only* then, I had a horrifying thought. My stomach turned. Oh my God, Saturday night was the 31st October — Hallowe'en — the old pagan festival of Samhain, the night of great magical potency when the powers of the Dark Goddess were at their maximum. It was *her* night — the night she was experienced and worshipped by the devotees of the past, *and* the present. If BA was going to try and manipulate the powers of the Dark Goddess, through Paphotia, then it would be on Saturday night without any shadow of a doubt. In other words, the day *before* we intended planting the new crucifix by the upturned tree stump.

Bernard just sank back in his chair and forced a worried grin.

It was obvious. Why hadn't I realised it before? Quickly, I gave him the chance to alter the burial date from Sunday afternoon to Saturday afternoon.

'No, leave it now.'

What! Why?

'I don't know,' he responded, indecisively. 'Curiosity, I suppose. Anyway, we've made arrangements for Sunday, so it's obviously meant to be.'

Yes, but wasn't that tempting fate?

'I know,' he said, with an uncertain smile. 'And what's more,

I shall be on my own all Saturday evening. Both the wife and the daughter are out that night.' He paused to contemplate the predicament. 'I'll give you a call if anything happens.

IF YOU WANT TO SEE THE TREES FOR THE WOOD AGAIN PLEASE HELP US NOW

THE NATIONAL TRUST TREES AND GARDENS STORM DISASTER APPEAL

On the night of 15th October, 1987, a disastrous storm hit 13 counties in East and South East England.

Perhaps one million trees and countless shrubs, bushes and rare plants were wrenched up by the roots, broken in two and smashed into and onto whatever stood in the way of their collapse.

The cost of the damage to National Trust property alone runs into millions of pounds.

Of course, we must re-plant and replace our trees, as quickly as possible. But first we have to clean and clear the way.

We have to work out a long-term forestry clearance programme, which may take 3-5 years.

And cost a large amount of money.

We also have to work with planners and landscape specialists to ensure that we re-create the balance of our landscapes for future generations.

Which also costs large amounts of money.

Finally, we will re-plant the saplings, young shrubs and bushes that will one day restore our heritage to its full, mature glory.

But it all costs money!

To fund the restoration work, we appeal to you to give generously of your money.

Simply send your donation to —

The National Trust Trees and Gardens Storm Disaster Appeal, PO Box 39, Bromley, Kent BR1 1NH.

YOU MAY ALSO DONATE AT ANY BRANCH OF BARCLAYS BANK OR THE WOOLWICH BUILDING SOCIETY

The National Trust's advert for its storm appeal which is still open and awaits all donations.

Twenty nine
The Sister of Zosimos

At home that night, in some photocopies of a book sent to me by a colleague named Clive Harper, I found my first reference to Theosopia. Taken from a recently published book entitled *Arcana Mundi,* written by a gentleman named George Luck (Crucible Books, Wellingborough, 1987), they gave a short account of Zosimos' life and works. Clive knew of my interest in the fourth century alchemist and had recently dropped them in the post.

The book referred to a Zosimos work entitled *On Completion* which, it said, had been dedicated to Theosebeia, whom it described as 'presumably a wealthy lady who was interested in Zosimos' alchemic researches.' There was no mention of her being his sister, and the spelling was different, although there appeared to be little doubt that this was the same woman that Bernard had been introduced to earlier that evening.

Turning to another book, *The History of Magic,* by Kurt Seligmann (Pantheon Books, New York, 1948), I found a further reference to Theosebeia, spelt Theosebia this time. Here she was clearly referred to as 'Zosimos' sister'. Nothing else was said about her, other than that she was an early female alchemist.

For a little while I went no further with my search, having satisfied myself that the lady Theo. had existed, and that she had indeed been Zosimos' sister. But then I remembered another book I possessed which featured Zosimos. It was a huge work entitled *Hermetica — The ancient Greek and Latin writings which contain religious and philosophic teachings ascribed to Hermes Trismegistus. Volume IV,* edited and translated by Walter Scott (1855-1925) (Shambhala Publications, Inc., Boston, Mass., 1985). It was a long, tedious and yet essential work which suffered much from something I hate most about old books—the constant use of original languages *without translation!* In other words, it was not very helpful unless you happened to read Greek, Coptic and Latin!

This somewhat pricey, specialist book I had purchased the previous year, as it contained a lengthy chapter on 'Zosimos Panopolitanus'. However, it had not proved of any particular use to me at the time as it did not contain any material on Zosimos' extraordinary vision concerning the priest named Ion, who sacrifices himself at a dome-shaped altar, which had featured heavily in some of the earlier Black Alchemist material.

Regardless of this, I began scanning its Zosimos chapter once more and soon found that the alchemist's greatest work — a series of short books on alchemy, each denoted by one of the characters of the Greek alphabet — had been addressed to Theosebeia. Indeed, it seemed as if the entire twenty eight volumes had been specifically directed at her, almost as if they had been personal letters of advice concerning the dos and don'ts of alchemy and Hermetica. Unfortunately, the various extracts taken from these books had been left in their original Greek, which was of no use to me at all. However, enough information could be gleaned from the accompanying notes, and the shorter, translated extracts from the passages, for me to get a pretty good picture of Theosebeia and Zosimos' advice to her.

The notes spoke of certain persons — corrupt priests, it seemed — who were trying to persuade Theosebeia to do something to which Zosimos clearly objected. They wanted her to raise 'daemons' who could be entreated and called upon for help by means of sacrifices. These 'daemons' said they would avoid hunger if sacrifices were made in their honour and promised to help anyone who would do this for them.

Theosebeia went on to invoke these foul creatures; something which had gravely concerned Zosimos, who pointed out that 'daemons' did not often keep their promises. He pleaded with her, in writing, to 'invoke the supreme God alone, and employ sacrifices, not to propitiate the daemons, but only to drive them away, or avert their malevolent influences.'

Later on in his books, Zosimos continued his advice on the matter by telling her that '. . . the local (daemons) are not only hungry for sacrifices, but are eager to devour your soul also, that is, they seek to destroy your soul by inducing you to offer sacrifices to them instead of worshipping the supreme God alone.'

So Bernard had been correct. Zosimos had tried, without much success, to persuade Theosebeia to stop calling up the local 'daemons' with sacrificial offerings. He had also warned her that, if she continued these foul deeds, then her soul would be in danger.

Perhaps, as Bernard had suggested, Theosebeia's soul *had* joined with that of her demonic Dark Virgin, Paphotia, after her physical death. The consequences of messing around with the black arts, I say!

So far, so good. However, I could not find any references to a Graeco-Egyptian female deity or demoness called Paphotia, or to a 'wizened' old corrupt priest named Nelos. For the time being they would have to remain unconfirmed, that was, until I could read classical Greek.

Thursday, 29th October. 'Saturday, 7th November, okay?' Terry DuQuesne suggested over the telephone, as he tried to find a convenient day for me to drop in to see him at his home in South West London.

That was fine. I could not make it that coming weekend as I expected trouble at Danbury. I would explain all when I saw him.

'Oh, now come on, tell me something of what's been happening,' he insisted. 'I may be able to help you.'

So I told him a little about what had taken place out in Danbury churchyard earlier that week.

'I haven't come across the name Paphotia before,' he said, after due thought. 'But Nelos, the name of this priest. Nelos is the Greek name for the River Nile.'

A significant point perhaps, since Panopolis, the Egyptian town in which Zosimos, and presumably Theosebeia and Nelos had lived, was on the east bank of the River Nile.

The rest of the story would *have* to wait until I saw him.

Thirty
Trouble at the Tree

Saturday, 31st October, 1987. A wrenching pain pulled at Bernard's stomach as the mantel clock passed 10.30 pm. Something was building up. It was time to leave the comfort and warmth of the lounge and move into the quieter surroundings of the dining room.

Sitting down at the large oak table in the centre of the room, he moved his notepad, pen and cigarettes into position, and waited.

Soon he sensed a presence, the increasing feeling of a supernatural entity steadily growing with intensity. It was a force; female, and connected with the power and use of magic spells. How he was aware of this, he did not know. So who was she? Paphotia? Theosopia? Hekate?

Suddenly, a beautiful vision crystallised in front of his eyes. He now saw an immensely powerful image, a deity, primeval and unblemished by time. Not good. Not evil. Just raw. An Ancient Egyptian goddess with the perfectly formed body and dress of a beautiful woman, but with the slim neck and head of a hissing snake. Long, flowing black hair fell away from an intricate royal crown of horns, feathers and silver. In her left hand was the Ancient Egyptian symbol of life — the Ankh — and in her right hand she held a tall lotus sceptre.

She was just there, present with him in the room, locked as one with his mind. Yet it did not disturb him.

Quickly, he sketched her radiant form, before trying to obtain her name. A hissing sound uttered vague, but undiscernable tonal notes which did not appear to match the word he then wrote next to his sketch.

Her name appeared to be 'Urtheku.'

Yet then, as promptly as she had appeared, the crystal-clear vision vanished from sight, like a light bulb extinguishing. However, he felt she was still around, in the air somewhere, and that whether they knew it or not, it would be her power that the practitioners of the black arts would be utilising and wielding that Hallowe'en night — the time of the Dark Goddess.

Slightly unsettled now, Bernard finished off his sketch and waited for something else to happen. Then, unexpectedly, his hand began to scribble down the words of a stern male voice who proclaimed:

Moses smeared bush with plant root to give instant fire at a touch.

He re-read his words. The statement seemed innocuous enough, and it was an interesting hypothesis as well. Instant fire would certainly have impressed the Israelite tribes, he considered, trying to recall the story of Moses and the burning bush.

Time ticked on. When Bernard next glanced at his watch it read 11.15 pm, or thereabouts. Patiently though, he waited for further psychic messages. The next one came shortly afterwards as he began to feel an urge to write once more. Words, this time from an unknown source, started to spray across the notepad:

Sword of Dardanus. Seven vowels. Harmony of the seven tones.

What was the 'Sword of Dardanus'? he asked himself. 'A rival of Solomon', came the clairaudient response. It did not make a lot of sense. However, he knew a little about using tonal notes and sounds to invoke magical forces, so that part he did understand.

Without warning, his hand then began to scribble down more words. He looked at what he had written:

Saraphara, Araphaira, Bramarapha.

No, these made no sense to him either.

Then came a distinct impression. He was back again on the seven vowels and seven tones, for some reason. The tones were not sung, but made with a hissing sound, he was being told. A bit like a snake's hiss, he suspected. Back to Urtheku perhaps? He wrote down the message.

Another voice then passed across the psychic airwaves and, as if recording a freak radio signal, his hand involuntarily moved again:

The sword will bend souls as is wished. It will torture. Engrave ACHMAGERARPEPSEI on stone. Burn Psyche. ACHAPA ADŌNAIE BASMA CHARAKŌ IAKŌB IAŌ Ē PHARPHAREI. Tie to tree and burn.

There was someone in Danbury churchyard. Messing about. But not BA. No, *a woman,* on her own. Not just a visitor either. There were strong vibrations coming from her energy form. She was up to mischief. Yet nothing heavy at least. No impressions of a ritual, or of her leaving anything; just walking around the church perhaps. Then the feelings ceased. She had gone.

Glancing at his watch he looked at the time. It was just past midnight. She could only have been in the churchyard for ten minutes or so. No more.

There was no point in ringing Andy as he would only shoot up there and find nothing. It could wait until he saw him later that day.

He received no more messages that night. Yet the overriding feeling left in his mind was that the female in the churchyard was, in some way, associated with the Black Alchemist. Not only this, but that he was using the 'Sword of Dardanus', whoever or whatever this was, to 'bend souls' in association with fire, or the element of Fire. How or why, he did not intend pondering upon. No, he would leave that for Andy to sort out.

As the Egyptian goddess 'Urtheku' stood before him in his home, Bernard sketched her radiant form.

Thirty one
The Arrowhead

Sunday, 1st November, 1987. The rural housing estates of East Hanningfield and Bicknacre passed out of sight as the car moved closer to Danbury. Already the tall spire of the church could be seen poking out of the tree-covered ridge of hills on which the village was situated.

I had expected a rather frenzied telephone call from Bernard the previous night. However, by 12.30 I had not heard from him, so assumed that I'd been wrong about the Black Alchemist hitting Danbury on Hallowe'en.

So, if not Hallowe'en, then when? The following weekend, the 7th and 8th November? These dates marked the actual quarter day period between the autumn equinox and the winter solstice. It was the precise point in the yearly calendar when, in the past, the subtle energies of the landscape were believed to have been at their most unstable. Although the eve of the pagan festival of Samhain, and the Christian festival of Hallowe'en, had eventually been fixed to the 31st October, some shrewd occultists and witches still carried out their rituals around the time of the old, original quarter day period.

Pulling up alongside the green in front of Danbury church, I locked the car and made my way to the upturned tree stump in the rear of the churchyard. It was three o'clock and, as Bernard would not be arriving until four, I decided to take a few photographs.

Bernard then appeared with a smile. He too had decided to arrive early, so, without further word, we set up several shots of the upturned tree stump and the hole in which the Christ figure had been found the previous week.

Looking at the charred earth at the front of the stump, I wondered where we were going to bury the new crucifix. In the same hole as before?

A guilty expression emerged on Bernard's face. 'I've forgotten to bring the cross,' he revealed. 'It went completely out of my mind.'

Could we not find a substitute at short notice?

'I'll look in the car,' he suggested, fumbling in his pockets for the car keys. 'I might have something in there we can use.'

He disappeared and returned a few minutes later, empty handed. 'No, there's nothing in there,' he said and shrugged. 'Oh well, it was obviously not meant to be. If I went home now, then by the time I got back it would be dark. I'm afraid it will have to wait until another time.'

He could be right. My friends, Carole and Ken Smith, had seen a lady actually metal detecting in the churchyard that week in the wake of the storm damage. It was highly possible that any new artefact buried would be discovered pretty quickly, especially if it was left anywhere near the upturned tree stump.

Changing the subject, I asked Bernard if he had picked up anything the previous night.

'Did you?' he responded, returning the question.

One or two things, perhaps, but they were of little consequence to the world. What about him?

'There was somebody up here last night,' he stated, his hands in his jacket pockets. 'A female; a girl, I think. But she didn't stay very long — only about ten minutes — so I didn't ring you.'

I wished he had. I might have caught her. In fact, if I had camped out in the churchyard then . . . No, I had to let my feelings rest. So, had he picked up anything else?

He stood balancing himself on the top of a sawn-up log from the tree, a contented expression upon his face. 'Oh yes. Loads'a stuff. It means nothing to me. You see what you make of it.'

Moving away, we entered the comparative stillness and warmth of the church's darkened interior and continued the discussion there.

He produced a bunch of folded sheets of lined paper and handed them over.

Unfolding them, I sat down on a pew in the north aisle and started to read their scribbled contents. Unfortunately, they made very little sense to me either. I had never heard of 'Urtheku', the 'Sword of Dardanus', the 'seven vowels', or of 'bending souls'. The only part which was familiar were the series of strange words he had written down. They looked like goetic barbarous names, similar to those on the Lullington and Rettendon spearheads. One was instantly recognisable, 'IAŌ', the title of the Gnostic Christian supreme being, which was also one of the words Terry DuQuesne had identified on the Rettendon spearhead. Yet Bernard knew nothing of barbarous names, as our conversation on the subject in the pub the previous Tuesday had, of course, been eclipsed by the dramatic revelations and events of that night.

So Terry had been correct. The Black Alchemist *was* using goetic barbarous names to call upon arcane magical forces over seventeen hundred years old. The only other word I recognised amongst them was 'ADŌNAIE', a very commonly used Hebrew divine name of power.

Turning to the subject of the girl, I asked Bernard what he could tell me about her.

'I know nothing more than what I said,' he responded, standing up and moving over to the medieval knight effigies set into recesses within the north wall.

I was almost ready to dismiss her visit. She could have been anybody. Remember, it *was* Hallowe'en and, let's face it, she could just have been a pub reveller who felt the impulse to walk around the church at midnight. On the other hand, there may have been more to her visit, so I suggested that we take a stroll around the exterior walls of the church to see if anything came to him.

Agreeing, we left the church and walked out into the cold air. Was there any particular direction she had taken around the building?

'Anti-clockwise,' he answered, giving us our own direction.

Widdershins. The witches' word for an anti-clockwise

perambulation.

'Widdershins,' Bernard repeated, mimicking what I'd said.

To him it was just a casual stroll. He picked up nothing. However, we did stop to study three parallel lines cut vertically into a large lump of sandstone, lying across an open drain in the water channel below the north-east corner of the church. Boot scuff marks, we concluded as we moved on.

After examining the interior of the north porch without a result, we moved back towards the upturned tree stump. I was beginning to give up. We had found nothing and Bernard had picked up no trace of the girl's presence in the churchyard. Perhaps she *had* just been a Hallowe'en reveller.

'No, if that was the case, then there would have been no reason for me to have picked up on her presence here,' he pointed out, as we strolled back along the gravel path. 'There must have been others who came to the church last night, but I didn't pick up on *them*.'

It was a valid point. He did not usually pick up on any old Tom, Dick or Harry who interfered with the church's energies. No, she was therefore in the churchyard for a specific reason. Perhaps we ought to take a closer look at the upturned tree stump again?

'I think she was sizing up the place. Casing it out for some reason,' he added, as we moved back on to the gravel path beyond the west tower.

At the tree, I put my hand down into the hole where the Christ figure had been found, but there was definitely nothing else there.

Bernard ambled around the stump and studied other cracks and holes by the main hollowed-out crater. He came to an inquisitive halt in front of a deep crevice around the other side of the stump.

What had he found?

'I don't know. Something perhaps.'

Did he get a feeling from there?

He shrugged his shoulders. 'Possibly. There seems to be a slight feeling, although it's very weak.' He moved his head about as if trying to find the correct angle to peer into its depths.

For him to say that there was a 'slight feeling' coming from the hole strongly suggested that there *was* something to be found. So, taking off my jacket and jumper, I rolled up my shirt sleeves, tore away at a few protuding roots, got on to my stomach and slipped my hand as far as it would go into the hole. If we knew what we were looking for and where it was, then it might help.

'Well, it must be small, and all I get is that it's down the hole,' he admitted, standing close by.

Dirt and stones came up by the handful. Yet then, as I unloaded another small pile on to the ground, our eyes caught sight of something out of place, and yet familiar. Staring in amazement, I snatched up the object and studied its form — it was an inch long, black, blunt-tipped flint arrowhead of the Mesolithic Age. Scratched into both of its faces were Black Alchemist-style magical symbols.

On one side were the words 'WE CAME', written in capital letters, above a conventional *Monas Hieroglyphica* symbol. And on the other side were the words 'TO TIE' on the left of an image which appeared to be a simple sketch of a tree. Below these were four of the usual magical symbols in a line, beginning with the much used CH monogram, and ending with a Greek epsilon, the letter E in our own alphabet. Lastly, below these was a roughly drawn picture of a sword with a flash effect above its hilt. This I took to be a symbol representing fire of some sort.

There seemed to be little doubt that this geniune 7,000 year old Mesolithic flint arrowhead — rather an odd artefact to use as a calling card — had come from the Black Alchemist. Yet one additional point was immediately apparent. They echoed the statements: 'Engrave . . . on stone', 'Burn Psyche', and 'Tie to tree and burn', picked up by Bernard the previous night.

Passing our new find between us, we wondered what to make of it. One of the Black Alchemist's colleagues — presumably the girl — had visited the upturned tree stump and left this calling card, despite the fact that Bernard had not felt that she had left anything behind. It almost seemed as if we had not been meant to find this arrowhead, especially as it was located over four feet below ground level. The chances were that if a small object such as this had been dropped into the crevice, it would have rolled even deeper into the uprooted tree's gouged-out socket.

So the Black Alchemist had finally targeted Danbury. But what was he up to? At my suggestion, the pair of us retired into the empty church interior and sat down at a suitable pew in the choir area to see what else he could pick up.

A short while passed before he began to speak. 'Well, whoever it was, they made notes as they walked around the church,' he started, in a low voice. 'There were three . . . two in a car . . . only the girl got out . . . She has dark shoulder-length hair and was wearing a full-length black coat and boots . . . She has a long face with sharp features, and is not tall. Medium height, I should think.'

As the author pulled up the stones and dirt from the crevice by the upturned tree stump in Danbury churchyard, the small black arrowhead, inscribed with Black Alchemist-style symbols, suddenly came into view.

Could he see the car? And was BA one of the two remaining occupants?

'No, I cannot see the car, only the churchyard. And no, I don't know if BA was in the car. I get no feelings of this.'

He paused for a moment. 'She was carrying a peculiar type of cross . . . quite big . . . I'll draw it.'

He did, in my notebook. It looked like a Christian Calvary cross with a double axe attached to each of its side arms; a symbol much used in the worship of the Goddess. But what did she do?

'She just walked around the church stopping at each corner and feeling at different heights, yet only at the corners,' he continued, as the fast-fading sunlight darkened the church the longer we remained there. 'I wonder if those three parallel lines on the boulder are something to do with it. We'd better get a picture of them.'

Another pause followed. 'She didn't go anywhere else, only went straight to the tree . . . I can see her using a little bottle of something . . . She's putting drops around the stump; at the four quarters, I think . . . it's like water; a clear liquid, at least. This was *after* the flint had been placed.'

So it *was* the girl who had planted the Mesolithic arrowhead the previous night.

A further period of silence was broken by the sound of someone slamming closed the west door, which — as it was so near sunset — we had deliberately left ajar for fear of being locked inside the church overnight. Jumping up, we hastily gathered together our belongings and headed towards the exit. Thankfully, the door was still unlocked.

Outside, we began to retrace the girl's path around the exterior walls of the church for a second time. I took several shots of the three parallel lines cut into the sandstone boulder by the north-east corner buttress as I tried to question Bernard more about the girl. For instance, how old did she look?

Turning his nose up at the thought of trying to predict her age, he threw out an answer: 'She looks as if she's in her mid twenties. However, I get the impression that she's a lot older. In her early thirties, I should think.'

So not really a girl. More a woman.

'Yes, I suppose so.'

Was she attractive?

He laughed. 'Yes, I think she is. Is that all you can think about?! Is she good looking?' He shook his head in dismay.

It was just a question!

She was obviously casing the joint for a return visit. That seemed obvious. If so, then they would probably return the following weekend, almost certainly during the evening of Saturday, 7th November.

As a kind of last word on the subject, I reminded him that if we were not able to put a stop to the Black Alchemist's activities here, at Danbury, then his next stop would be Bernard's home. I was sure that his wife and daughter would not be amused to see a group of figures in black cowled robes carrying out a ritual in his back garden!

Showing his teeth, he grinned inanely at the thought. 'No, I don't think so, either!'

We had to stop him this time.

He smiled at my concern. 'I don't think I'm taking this seriously enough. Am I?'

No, he wasn't. However, we had one possible advantage.

'And that is?'

There was a new slant to the activities of the man we knew as the Black Alchemist. He was now allowing his minions to carry out his ritual work on his behalf; and that could turn out to be his biggest mistake so far. For although *he* was careful, well calculated, shrewd and extremely psychic, minions have a tendency of making mistakes.

Bernard was pressing to leave, but before he went I had one final question: how could the Black Alchemist have known that the fallen tree was particularly special to us? It had not been mentioned in *The Knights of Danbury,* and I could not recall telling any of my questing associates about its existence. So how had he known?

'He didn't need to know, did he?' he responded. 'Like us, he was intuitively drawn to the site's psychic epicentre. The tree controlled the entire energy field within the circular earthwork and therefore had to be captured and used to his advantage. He didn't need to know of our interest in it.'

However, this answer also implied that BA had probably picked up the existence of the tree on a psychic level, either directly from the site, or from our own minds. If that was the case, then it meant that our very thoughts were no longer impenetrable. We would *both* have to be on our guard.

Sitting at home that evening, I studied Bernard's psychic material from the previous night and looked thoughtfully at our latest retrieved artefact.

Starting with his vision of the snake-headed goddess, going by the name of 'Urtheku', I searched for any references to her existence in my books on Ancient Egyptian mythology and religion. Eventually, I found her.

'Urtheku', it seemed, was a title composed of two Egyptian words: *urt,* meaning 'powerful one' — in the feminine — and *hekau,* translated as 'magic power' or 'spells.' So together, the correct translation of Urt-Hekau, as it was more correctly written, was Great Lady of Magic Power and Spells. As Bernard had said, she was a primeval magical force of immense potency invoked and wielded for the success of spells and enchantments. She was, in fact, just one particular form of another, much more well-known Ancient Egyptian goddess named Isis.

She was also associated with the Egyptian snake or serpent symbol known as the Uraeus. However, although I could find no depictions of Urt-Hekau with a single snake's head, I did discover a picture of her with three snake's heads.

More significantly, certain scholars of classical and Ancient Egyptian mythology believed that Hekate who, despite being a Greek goddess, was originally worshipped in Egypt, derived her name from the Egyptian word *hekau* — magical power.[1] Indeed, one of Hekate's own titles was Mistress of Magic Spells, and one of her three heads as the Triple Goddess was that of a savage snake. If this was the case, then it meant that

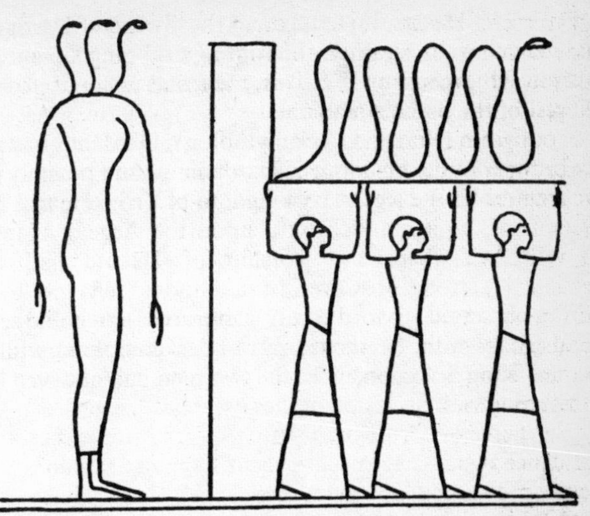

A drawing from Ancient Egypt showing the goddess Urt-Hekau, with three snakes' heads, standing before three initiates calling upon the cosmic force of the serpent.

Urt-Hekau was an original, primeval form of Hekate.

We were therefore back to the same Dark Goddess aspect that had haunted the minds of many over the night of the hurricane, and the same force that the Black Alchemist had utilised to punch a hole in the normally stable energy matrix present in Danbury churchyard. So, she was still around. Hekate, Theosebeia, Paphotia and now Urt-Hekau. How many more forms could this ancient magical force take upon herself?

Still, in Bernard's words, it appeared that Urt-Hekau was the most ancient and powerful form of the Dark Goddess we had so far encountered. Her presence had shown her to be more radiant, more awe-inspiring, more unblemished and far more beautiful than any other guise she had used. Perhaps Urt-Hekau was the true identity behind the many masks of the Dark Goddess.

From Urt-Hekau, I moved on to the 'Sword of Dardanus', skipping over the message about Moses rubbing a plant on a bush to achieve instant fire. This, I felt, was unconnected with the rest of the psychic material.

I soon found that, in Greek mythology, Dardanus had been the founder of the kingdom of Dardania — and possibly even the founder of the legendary kingdom of Troy. He was born the son of Jupiter and Electra upon the Aegean island of Samothrace, where the worship of Hekate had been particularly strong. However, I could find no reference to him having possessed a sword of any significance and could see no good reason why he should have been compared with the Biblical King Solomon, since the two men had not even been contemporaries.

I carried on.

Seven vowels. Harmony of the seven tones.

What did this mean? I found the answer in Richard Cavendish's excellent book *The Black Arts,* for it seemed that — in Graeco-Egyptian magic — great importance had been attached to the use of the seven vowels of the Greek alphabet when chanting goetic barbarous names. Each had been used to invoke seven individual aspects of cosmic power. 'The seven tones' was probably a reference to the seven chakras, or energy centres, said to be present in the human body, which could be activated by the use of tonal notes and words of power.

Next up in Bernard's psychic material were the three nonsensical words:

Saraphara, Araphaira, Bramarapha.

Were these yet more goetic barbarous names? I did not know. However, they almost had a Hindu flavour about them, especially the word 'Bramarapha'.

After this Bernard had noted 'Tones were not sung, but made with a hissing sound.' Snake-like, I suggested to myself.

Then he had written:

> **The sword (presumably the Sword of Dardanus) will bend souls as is wished. It will torture. Engrave ACHMAGER-ARPEPSEI on stone. Burn Psyche. ACHAPA ADŌNAIE BASMA CHARAKŌ IAKŌB IAŌ Ē PHARPHAREI. Tie to tree and burn.**

All this had come through at the same time that the Black Alchemist's female accomplice was actually in the churchyard. They looked to be words she had said as the ritual was conducted around the upturned tree stump. The words also corresponded with the symbols found on the Mesolithic flint arrowhead left in the crevice.

The statement 'WE CAME' on the arrowhead merely indicated their presence at the site, whilst the use of the *Monas* symbol was, I felt, implying some sort of emblem of office for the Black Alchemist's activities.

I could go no further. The rest would have to wait until I saw Terry DuQuesne the following week.

Sitting back, I poured a glass of red wine and pondered over the situation. The Black Alchemist had struck again. The Mesolithic flint arrowhead appeared to confirm this without any possible doubt. So what was he up to this time? It was obvious that he intended moving again pretty soon, and it seemed to be Bernard that he was after. Unfortunately for him, he was a very sensitive and vulnerable psychic who could easily be affected by occult rituals on both a physiological and psychological level. The killing bone would have great difficulty affecting my thick brain, but it could kill him — and that was no joke.

Yet the approach was changing. For the first time, the Black Alchemist had allowed one of his minions, a woman in her thirties, to conduct a simple ritual on his behalf. She was obviously trusted by him and fully accepted his warped attitude to ritual magic as well as his apparent hatred of us.

I thought carefully about this woman. She had to be more than just a minion to the Black Alchemist. Maybe she was his new girlfriend or his female accomplice. Perhaps she had even influenced him to invoke the powers of the Dark Goddess during the hurricane. I didn't know. However, I had an uncanny feeling that she was going to crop up again in the not too distant future.

Thirty two
Maria's Calling

Wednesday, 4th November, 1987. Bernard was on the move, walking aimlessly through a dense, foreboding wood in pitch darkness. He was not sure how he had got there, or where he was, so he just kept going.

Gradually the trees parted to reveal a large clearing. Smoke from an unseen fire drifted up and filled the air.

Through the thick, curling cloud of greyness he beheld the form of a woman clothed in a black cowled robe; its floppy hood leaving her with only a shadow for a face.

She stood before the open mouth of a deep cave amid a moving carpet of writhing, black eel-like snakes.

Looking in his direction, she slowly slid her hands over a swollen belly to show and emphasise that she was pregnant. 'Soon he comes,' she rasped, with a self-gratifying sense of pleasure.

He did not reply, but merely stood there dumbstruck at the unpleasant sight, inquisitively scanning her image for an identity. She was not Paphotia. So who was she?

'I am Maria the Jewess,' she proudly announced, as if he should recognise the name.

But the title meant nothing to him.

Turning around, she entered into the uninviting cave, as if expecting him to follow.

He did so, not because he wanted to, but because he could not stop himself.

The darkness began to engulf him and gradually he lost consciousness.

When his eyes re-opened, a horrifying experience possessed

him. He was hanging by his throat from a noose tied to a tree, slowly choking to death.

Violent gale-force winds swung his limp body back and forth within the terrifying darkness.

Momentarily his eyes glimpsed a fiercely burning bonfire in front of a group of orange-tinged, silhouetted trees; their branches twisted nearly sideways by the sheer force of the intense winds roaring and hissing across the bleak hilltop, which he now recognised as Danbury churchyard.

Little by little he was losing the will to live as the darkness which accompanies death began to swamp him. Yet not before the noose had twisted around sufficiently enough for him to make out two characters — men, he felt — who were staring up at the proud sentinel-like church with its tall conical-shaped spire.

The scene blurred and, once again, he lost consciousness.

A sudden bang awoke Bernard and brought an abrupt halt to the sickening nightmare. His head throbbed, his neck burned with pain and he knew he must not return to a sleeping state, lest he begin to relive or continue the frightening experience. He had to get up.

Climbing quietly out of bed, he moved downstairs and switched on the kitchen light. It was too bright for his eyes, but at least he was in familiar surroundings. He noted the time — it was 3.30 am.

Lighting a cigarette, he filled the jug kettle and plugged it in. Only then did he start to think about the disturbing nightmare. It had been symbolic; that was obvious. But who had made him dream such a thing? It was not from 'our' side, he assumed. The woman in black — someone called 'Maria the Jewess' —appeared to be yet another form of the Dark Goddess; or more accurately, a form of Dark Virgin; a corrupt antithesis of the pregnant Virgin Mary. It was not natural. However, she had emphasised the fact that she was pregnant with the words: 'Soon he comes.' Soon who comes?

He frowned as he stood over the kettle waiting for it to boil. The cave symbolised a womb, he believed. So he had therefore entered a womb — her womb — and re-emerged in Danbury churchyard hanging by a noose from a tree. He thought for a moment. The tree in the dream had been positioned at the same spot as the upturned tree stump. This therefore implied that someone saw this area of the churchyard as symbolising a womb and was using it as a site to germinate something into life. No, it did not make sense.

The matter was dropped in favour of a cup of coffee.

At work that day the vivid memory of the macabre nightmare had kept recurring in his mind, like something distasteful he had eaten. Its implications were clear enough, but he wanted to know a little more, and the only way he knew how to do this was to tempt fate and recall the dream to mind later that evening. He knew it had not originated from a friendly source, so this would therefore be a dangerous exercise. He might even open up his mind to someone, or something, which meant him harm. But he decided to take that chance. He needed to understand what was happening to him.

As Bernard waited for the right opportunity to retire quietly into the solitude of the dining room, the telephone rang. It was Andy wanting to make sure everything was okay.

He needed to tell him about the dream, but his wife and daughter were in the vicinity and he had purposely kept them from knowing anything of the Black Alchemist affair. So he talked to his friend in a low voice.

'I've had a D-R-E-A-M,' he whispered. 'Can't say much, but it's very symbolic, although it doesn't make much sense to me. It might do to you.'

Andy understood his predicament.

'I'm going to have a little delve later, when I'm on my own. If anything happens, I'll give you a ring.'

It was not until 10.30 pm that Bernard finally found himself on his own with time enough to recall the vivid memory of the dream.

Slipping into the dining room, he readied himself with pen and paper in front of him on the great oak table. Following a simple protection ritual, he started to concentrate on the dream.

Clearing his mind allowed the image of the dense wood to return and, once again, he found himself moving swiftly out of the darkness and into the smoke-filled clearing. Yet upon looking about, he realised that, this time, he was on his own. Maria the Jewess was nowhere to be seen. So, with some slight hesitation, he moved into the cave without any resistance. Once more, an overwhelming darkness obscured his vision leaving his psychic eyes without any images at all.

Then a familiar sensation began to pulse through his body, like a shot of adrenalin; an impulse to involuntarily put pen to paper. But who was overshadowing his senses? He could not be sure. As the impulse increased, he scribbled down his feelings.

'I could stop now,' he wrote. 'Maybe I should. Writing becoming scrappy which usually means something is coming.'

He waited for a moment before scribbling down further impressions: 'Black forms. Human. Number not known.'

Then he lost control of the situation and, involuntarily, his hand began to scrawl strange words:

The waters visit the corpse lying in death and darkness, and the waters will rouse from sleep and they rise anew. Where you take the stones and relics from their resting place they are not mature until the fire has tested them. They are nourished in the fire and the embryo grows nourished in its mother's womb.

At the appointed time the new child will come. The spirit of the blackness appears and rises up and encircles the child. A cry of awaken from Hades (the Greek form of Hell) will be heard.

Arise from your tomb and the pit. Clothe yourself, the

voice of resurrection has sounded and life has entered you. The soul will cling to the body. Darkness will become your triumph and your dominion and they will suffer for an eternity. The body and soul united become one. The union of the mystery is complete. Its dwelling place is sealed. Fire has changed them from the womb. They have gone forth. Fire brought them from darkness, from death into life.

The pen stopped and Bernard felt sick. He could no longer hold back his physical revulsion of what he had just written. Getting up, he stumbled into the kitchen and vomited in the sink.

Washing away the unsightly mess, he tried to regain his composure. Lighting a cigarette to take away the foul taste, he switched on the jug kettle before walking into the warm lounge to pour himself a glass of whisky. He needed to ease his nerves.

Where was this disgusting stuff coming from? It was not from any of the Dark Goddesses who had been around in recent weeks. No, it was from a man. He had heard his voice and a vague impression told him that he was an 'ancient priest' of some sort. That was all he knew.

As the kettle boiled and clicked off, he downed the rest of his glass of whisky. He felt unsteady, but not because of the alcohol. He still felt sick as well. He needed advice, so should he ring Andy? No, it was 11.15 pm and what would he say? An ancient priest had just made him write a disgusting automatic script? Bernard threw out the idea. It would have to wait.

As he ambled back into the kitchen to make the coffee, he thought again about the situation. The incident that evening quite clearly meant that his senses could be controlled relatively easily by malevolent forces. So why had the simple protection ritual not worked?

He shook his head as he began to admit that he was losing. A few more incidents like that and it could destroy him; and he knew he was not fooling himself.

Thirty three
The Griffin

Thursday, 5th November, 1987. Having returned to the office after completing the advertising copy for the next edition of the *Leigh Times,* due out the following week, I sat on a desk and tried to find the effort to leave for home. It was five o'clock and *Top of the Pops* and *Eastenders* were on later, so a quiet evening in was the order of the day.

The telephone rang and Brian Fenning picked up the receiver and read out the number before remaining silent as the caller had their say.

'Andy, it's for you,' he said, a look of puzzlement on his face. 'Someone called . . . Bernard?'

He did not recognise the name. And no wonder. It was the first time that Bernard had ever rung the office, so something had to be drastically wrong. Leaping across to the phone, I acknowledged my presence.

'I'm going up to Danbury,' he revealed, in what sounded like an agitated tone of voice. 'I was violently sick last night when I tried to attune to the dream. I've also been getting all sorts of strange feelings and impressions of the churchyard this afternoon.'

He paused for a moment as if searching for words to express his feelings.

'I don't know what's going on. I really don't. But something's happening up there.'

Accepting his concern, I promptly arranged to meet him at The Griffin around seven. However, I made him promise not to venture into the churchyard alone, *whatever* happened. He was to wait for me before doing anything.

He understood.

Putting down the receiver, I rushed home in a state of virtual panic. Flying around the house, I kept on my shirt and tie, put on a large tweed overcoat, picked up various magical and physical items of protection and dashed towards the front door.

Yet then I remembered the swordstick given to Bernard the previous November by the Indian mystic at the antiques and collectors' fair. To date, it had not been used for anything other than blasting open the south door of Danbury church, so perhaps it would come in handy that evening.

As the car clock showed 6.35 pm, I entered The Griffin's car park. Not seeing Bernard's Orion, I picked up the swordstick and decided to take a little walk around the churchyard; just to make sure nothing looked out of place.

Not a little apprehensively, I crossed the green, passed the church and entered the brightly-lit churchyard.

The brightly-lit churchyard. Of course, *it was a full moon that night*. Looking up at the glowing white orb hanging motionless in the indigo sky, surrounded by an array of twinkling stars, I knew this was the answer. Yet then, as if to add to the situation, an orange firework rocket careered into the sky and exploded in a mass of coloured light. Of course, it was also 5th November — Guy Fawkes' Night.

I had fully expected the Black Alchemist to make his next move on the quarter day, Saturday, 7th November, and not *that* evening. Yet, as I already knew, Hekate was often worshipped at the time of the full moon so, in a way, it all made sense for him to have struck that day.

However, the deathly silence of the moonlit churchyard said it all. A thick blanket of mist hung low over the gravestones and box tombs. Yet aside from this everything was still and quiet. No one appeared to be around and nothing seemed to be out of place. But something must have happened or else Bernard would not have rung me in such an agitated state.

Anyway, he would arrive shortly, so all would be revealed then.

Walking back across the green to The Griffin, I saw Bernard now standing in the car park awaiting my return. He too had arrived early. So, after putting away the swordstick, we disappeared into the pub and ordered drinks.

Sitting down, he took out a few pages of folded notes and asked me for my comments. They concerned the strange dream he had experienced the night before last and the automatic writing scribbled down the previous evening.

After several minutes silently reading and digesting their contents, I told him what I knew about Maria the Jewess. She was a female alchemist mentioned in many of the early Graeco-Egyptian treatises on ancient alchemy, including those by Zosimos of Panopolis. However, no one rightly knew her true identity, as the title Maria the Jewess was thought to have been a pseudonym. Some early scholars of alchemy even believed that she was Miriam, the sister of Moses, for some inexplicable reason. Later classical scholars considered that Maria the Jewess was purely the Gnostic Christian, or alchemical form of the Virgin Mary, a fact almost certainly relevant to Bernard's dream.

Although quite obviously symbolic in content, it appeared that someone — BA most probably — was warping the traditional associations of Maria the Jewess with the Virgin Mary and the Divine Birth. Instead of a pure, young maiden who, by way of divine conception, gave birth to the Son of God, she was being seen, like Paphotia, as an antithesis, a barren old crone who achieves diabolic conception in a corrupt and unnatural manner.

If this was so, then it implied that the Dark Virgin of his dream was carrying some form of Antichrist, a new dark power of immense magical potency which was soon to be unleashed into the world.

Earlier that year Bernard had picked up certain information which had suggested that the Black Alchemist believed that he was the Proclaimer, the one preparing the way for the coming of Antichrist. If the Maria the Jewess dream *had* been influenced by the Black Alchemist, then it looked very much as if he and his associates considered the appearance of Antichrist to be imminent. That was their belief at least. Whether any of this had any basis in truth was a different matter altogether.

However, like Bernard, I had no real idea what the rest of his dream, or the automatic script, actually meant or represented. Of more immediate concern was the current state of affairs out in the churchyard. What was happening out there?

He pulled a funny face, as if to mask his obvious concern over the simple question. 'I don't know yet,' was his cautious reply. 'I just keep receiving glimpses of the churchyard. Something's afoot, so I thought I'd come up here.'

So nothing definite?

He shook his head as he picked up his pint of Kaliber and took a sip. 'No . . . just feelings. That's all.'

Frowning, I decided to put forward my plan of action assuming, that was, that someone *had* been up to mischief out in the churchyard. Bernard, I suggested, should try to gain mental communication with his spirit guide, the Elizabethan alchemist, and then get *him* to tell us what was happening out there. If there *was* something to be found, then I would find and remove it on my own, safe in the knowledge that he was still in the warmth and comfort of the pub, away from any possible psychic danger.

Bernard thought this a good idea so, picking up a pen, he glanced about for some notepaper. There was none. In our blind panic to get to Danbury, neither of us had remembered to bring any paper!

'I'll use the back of these,' he decided, turning over his written account of the Maria the Jewess dream and the automatic script from the 'ancient priest' received the previous night. Waiting for some form of response from his guide, he felt he should sketch an aerial view of the church and churchyard in case he needed to mark a specific spot. Soon the Elizabethan alchemist began his message as Bernard's hand wrote:

Two they were. During afternoon.

So, two people had apparently visited the church that very

afternoon. Were they the two men that Bernard had seen staring up at the silhouetted church during his dream? It seemed possible.

'Go round church', had been the guide's next instruction. Taking this to mean that he was to go round his little sketch of the church, Bernard began to move his right index finger slowly around its exterior walls. It came to a halt at a spot below the middle of the east wall, an obvious place for the Black Alchemist to have left an artefact. Marking an X on the spot, he then intuitively drew a continuous line which completely encircled the church. More words then explained this circular line:

> **Placed at east (the east end of church). Picture on stone. Church sealed. No entry to church. Energies sealed.**

Bernard interrupted the communication to give his own feelings on the situation. 'Well, I understand this to mean that these two characters have placed a stone — on which is a picture — below the east wall of the church. This has apparently sealed off the energies of the church in some way.'

It would be a simple task, therefore, to go out into the churchyard, find the inscribed stone and destroy its magical hold over the church by dousing it with holy water and removing it from the spot. Was it on the surface, or was it buried?

'On the surface, I think.'

And was it up against the wall, or away from it in the grass somewhere?

He thought again, as if waiting for an answer to the question. 'Away from the wall.'

Rising from my seat, I told him to stay exactly where he was and await my return. I would not be more than ten minutes. In the meantime, he could try and find out what else was happening out there.

'I'll give you five minutes before I send out a search party,' he quipped, amused, as always, by my actions.

Ten minutes, I told him, as I disappeared from view and walked out into the cold November night.

Thirty four
The Heart of the Quest

Unlocking the car boot, I took out my camera, my torch and the Indian swordstick, before crossing the busy main road towards the church.

As I looked up, another firework rocket wooshed up into the clear moonlit sky and burst into a noisy galaxy of glittering multi-coloured stars which fell slowly to the ground.

The church green was now buzzing with activity. More than a dozen cars were disgorging their occupants for an evening service inside the church. People milled about greeting friends, laughing, talking and gradually moving towards the entrance door below the stone tower.

It must have seemed a strange sight to them: a lone figure swinging a swordstick in John Lennon glasses, a shirt and tie, and a long, baggy overcoat. Yet all I could do was stroll through the parishioners and just hope that they did not ask any pertinent questions.

Reaching the churchyard, I moved swiftly across to the building's east end and disappeared into the long shadow cast by the towering edifice. Switching on the torch, I scanned the ground at the spot indicated on Bernard's crude sketch map.

Several minutes of searching and I had still not located the inscribed stone. Bernard would be wondering where I had got to. It was no good, I would have to go back and enlist his help.

Shortly after Andy had disappeared, Bernard had received a further message from the Elizabethan alchemist.

In answer to the question: 'What's going on?' he had been told:

> **To ensnare. Your energies strong. A wish to control. Beware of a stumble in the dark. Soul can be used after death.**

He was not sure what this meant. However, it was then eclipsed by another, more decisive message from the guide, who stated:

> **At the tree. Very strong.**

With this had come the overwhelming impression that, out by the upturned tree stump, a second artefact lay concealed which had to be removed as quickly as possible. It was an impulse, an urge he felt he could not ignore, despite what Andy had said. Anyway, he said he would only be ten minutes and over fifteen minutes had now elapsed since his departure from the bar. So he would have to warn him; tell him what was going on.

Picking up their belongings, he finished off his drink and walked out of the pub.

Walking briskly back across the green, I saw Bernard coming towards me. As he approached, I lightly chastised him for not having remained in The Griffin. Yet, in a way, I was glad to see him as I admitted that I had been unable to locate the inscribed stone on my own.

'And there's something else out by the tree,' he eagerly told me, pacing about on the spot. 'I think we'd better see what's there.'

He obviously wanted to join me in the search for both artefacts so, a little reluctantly, I accepted the situation. However, I did stress, as usual, that before we went anywhere near the church, or the tree, we should carry out our normal protection ritual, just to make sure he did not get into any trouble.

Walking along the side alley next to the eastern edge of the churchyard, we came to a halt by the old Victorian wrought iron gate and carried out the protection visualisation. Once this had been completed, we moved swiftly across to the church's east wall.

Our eyes followed the torchlight as it illuminated different sections of the grass and concrete below the stone wall. Still there was no sign of any inscribed stone.

'Perhaps it was just a mental incantation,' Bernard concluded, attempting to justify his earlier feeling that a physical artefact had been left at the spot.

A minute or so later we found what we were looking for. It was a large piece of sliced slate, some four inches in length and three inches in width. It had been resting on the angled slope of the concrete drainage channel, exactly below the midway point of the east wall. Flicking it over, we saw its 'picture'. It was an updated *Monas* symbol, encircled by a fat Ouroboros serpent biting it own tail, carefully scratched into its face with a fine point.

Just in case it was dangerous, Bernard moved away as I rapidly slid out a plastic flask of holy water and doused the stone to break its psychic hold over the church's energies. Then, taking out my camera, I snapped a couple of shots of it *in situ,* before slipping it into my pocket and catching up with Bernard.

He appeared to be none the worse for the discovery, so we moved on to our next destination.

Within thirty feet of the darkened mound which indicated the position of the upturned tree stump, Bernard came to a halt and stared. 'Ah, it's just there; in front of us,' he remarked, not having realised how close we had come to the tree without any adverse reactions.

Confirming his apparent fear, I asked him if it was safe to go near the stump.

Still he stood and stared. 'I see her standing between us and the tree,' he pronounced, clearly quite concerned by the sight.

Who?

'The same woman that was in the dream; dressed in a black cowled robe.'

Who? Maria the Jewess?

'Yes; no, they're all the same. Maria the Jewess, Paphotia, even Hekate.' He paused to listen before turning around with a very worried expression upon his face. 'She's saying "Come, come, come, come, come to me."' He paused for a moment to listen to her call. 'Now I hear giggling laughter,' he continued, feeling that it was time to put some distance between him and the source of his discomfort.

Stopping on the edge of the gravel path towards the southern edge of the churchyard, he spoke again with a note of acute anxiety in his voice: 'There's a deep pulling in my chest. She's pulling me back towards the tree.'

His apparent torment was confirmed as he slowly began to sink towards the ground, holding his hands across his chest.

I had to act fast. The protection ritual was obviously not working, so what could I do? Yes, a banishment ritual. I would try to banish Maria the Jewess' presence from the churchyard. So, waving the swordstick around, I used my limited magical capability in an attempt to dissipate the malevolent supernatural form. It was a hastily conducted ritual which I just hoped would work.

Running back across to where Bernard was now a crumpled heap on the path, I found him seemingly in great pain and muttering something about 'You're disgusting. How could you do that?'

I stood and stared. It was apparently a statement being made to the female apparition still standing by the tree. My banishment ritual had obviously *not* worked. But *what* was disgusting?

'JUST GET RID OF IT,' he pleaded, the pain clearly showing in his voice. 'I . . . I can't move . . . *GET IT OUT.'*

What? Where?

'Same place as before . . . Something.'

The artefact. In the same hole as before, where we had located the arrowhead the previous week. I had to remove it. Quickly, I dashed over to the upturned tree stump and shone the torchlight down into the crevice.

Shit. What I could see stunned even me. It *was* disgusting.

Below the eastern wall of Danbury church, Bernard and the author finally located the source of the problem — a piece of slate inscribed with an Ouroboros serpent encircling a *Monas* symbol.

But what was I to do? There was no way that I was going to reach down into that hole and touch them. I needed to speak to Bernard, immediately.

Racing back across to the psychic, I found him now in a terrible state, bent double in tortuous pain and looking as if he was fast losing consciousness. He was not going to like what I'd discovered.

'JUST GET RID OF IT,' he cried out in sheer desperation, as he slumped even further down on to the gravel path.

Couldn't he perhaps get up and move out of the churchyard whilst I dealt with what was in the crevice?

Without waiting for an answer, I lifted the psychic on to his feet and pushed him in the general direction of the wrought iron gate on the eastern edge of the churchyard. He remained on his feet as he staggered like a drunken old man towards safety and I made my own way back to the tree stump.

Shining the torchlight into the deep crack, I looked again at the vile sight. Resting on a ledge, about eighteen inches into the hollow, was a large, blood-soaked heart into which was speared a black dagger, its handle carved into a crouching monkey. Realising that nobody was ever going to believe this, I took out my camera and used the flashgun to snap a few shots of the two items in position. Then, slowly reaching down into the hole, I grabbed hold of the dagger's carved monkey handle and levered the heart up into the air, trying to make sure that it did not fall off and tumble back into the depths of the crevice. Placing them on the ground, I took more photographs.

Pulling out the plastic flask of holy water, I doused both the dagger and heart and then sat back for a breather. What was I to do now? Showing them to Bernard would only send him into further fits of revulsion. No, I would have to hide them in the grass — for the moment at least.

So where was he? Picking up the dagger, with its bloody heart still impaled on its tip, I walked towards the gate and located a suitable spot to conceal the macabre evidence. I found him by the gate still doubled up and mumbling something about terrible pains in his chest. Hoping to alleviate his suffering, I told him that I had removed the offending items, so they should give him no further problems. Perhaps we should now leave the vicinity and go back to the pub.

'I can't,' he stated, in a low, frightened voice. 'I . . . I can't move.'

He sounded like a child who could not face being left alone in the dark. Attempting to act logically, I told him to follow me.

Instead, he just stood up and stumbled blindly out into the open field to the south of the churchyard.

We clearly had problems. Reaching him, I saw that his internal pain and torment still showed on his contorted, moonlit face. He was fighting possession.

Somehow, I had to stop it. Remembering the large crucifix I had in my coat pocket, I yanked it out and thrust it into Bernard's hand. I just hoped it would have some sort of effect. Yet he merely stood there, totally unaware of its presence, engulfed in his own inner conflict.

Suddenly, his hands began to shakily rise with the crucifix, as if he was beginning to fight back against his uncontrollable actions. I watched cautiously as they gradually came to rest upon his throat.

For a moment there was no movement, but then the large wooden crucifix and another small brass crucifix he had been wearing on a chain around his neck, were both thrown forcefully into the long grass.

He was losing his will to fight. I wanted desperately to save him. Banishment rituals spewed from my mouth, but they were useless and had no effect whatsoever. I ran out of ideas.

'Your Christ is nothing,' a deep, mocking voice then unexpectedly exclaimed from Bernard's mouth.

Possession. That was all I needed. He still appeared to be fighting this barbaric intrusion within his mind, so I had to think fast. Picking up my own crucifix, I placed it on his forehead and held it there with both hands.

'Your crosses are worthless,' the foul voice announced, with a nightmarish gutteral laughter. 'Fool.'

It obviously wasn't working. A different tactic was needed. I knew. I would tell the intruder that if he had something to say, then I would only listen if he stopped tormenting Bernard's mind and body. It could work, so I said it out aloud.

It did work. The contorted expression disappeared from his face, even though he still stood there, his shoulders stooped as if he were a hunchback, and his arms moving about as if they had life of their own.

'Darkness will always conquer light,' the intruder began, in a slow, decisive tone. 'You will never stop our power. We are too strong for you.'

I heartily disagreed, in a friendly voice. Anyway, who says so?

'Comarius,' came the proud, but almost inaudible response.

Who? Temarios, did he say?

'COMARIUS,' he bellowed at my insolence. 'High priest, sage and prophet.'

I still didn't get his name. Anyway, what did he want with Bernard?

'His soul.'

But why his soul?

'It is strong,' he responded, as if relishing the sensation of being inside a human body. 'I have it.'

Do you?

'Red plus white equals black. The new child will come, and blackness will rise up and encircle it. Darkness will be his triumph and his dominion.'

I recognised those statements. They were similar, if not the same, as the sickening automatic script Bernard had received from the 'ancient priest' the previous night. The two sources were undoubtedly the same. But who was this man? Presumably one of Theosebeia's mates.

Leaving the intruder to continue his rambling monologue, I took time to think again about the situation. Trying to banish him using the same old ritual would almost certainly only result in more mental torment for Bernard. I could let him continue until he left of his own accord, but that didn't seem the right thing to do.

Comarius reiterated on the automatic script of the previous evening and kept making references to the 'new child' who, I

Shining the torchlight into the crevice by the upturned tree stump in Danbury churchyard, the author was revolted by what he saw — a black dagger speared into a blood-soaked heart, left as part of an obscene black magic ritual.

Lifting out the bloody heart impaled on to the black dagger, the author doused the macabre discovery with holy water as Bernard gradually lost consciousness.

had to assume, was a reference to the coming of Antichrist. But I had heard enough. I had to get rid of him.

'. . . the path of darkness you will follow . . .'

No we won't. He was barking up the wrong tree with us as there was no way that we would ever change sides. The forces of light would always vanquish the powers of darkness in the end. However, I wished him no immediate harm and suggested that if he did not leave whilst the going was good, then I would banish his soul essence forever.

'. . . the serpent will rise and great power will . . .'

He was obviously not listening and, at that moment, Bernard fell to his knees as if being compelled to do so and almost inaudible words began to issue forth from his mouth. One I caught was the name 'Septemos,' whoever, or whatever, that meant. Now I really had seen enough. I also had an idea. The Indian swordstick. That was the answer. If the powerful imagery and symbols of the Christian faith had no power over this supernatural intelligence, then I would have to use the primeval, spiralling serpent energies supposedly inherent within the swordstick.

When Bernard had been given the swordstick by the ageing Indian mystic and his grandson, he had been told that it was to be used by me and that it would protect and give 'protection of the seven.' At the time, we had not understood why it had been given to us. Nor did we know who, or what, 'the seven' were supposed to be. Now I knew. It was a reference, I felt, to the seven energy centres of the human body, the so-called chakras, as they were referred to in Hindu mysticism. Each one was positioned within a vertical column of energy which ran down the length of the spine and controlled a different aspect of the physical and spiritual body. In cases of possession, it was these that an alien force took control of to inhabit a human body. The power of the swordstick could, I now realised, be used to purge the body of the uninvited intruder. So I knew exactly what to do next.

With renewed enthusiasm, I approached Bernard, who was still in a kneeling position, and clasping the swordstick with both hands I began to visualise spinning bands of rainbow-coloured light pouring down the length of the rod and shooting out from its metal tip, like a psychic lazer beam. Slowly, I brought it down on to his neck and saw radiant energies flowing down his spine which burst into balls of vibrant, coloured light as they touched and engulfed each of the seven chakra centres.

This was real serpent power, I told the intruder, not his writhing black snakes.

For what seemed like an eternity, but was probably only about five minutes, I continued the powerful visualisation. Eventually, the high priest fell silent. It was working.

Bernard began to flex first his hands, then his arms, and then his head. But was it Bernard?

'Yes . . . It's me,' he uttered in a low, tired voice.

I removed the swordstick from his neck. He was back in the land of the living.

For a while he just knelt there, staring around at the field, as if it was totally alien to him. 'How did I get here?' he asked, a slight note of amusement in his question.

Couldn't he remember?

'The last thing I recall was being somewhere up by the tree with these stabbing pains in my chest.' Pushing himself off the ground, he took out and lit a cigarette.

A terrible thought suddenly crossed my mind. Pains? In what part of the chest?

'About here,' he replied, prodding the centre of his rib cage.'Around my heart.'

My own heart sank as I realised what I should have done upon discovering the dagger in the heart. Why had I not thought of it before? It had undoubtedly been set up at the tree with the purpose of harming Bernard, like some sort of black magic wax effigy pricked with a needle. As he had attuned his mind to the tree, the effect of the dagger speared into the heart had given him severe pains in his own heart. It was a very nasty trick which could quite conceivably have killed him.

I should have removed the dagger from the heart. If this had been done, then he would not have suffered the pains in his chest or experienced the diabolic possession out in the field. It just went to show my inadequacy in magical matters such as this. In many ways, I actually felt I had let Bernard down to the point where the opposition had been able to twist us around its little finger. Our protection rituals and banishments no longer worked, so we were now defenceless against any further attacks and confrontations.

In many ways we had lost the day.

Yet then I remembered that Bernard had still not seen what I had unearthed in the crevice. So, leading the way back into the churchyard, I took him across to the grave concerned, pulled away the loose grass and shone the torchlight on to the dagger plunged into the heart.

Bernard smiled wryly and shook his head in mild disbelief. 'What do you intend doing with *them,'* he queried, intrigued by the possible answers.

Take them home.

His jaw dropped. 'You can't take that heart home. Bury it somewhere. Out in the field, anywhere. But don't take it home.'

Accepting his more sensible solution, I dug a shallow hole in the grassy earth, by the spot in the field where Comarius had possessed Bernard, and dropped in the fleshy heart. Having replaced the turf, we both left the vicinity and made our way back to The Griffin.

Thirty five
The Perfect Master

After washing our hands and grabbing an available table in the crowded bar, Bernard and I scrutinised our latest retrieved artefacts.

Firstly, we passed the piece of inscribed slate back and forth between us, studying its symbols. Its fat Ouroboros serpent was a familiar design I had seen before in various books on alchemy.

Getting bored with this, we moved on to the dagger itself, which I had already washed thoroughly under the tap in the pub's toilet. It was a hand-carved African tribal knife, made of ebony wood, which looked as if it had been produced as a letter opener for the tourist trade. However, it was by no means a cheap and nasty piece. It was a finely-carved example of tribal art of the sort which often turned up in antiques shops at fairly reasonable prices.

It was also easy to see why the dagger had been chosen as a ritual item. The shiny dark wood finish made it ideal for use as the so-called black-hilted knife, or 'athame,' during magical ceremonies. However, it was likely to have been chosen by its former owner because of its crouching monkey handle. To them, this would probably have represented the cynocephalus, a type of sacred baboon which, in Ancient Egyptian religious tradition, symbolised the dark or waning phase of the lunar cycle, the period most commonly associated with the Dark Goddess.

Drawing the dagger a little closer, I looked at its inscription and symbols. On one side was a two line inscription scratched into the blade with a fine point, which read:

All haile to the noble companie
A parfet master made them call

The style of writing was, in my opinion, quite clearly the handiwork of a woman; not a man. It was nothing like the writing we had seen on earlier Black Alchemist artefacts, like the 'To touch is to enslave' message on the inscribed stone found in Shenfield Common the previous year. So it seemed that this ape dagger's previous owner had very possibly been a woman.

Yet who were the 'noble companie'? And who was the 'parfet master"? Parfet being a Middle English form of the word perfect.[1]

The only other image on that side of the blade was a crudely-scratched circle to the left of the inscription which, I assumed, somehow symbolised the full moon that night and perhaps showed it significance to the evening's preceedings.

On the other side of the blade was a series of the usual Black Alchemist-style symbols, beginning with a clear CH monogram and ending with an updated *Monas* symbol, which was on its side and close to the tip. The only out of place symbols were what looked like the astrological sign for Taurus, just before the *Monas,* and the planetary symbol for Saturn on the edge of the handle. Why these should have been added to the normal line of undecipherable symbols, I could not say.

Concluding my scrutiny of the ape dagger, I asked Bernard whether he thought it *had* been owned by a woman; and, if so, whether it was the same person who had visited the churchyard on Hallowe'en.

He huffed and thought about the question for a few moments as he picked up the dagger again. 'Well, I feel that, although it was apparently placed in position by two men, I believe it actually *belonged* to a woman.'

The same one?

'Possibly, I don't get any definite feelings,' he said, still twiddling the ritual item around in his fingers.

I felt it *was* the same woman. If so, then big questions needed

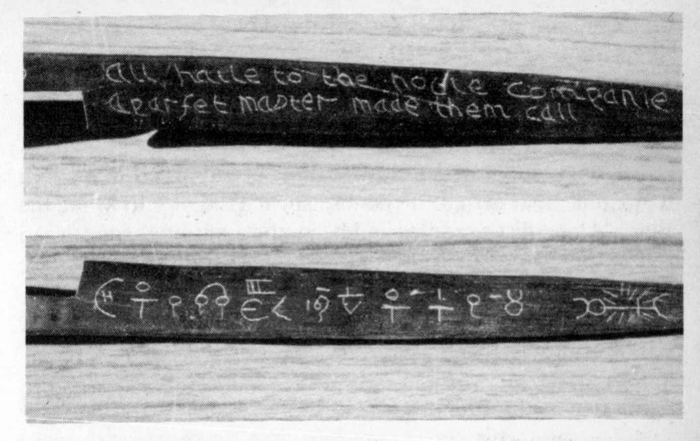

On one side of the ape dagger found in Danbury churchyard was an inscription, and, on its reverse, were familiar Black Alchemist-style symbols.

answering. Such as: where was BA? Why had he not visited Danbury himself? And who was this woman who was taking over the duties of the Black Alchemist? She was obviously trusted by him, so what was her role in all this?

I wasn't sure. However, the one thing I did know was that leaving the ebony ape dagger for us to find was probably the biggest mistake the Black Alchemist had made so far. In the past, he had always left artefacts fashioned specifically for the ritual concerned. Never before had he left a ritual tool which would almost certainly have been consecrated and psychically charged for use in magical operations by its previous owner *before* they chose to leave it speared into a fleshy heart in Danbury churchyard.

On a magical level, the dagger could now be used as an effective tool to counteract or manipulate the very forces it was originally intended to wield. Not only this, but at some later date the ape dagger could be psychometrised by Bernard to see if he might pick up any information about its former owner. Unlike the Black Alchemist who, we knew, could successfully block out any attempts to attune directly to him, or his home, this woman might not be as adept at doing the same.

So, where were we to go from here?

'I know where I'm going,' Bernard responded. 'Home! I've had enough for one day.'

I strongly suggested otherwise. We needed words of wisdom from our Elizabethan alchemist spirit guide as to what the Black Alchemist's cronies had been up to out by the upturned tree stump. We also needed to know whether they would strike again in the near future.

Bernard was not very keen on the idea. 'I really don't think you'll get anything else.'

Yes, Bernard.

He frowned at the thought of more psychic work. 'Alright then,' he said, with some reluctance. 'We'll go out into the car.'

Sitting in his Orion, Bernard closed his eyes and mentally contemplated the presence of his spirit guide.

Moments passed as I waited patiently in the darkness, a pen held up against a clean sheet in my small pocket notebook.

A group of youths passed by the front of Bernard's car and walked up to their own vehicle parked on the opposite side of the small car park. Suddenly, its engine burst into life as the headlights came on.

'Right,' he said, taking in a deep breath to open the proceedings. 'The ritual out by the tree stump here today. It had something to do with the tree in connection with alchemy.'[2]

I see.

With its wheels spinning wildly on the spot, the other car tore out on to the main road in front of the pub and was lost from view.

'The idea was to leave the ape dagger speared into the heart at that spot, with the church's energies blocked, so as to increase the potency of the ritual.'

Rapidly, I scribbled down his every word. Yet surely they

expected us, or someone else, to have found it. There was no way that anyone looking down into that crevice would not have seen the dagger stuck into the heart.

The psychic did not answer. He was now on to other topics. 'The high priest's name. It's Comarius.'

Before this, I had only remembered his name as Temarios, or something similar. I had not come across the name Comarius before.

'He was high priest, sage and prophet to Maria the Jewess and denounced biblical assertions of the True Cross and the Virgin Birth . . .'

His words were becoming lighter, slower and more monotone. His bodily movements had now ceased and, with his eyes still firmly closed, I realised that he had fallen into a trance state. He was being overshadowed, not this time by a malevolent intruder, but by our Elizabethan alchemist friend.

I just let him carry on as I attempted to scribble down the psychic communication in the pitch darkness.

'The cave and the bower are the same. His (Comarius') writing interprets as red and white to black, which is written as menstruation, fertility mixing to give new life form which is interpreted as only a dark form and is not increased by fire to become white and gold, but reduced further and combined further with water to produce black life which grows if hidden.

'This practice has always met with disaster, but many have tried and will do the formation of chemie . . .'

My pen slipped a few words as I frantically tried to scrawl down the message.

'. . . other names given are Bolos[3] and Septemos . . . both very early practicers of chemie.

'They say is early chemie but these (ie. BA and his cronies) still wish to bring forth the white and gold, and many are given in papers (of) which some (still) exist and some are lost.

'Also, Comarius used stones with wording which he says were obtained from sealed tombs and so give the right to invoke darkness. Set form also used; but he is wrong. These precious stones and tablets were only usually placed with kings and royalty to assist a thought progress (through) darkness, and (supply) main knowledge to afterlife.'

There was a brief pause. My hand ached like mad. However, I had to seize the opportunity to ask a question more relevant to the situation at hand. Such as: what was the Black Alchemist really up to at the moment?

The monotone voice recommenced its dialogue: 'He seems to use several ancient types of chemie writing, and combines to attempt to find what he considers the final form of growth.'

There was another short pause, long enough for me to get in a second question. What moves could we expect from the Black Alchemist in the near future?

'Future not certain. But (he) will withdraw to practise again and possibly discover new formulation (of) calcination at which point he seems to stop and place (his inscribed stones and artefacts).'

Who were the 'noble companie' mentioned on the ebony ape dagger?

'This would be a new form of brotherhood. Again, very subservient to darkness hoping for a new king form to worship. Hate is involved against all so-called pure religious practices. This also includes many practices of different nations.'

Then came a prolonged silence. Our Elizabethan alchemist was suddenly no longer with us. Soon afterwards, Bernard began to open and close his hands and move his arms, before finally opening his eyes. 'He wears a floppy hat. Like a floppy beret,' he announced, none the worse for his trance state. 'And he has white hair.'

I wrote this down.

'Anyway, I'm off now,' he exclaimed, knowing full well that his psychic commitment for the evening had well and truly been fulfilled and that he could justifiably leave for home.

I said I would give him a ring.

Thirty six
The Demonic Connection

Friday, 6th November, 1987. The bizarre events of the previous evening put me into a rather subdued mood all day at work. I felt as if I did not want to tell anyone about what had happened, and what we'd discovered in the crevice by the upturned tree stump. No one was going to believe what had taken place in Danbury churchyard, never mind understand its implications.

Still despondent by the time I reached home early that evening, I decided that I had to tell someone, so invited Carole and Ken Smith across to my home. I had been keeping them up to date on the various developments in the Black Alchemist affair and valued their comments and constructive criticisms.

The sound of the door bell announced their arrival around half past seven. Even before I had a chance to tell them my news, they attempted to confront me with a hardback book, with a blue dust jacket, which they seemed eager for me to take.

'I think you should read this book, Andy,' Ken emphasised. 'Carole and I found it today in Southend library.'

There were more important things to tell them. The book could wait for a while.

But Ken was insistent. 'It's called *The Demonic Connection* and it's by someone called Toyne Newton,' he stated, as they moved into the lounge. 'It was only published earlier this year by Blandford Press and it's about modern-day black magic and Satanism in Sussex.'

Ken sat down on the moquette-covered art deco sofa with

the book still in his hand, as I went to fetch the psychic material from the previous evening.

'Andy,' Ken started again, trying to keep my attention for a moment. 'I feel the contents of this book may link with the activities of the Black Alchemist.'

Why? I asked, as I sorted through the papers on the great wooden table by the window.

'It concerns the activities of a black magic organisation called the Friends of Hekate who operate out of a place called Clapham Wood, near Worthing,' he continued. 'The group has been linked with four mysterious deaths, along with the disappearance of a number of dogs and all sorts of strange paranormal events in the area.'

Carole sat down on one of the matching armchairs and offered me a Marlboro, before taking one out herself. 'You really should take a look at this book,' she said, echoing Ken's own words and sounding like an authoritative sister.

I stopped in my tracks and looked at the book. Clapham Wood. Hekate. Dog disappearances. Unexplained deaths. Things were beginning to ring bells. That was the place Bernard had picked up during the Running Well confrontation the previous year. He said he had seen some woods at a place called Clapham, in Sussex, which he felt were connected with the Black Alchemist's activities. He had also seen a church reached down a long, winding road.

'That must be Clapham church,' Ken suggested. 'It's approached by a long, winding track and it's next to the entrance into the woods.'

'Wasn't Hekate the Dark Goddess experienced by several people during the night of the hurricane?' Carole asked, reclining into the seat.

Indeed it was.

'These people are using the power of Hekate. Didn't the hurricane move north-eastwards from Sussex, through Kent and into Essex?' she asked.

Ken cut across her words. 'Perhaps this has something to do with why BA chose to use the Dark Goddess to strike at Danbury during the hurricane.'

Yes, I saw his point, as I read the book's front cover blurb:

> **THE DEMONIC CONNECTION — An investigation into Satanism in England and the International Black Magic Conspiracy.**

'They're into heavy stuff,' Ken warned. 'One of these deaths was a retired rector who disappeared on 31st October, 1978. On Hallowe'en, the time of Hekate. An anonymous letter received by the author implied that he had been used as a human sacrifice. You must read this book. It's really good.'

I felt uneasy. Getting up, I told Carole and Ken that I would try to find Bernard's original psychic notes concerning Clapham Wood to see what they actually said. Leaving the room, I moved into the study and began searching through a file full of psychic notes made over the years by Bernard. I soon found what I was looking for — the notes he had made at the Running Well on Tuesday, 14th October, 1986. And there it was, the very last thing he had written that evening: 'Sussex. Clapham. Church. Winding road.'

I tried to recall our conversation. Upon asking him what he felt about this place, he had replied: 'I see some woods. Something's been going on there; ritual, I think. I also see a church nearby, reached down a long, winding road. Not a very good feeling from the place,' he had stressed. 'Best left alone, as it's not important to the current situation,' or words to that effect. I had not even bothered to follow up this information, for some reason. However, I had remembered to tell him about my trip to nearby Angmering to investigate various UFO sightings during 1976.

Pondering over this new and rather disturbing development, I glanced through a few more of Bernard's original psychic notes and scribblings concerning the Black Alchemist affair. One set caught my eye. It was the notes I had made at the St Anne's Castle public house, at Great Leighs, shortly after the Shenfield Common sketch during May the previous year.

I read them and remembered:

Stinking real heart. Blooded. About. St Mary. Wombs. Birth. Blood. Not working. Mercury. Circle closing. Message. Squeeze circle. Strong enough. Heart stops. Something coming up. Change.

My God. So many of these statements appeared to have been portents of events which had since taken place and I had completely forgotten about them. The 'Stinking real heart' seemed to have been a reference to the heart found in Danbury churchyard the previous evening. The mention of St Mary may have been a reference to Runwell church's dedication to St Mary. The use of a Mercurial force had featured prominently in the Running Well confrontation the previous year, and the 'Heart stops' statement, well . . . I immediately felt bad when thinking about its implication. What if Bernard's heart *had* stopped beating out in the churchyard?

Frowning at the thought, I left the room and rejoined my guests in the lounge. Having shown them the Bernard material relating to Clapham Wood, I promised that I would read *The Demonic Connection* and give them my comments.

With the subject of the book now out of the way, I got down to telling Carole and Ken about the events of the past few days; everything from the Maria the Jewess dream to the automatic script from Comarius, the discovery of the artefacts, and the possession out in the field behind the churchyard the previous night.

At the end of the dramatic account, both guests were clearly disturbed by what they had just heard.

'Bernard and you are in grave danger. Don't you see,' Ken tried to emphasise. 'If what you've told us is true, then you are obviously dealing with complete nutters. They're maniacs who will stop at nothing, even ritual murder, to protect their secrecy.'

Okay, so they were dangerous people, but we could handle them without too much problem.

'And you just can't leave that heart,' Ken stated, incredulous at the very fact that it had been buried without first being identified. 'What if it's human?'

I hadn't really thought of that.

'It has got to be retrieved at the earliest convenience. Tonight, if possible, before it has a chance to decay.'

Accepting his word, I suggested that we go there later that night.

'Fine,' Ken said, satisfied that I had come to my senses at last.

Carole picked up the ebony ape dagger and began to study the inscription and magical symbols along its blade. 'This symbol here,' she began, attracting my attention. 'Before the commencement of the inscription. That represents the full moon, doesn't it?'

Yes, but why, was it of significance?

'Well, on the other side is another "loose" symbol — the sign used for the planetary influence of Saturn.'

Okay, I knew that as well.

'Do you feel it shows some sort of link between the full moon and Saturn?' she asked, still holding the ritual object.

I wasn't sure. However, Carole was a first class astrologer and I began to see what she had in mind.

'This could refer to what is known in astrological terms as moon conjunct Saturn,' she decided, lighting up another cigarette and exhaling smoke with a little puff.

Moon conjunct Saturn. What was that?

Carole was eager to tell me. 'In astrology, when two planets conjunct their individual aspects and influence upon the human mind changes into a new, third influence with new characteristics,' she explained. 'The aspects of moon conjunct Saturn are usually associated with matters such as ageing, darkness, sorrow, harshness, coldness, sterility and a lack of love. It is generally a very bleak influence or aspect, and is often symbolised by an ageing crone or hag; cold, harsh, sterile and terrifying in appearance. Very much Hekate in her crone aspect.'

Another link with the Hekate/Dark Goddess influence. I asked her to tell me more. What about the association of the *full* moon with Saturn? Was that the same?

She nodded. 'As a planetary influence, Saturn can relate to

the bringing of things into manifestation.' She searched for words. 'And the full moon is very much associated with the completion of pregnancy and childbirth.

'As most midwives will tell you, more babies are born at the time of the full moon than at any other point in the twenty eight day lunar cycle. So, if someone was going to set up a ritual where they wanted to germinate, bring into manifestation, or "give birth" to a concept, an idea, a force, or a being, then the full moon would be the best time.

'Combining this full moon influence with the moon/Saturn conjunction would crystallise a force or influence symbolised and seen as an old, sterile, yet pregnant hag giving birth, almost against the laws of nature. A corruption or antithesis of the Virgin Birth; Paphotia or Maria the Jewess again,' Carole concluded.

'It looks to me as if the Black Alchemist was attempting to germinate something rather unpleasant out in Danbury churchyard last night,' Ken added, summing up the situation.

I had feared this. It explained why, in Bernard's dream, Maria the Jewess had emphasised that she was pregnant with the words: 'Soon he comes.' The ancient priest named Comarius had said virtually the same thing the evening after the dream. We had taken this to mean that the Black Alchemist considered Antichrist's appearance as imminent and that he was preparing the way for his coming. So what had he been trying to manifest out there in Danbury churchyard?

'I will check my *Emphemeris* when I get home to see whether the moon did actually conjunct with Saturn yesterday, around the time of the full moon,' she said, placing down the ebony ape dagger. 'Anyway, I told you all this last month, just after the hurricane.'

What? I looked at Carole as if she was mad. What did she mean — she told me last month?

'That psychic reading I gave you. Don't you remember? That was all about wombs, something coming out of the ground and an ancient priest.'

No, I didn't. Hold on. Yes, I vaguely recalled the reading but could not remember when it had taken place, or what she had come out with. But I had her original notes somewhere.

Leaving the room once more, I searched through my miscellaneous file, which was where I dumped any psychic material which did not check out with anything I was working on at the time. Finding her notes, I suddenly realised their extraordinary accuracy in respect to the events of the past few weeks. And the date on the notes — it was the afternoon following the Thelemic conference — Sunday, 25th October; around the same time that Bernard had found the Christ figure in Danbury churchyard.

Sitting with Carole in her living room, she had suddenly felt the compulsion to scribble down various psychic impressions she was picking up concerning the future situation of the Black Alchemist affair. She had written:

> **Waiting — in the womb — darkness all around. Drawing the chosen body to the womb. Rendering open — from darkness — death — to rebirth — holding in command the chosen body — the preparing.**
>
> **A great fire — a high flame (the will). To die in the high place of the womb — the higher womb and be reborn in the prepared one. An old body burnt — no trace.**
>
> **Can see a face. A man — a priest. He has a bald head and coarse round features. About fifty years old — he commands great fear. I see his head as being born (not) through a woman but through two pillars inside a temple instead.**
>
> **About being or playing the role of God — choosing the spirit and body and commanding as if God and, in that sense, seems diabolical.**

I attempted to interpret its meaning. 'Waiting — in the womb — darkness all around' could be taken as a reference to the recent situation in Danbury churchyard. Bernard's Maria the Jewess dream had implied that someone was viewing the upturned tree stump as a symbolic womb, a fact supported by Carole's words concerning the full moon/Saturn conjunction link with the ape dagger.

Next, Carole had written: 'Drawing the chosen body to the womb. Rendering open.' Who was the chosen body? 'Rendering open' was perhaps a reference to the gateway of this 'womb' that had appeared in the churchyard after the hurricane. She had also mentioned 'A great fire — a high flame (the will)'. Was this a reference to the fire that had consumed the upturned tree stump, rendering the gateway open?

She had even mentioned that she could see the face of an ancient priest who could, conceivably, have been Comarius. The rest of her psychic message also made a lot of sense. Reading between the lines, it appeared to confirm our belief that the Black Alchemist had been attempting to manifest something unholy out by the upturned tree stump. Yet, for some reason, I had completely forgotten about it. So much so that I had not even mentioned it to Bernard.

As the midnight hour passed, two shadowy figures carefully surveyed a small area of field to the south of Danbury churchyard. Sudden movement in the driveway of a nearby house sent them diving for cover and meant that they would have to continue their search in complete darkness.

For over an hour, Ken and I looked desperately for the buried heart.

Getting down on my hands and knees, I scoured every square yard, still without the use of a torchlight. Then I found the clue I was looking for — a piece of loose turf no more than six inches square. Pulling it away, my fingers crept into the tiny hollow and made contact with our goal. It felt cold and spongy.

Lifting out the large heart, I slipped it into an old rag and replaced the piece of turf. Without further word, we left the churchyard and made our way back to the car.

'I have checked my *Ephemeris* for Thursday, 5th November, 1987,' Carole said, as she hovered around Ken and I upon our return to their house, following the retrieval of the heart.

Ken disappeared off to make a cup of tea as Carole and I sat down in the living room.

'Unfortunately, there was not a moon/Saturn conjunction on the 5th,' she sighed, feeling she may have partially let me down. 'However, the use of the full moon and Saturn symbols on the ape dagger was almost certainly an attempt to invoke the same aspect, or influence, of the conjunction by magical, instead of astrological means. So the barren hag-like Dark Virgin giving birth to something unholy still stands.

'On the other hand, I did find something interesting about the astrological influences around on 5th November,' she continued. 'At the exact time of the full moon — at 4.46 pm that afternoon — the moon was at twelve degrees Taurus. And as the only other unusual symbol on the ape dagger, aside from the full moon and Saturn symbols, was the zodiacal sign for Taurus, it implies that whoever inscribed it must have been aware of this fact.'

I felt I understood what Carole was saying. It also seemed quite clear that there had been an awful lot more to the Black Alchemist's dagger-in-the-heart ritual than either Bernard or I had at first realised. However, whether or not we would ever know the full story was another matter altogether.

Thirty seven
The Friends of Hekate

Sunday, 8th November, 1987. After a bath, a bowl of muesli and three cups of tea, I lazed about in the kitchen trying to find further excuses not to get down to the housework.

Having established that the heart was either that of a large pig or a small calf — according to the local butcher I had shown it to the previous day — the pressure was now off. Had it turned out to be human, I don't know what I would have done.

So where was I to go from here?

Toyne Newton's book, *The Demonic Connection,* lay unread upon the kitchen table. It looked tempting, and it was an excuse. Carole and Ken had felt it may lead me to the Black Alchemist, even before they had known that Bernard had already picked up on the strange goings-on taking place inside Clapham Wood, the book's main focal point.

Pouring out a fourth cup of tea from the teapot, I pulled across the hardback book and began to read it.

The curious saga had begun during the mid seventies when the woods around the isolated village of Clapham, just outside Worthing, had unexpectedly become the focus of all manner of unexplained incidents. Dogs began to disappear without trace, whilst others had become 'desperate' or 'distressed' in the woods. It was even claimed that a horse had vanished there under somewhat peculiar circumstances.

Visitors to the woods experienced odd presences, 'psychic

barriers', strange amorphous mists, as well as inexplicable physiological effects, such as fainting, nauseous stomach pains and unaccountable muscular spasms.

There were also reports of mysterious fires, strange footprints and the lingering smell of sulphur in certain parts of the woods, all apparently without suitable mundane explanations.

As I remembered only too well, Clapham Wood had then become a Mecca for UFO buffs, after a number of strange lights were seen over or very near the vicinity of Clapham Wood. This had generated a lot of media coverage which had eventually led the flying saucer enthusiasts to conclude that the woods were haunted, not by ghosts and supernatural forces, but by aliens who were using the area as a base camp!

The Demonic Connection also spoke of four mysterious deaths which had taken place in the 1970s and early 1980s, one in the woods, the other three on downland not far away.

The first of these was the curious death of PC Peter Goldsmith who had disappeared on the South Downs, not far from his home at Steyning, on 2nd June, 1972. Despite an extensive search of the area, it had taken six months for the policeman's decomposed body to be located in thick undergrowth at nearby Pepperscombe. The coroner had returned an open verdict on the mysterious death.

Even more curious was the controversy surrounding the disappearance of the Rev. Harry Neil Snelling, the 65 year old retired vicar of Clapham and Patching. He had disappeared during the afternoon of 31st October, 1978, following a dental appointment in nearby Goring-by-Sea. He had seemed in good spirit when he had telephoned his wife to say that he was about to walk from the village of Findon, across the South Downs, to their home in Steyning.

But the Rev. Snelling was never to be seen alive again. Despite an extensive search of the area by police with tracker dogs, it had taken three years for his skeletal remains to be located under strange circumstances in prohibited woodland, near the village of Wiston. As in the case of PC Peter Goldsmith, it was an area which had been thoroughly searched at the time of his disappearance. Even though there had been no indication as to the cause of his untimely death, it was assumed that he had died of a sudden, fatal heart attack. However, as with PC Goldsmith, the coroner had returned an open verdict.

Such was the state of affairs when, in 1978, sales assistant and paranormal investigator, Charles Walker, had decided to take an in depth look at the ever-deepening mystery of Clapham Wood. Using local newspapers to announce his intentions, he requested that if anyone could help him with his research then they should contact him at his home address in Worthing.

Calls and letters had resulted — mostly from time wasters. Then, one evening in early November that year, Charles had received an unexpected telephone call. It came from a well-spoken gentleman who would not give his name. He suggested that if Charles wanted to know what was really going on inside Clapham Wood, then he should be at a spot in the woods, called the Chestnuts, in half an hour.

It was a location Charles knew well. Here a signpost marked the convergence point of various footpaths. So, without even time to contemplate the possible consequences of his foolhardiness, he decided to keep the shadowy rendezvous.

At the appointed time, as he stood in the pitch darkness at the Chestnuts, slightly fearful of what might happen next, a voice had addressed him from within the nearby undergrowth. He instantly recognised it as the same well-spoken gentleman who had made the anonymous telephone call.

'Don't attempt to look at me,' Charles was told. 'For your safety and mine, it is imperative you do not see who I am.'

He froze for a moment, yet not wishing to provoke danger, Charles had simply responded with the words: 'All right.'

The invisible speaker had then proclaimed: 'I am an initiate of the Friends of Hekate, a group formed in Sussex.'

What sort of group? Charles had asked.

'The nearest I can describe our activities to you is that we are followers of Satanism,' he was informed. 'At every meeting we hold we sacrifice some animal or other. My fellow initiate, who is with me tonight, will confirm that if you doubt what I say.'

So there were two of them in the undergrowth, not one, Charles had realised at that point. He assured the owner of the voice that he did not doubt his word.

'We hold meetings in Clapham Wood every month and dogs or other domestic or farm animals are sacrificed,' the voice revealed. 'It all depends on what is easy to obtain at the time.'

Charles had then remembered the various dog disappearances in the woods. Were any of these connected to their activities?

The response was sharp. 'We have already told you that our cult demands a sacrifice at every meeting. You are very close to a site that has been used.' However, the initiate added: 'But if the weather is bad we make other arrangements.'

So how long had the Friends of Hekate used the woods? Charles asked next.

'We have been using this area for ten years and plan to continue using it for another ten,' was the response from the dense undergrowth. 'After which time we will select other areas in which to spread the word. We use Clapham Wood because it is the most convenient for our members and because the atmosphere of the wood is right for our purposes.'

Exactly what *were* their purposes? Charles had queried, feeling that such a question might be pushing his luck a little bit too far.

The answer came in the form of a stern warning: 'There are people in high places holding positions of power and authority who are directly involved and will tolerate no interference. We will stop at nothing to ensure the safety of our cult.'

Then there was only silence. No further statements came from the concealed initiate, implying that the meeting was now over and that Charles should go.

The peculiar nature and content of the clandestine meeting, coupled with the serious tone of the well-spoken male voice, convinced Charles that it had been no hoax or prank. He felt he really had been speaking to an initiate of a dark group who appeared to be using Clapham Wood for their warped magical activities, which included blood sacrifice. As to why they should want to divulge details of the group's existence to him, he could only guess. All he could surmise was that it had been a firm warning for him to lay off the subject.

For Charles, this assumption was to become a nightmarish reality later that same month when, cycling home from work late one afternoon, he was deliberately forced off the road by a hit-and-run car driver. He had known nothing about the oncoming danger until a sudden bump had sent him crashing on to a concrete pavement as the unidentified vehicle sped off and disappeared out of sight.

He suffered head and back injuries as a result of this 'accident.' It also left him partially paralysed and unable to attend work for several weeks.

In Charles' mind, there was a firm link between this incident on the road and his shadowy encounter with the initiate of the Friends of Hekate only a few weeks beforehand.

Following the mysterious bicycle 'accident,' he had decided to put the Clapham mystery to one side for a while. However, this did not prevent him trying to find out as much as he could about the group's patron deity, Hekate, the Greek goddess of the underworld. He soon found that one of her three forms as the Triple Goddess was that of a 'frenzied bitch,' and that dogs, hounds and wolves were the animals most sacred to her dedication. He also discovered that dogs were often sacrificed in her name, either at the time of the full moon, or on Hallowe'en, the time when she was at her most powerful.

It all appeared to confirm the words of the initiate, as well as his own fears, that at least some of the dog disappearances in the woods were linked with the group's sickening activities.

Charles had reopened his case book on Clapham Wood the following spring by revisiting Clapham's mostly thirteenth century church of St Mary, close to one of the entrances into the woods. As he stood in the churchyard looking across the fields, he had recalled one of the statements made by the initiate the previous November: 'But if the weather is bad we make other arrangements.' Immediately the presence of the unoccupied manor house, amid the cluster of farm buildings and outhouses, some 150 yards away to the south, now took his attention.

Wondering whether this might harbour any clues as to the activities of the Friends of Hekate, Charles had decided to investigate. Moving to a spot along the winding track which led up to the church — the one seen psychically by Bernard — he scaled a low brick wall and a barbed-wire fence. Once inside the grounds, he walked swiftly across the muddy forecourt — which was being used as a pigsty — and approached the empty building. Hesitantly, he pulled open the front door and slipped inside. Looking behind him in one of the downstairs rooms, a startling sight greeted his eyes — for covering the entire wall, to the left-hand side of the door, was a hideous, yet mesmerising demonic mural in brightly-coloured paint and crayon.

It depicted, in vividly-fine artistic detail, the profile of a crouching demoness amid a backdrop of red and yellow

Once inside the disused manor house, close to Clapham church, in West Sussex, Charles Walker turned around to see a demonic mural completely covering the wall (Photograph: Charles Walker).

flames. Its blue and white squat body, which was covered with reptilian scales, ended in a devilish, forked tail curling up into the rising flames. In its claw-like hands, with razor-sharp talons, was a religious orb surmounted by a blue eight-armed cross.

Yet it had been the mural's hypnotic head and face that had momentarily held Charles' gaze. It showed a yellow, clearly feminine face with a bald head, long ears and curled blue horns, which stared open-mouthed over and beyond the cross. Across her left cheek were painted black stripes and daubed bright red patches which were undoubtedly meant to represent smeared blood.

The image had not, Charles realised, been painted either by kids, or by someone simply dabbling in primary text book magic. It was a complex, awe-inspiring work of art created for a specific purpose. As to who it represented, he could not say. Was it Hekate? Or was it some demoness unknown to him? Or was it just some sort of abstract representation used as a backdrop for magical rituals?

Taking out his camera, Charles snapped three shots of the mural before promptly leaving the building, fearing for his safety. As he scurried back towards the boundary wall, a man appeared out of nowhere, shouting abuse and brandishing a shotgun. Since he was trespassing on private property, he did not stop running until he had scaled the wall and was once more on the track that would take him back to the church.

Despite his hair-raising experience, Charles was pleased as he now had further evidence for the existence of the Friends of Hekate. Two out of three of the colour photographs came out perfectly, and one of these was there to be seen in *The Demonic Connection.*

Time then passed and, by 1981, Charles had begun working with a freelance photographer and writer named Toyne Newton, who shared his interest in the Clapham mysteries. That year Toyne wrote a series of three articles on the subject for *The Unexplained,* a popular news-stand magazine on paranormal mysteries. Each had featured the strange goings-on taking place in Clapham Wood and another nearby site called Chanctonbury Ring, a Bronze Age ditch and rampart earthwork perched high on the ridge of the Sussex Downs, not far from Steyning.

Toyne's articles had concentrated more on the alleged paranormal and UFO activity associated with both sites, and avoided going into any detail concerning the black magic activity the two investigators believed to be taking place inside the woods. They did not mention Charles' meeting with the initiate in 1978, nor his discovery of the demonic mural in the old manor house during the spring of 1979. Most importantly, they made no reference to the Friends of Hekate. All this was deliberately left out as Charles and Toyne wanted to see what sort of response the articles might generate.

For this reason, a letter that Toyne received, via *The Unexplained,* during March 1982, took on a rather significant role in supplying them with their next piece of the jigsaw concerning the clandestine activities of the so-called Friends of Hekate.

Unsigned, badly typed and with odd spacings and spelling errors, it read as follows:[2]

H. Howard and T. Newton.
The Unexplained.

Dear Sirs,

In your article on Clapham Woods you ask if the mysterious events are linked to a black coven? I can tell you they are but it is much more than that. A few years back a friend of mine joined them, they are called the friends of Hekate, they meet in the woods and barn up by the church and make ritual sacrifices at the time of orion and the archer.

Lots of Patching and Clapham people are in it but the top ones come from London, two women and a man, the man is a doctor, about 45, the women about 30 and 60.

They always go back to London after the meetings so no one knows who they are or that they are connected with what goes on, I think this is when there is a human sacrifice.

My friend said there are other groups the same in Winchester and Avebury, a big group in London, I can't remember them all but lots of people are involved as there are different grades, and thousands of members in the outer one but only about 200 at the inner circle. It is all very secret, the inner core members are protected by the others who they use as spies and guards to make sure everything is kept secret.

At Clapham there is about 30 members, who they are I don't know, it is only because my friend has gone to live abroad I can tell you about it. He was sick of it all especially the sacrifices. He was very frightened when the police (were) looking out for the vicar you mention (Rev. Harry Neil Snelling) and when I said I was going to join the search party on the downs he said no need, they'd got him. I thought he meant the police had found him but they had'nt, and when I asked him later on what he meant he told me to shut up.

People get headaches and strange feelings at Clapham because the place is right for building up the best vibrations so as they can get the force they want. It affects people and also dogs like you say and can be left about after like a force wall, and the reason for it is to do with the 3rd army and to break people's resistance mentally so as to get control of them and situations.

Sometimes this strange force starts fires and has interrupted people's car electrics and there has been some accidents and fires in Long Furlong but everything is hushed because they use anybody so as to get what they want.

They can make people do what they want and could make a politician ask over a terrorist group who he was only arranging to talk with, so as to cause trouble, and things like that.

I can't sign my name but be warned, they are much more powerful than a black coven.

The shocking implications of the anonymous letter were obvious, for it inferred, rightly or wrongly, that the Rev. Harry Neil Snelling, the retired vicar of Clapham and Patching, had been abducted on 31st October, 1978, and ritually murdered as a sacrificial victim by the Friends of Hekate.

He had been used as a blood sacrifice to Hekate on the night most sacred to her, Hallowe'en, when her power was at its maximum. And what a catch — a retired vicar who would have been seen as a powerhouse of Christian magical energy which, if released through ritual murder, would have been perfect to recharge the group's strength and gain the favour of the goddess. And it was not just any old vicar, either. For many years he had been the rector of St Mary's church, Clapham, the Christian edifice which dominated their *own* territory.

It made total sense. The Rev. Harry Neil Snelling had been a grim human sacrifice; according to the author of the anonymous letter at least. Yet could this single, ill-written document be trusted, or even believed?

It was possible that the letter writer had purely been scare-mongering as there was no positive indication that the Rev. Snelling had died from anything other than natural causes. However, the letter did contain certain points that its author should not have known about. Like the title 'the friends (sic) of Hekate', for instance. Toyne and Charles had purposely kept this name to themselves in the hope that someone would eventually mention it independently. Now it had happened and, curiously enough, the name Hekate had been spelt in its original Greek form with a K, and not with a C, its more usual, modern-day spelling.

The letter had also mentioned the barn 'up by the church' as one of the meeting places of the 'black coven'. The barn referred to — the one next to the old manor house where the demonic mural had been discovered — had already been cited as another possible location used for black magic purposes by a talented psychic working with Toyne on the Clapham mystery.

In addition to all this, the letter made some curious statements which begged attention; such as, they meet 'at the time of orion and the archer.' As Toyne soon realised, this was clearly a reference to the visibility of star constellations in the night sky. Orion was prominent in the heavens during autumn, whilst Sagittarius — the Archer — was prominent, in astrological terms, from mid November through to mid December. From this Toyne had deduced that the Friends of Hekate concentrated their magical operations around the autumn and winter months, the time most associated with the worship of Hekate.

On a more sinister note, the letter implied that the Clapham-based Friends of Hekate was merely a cell within a much larger network of similar groups in different parts of the country. These were apparently controlled by a powerful London-based organisation.

The letter writer had also claimed that the Friends of Hekate consisted of about 30 members, some of whom actually lived in the villages of Clapham and nearby Patching. However, it was allegedly run by three shadowy figures who travelled down from London especially for the meetings. One was a male doctor, aged around 45, one was a woman, aged around 60, and the third was a younger woman, aged around 30.

Toyne believed it was the elder of the two women who had originally set up the group around 1968. Around this time there had been a great revival of interest in witchcraft and the occult, due principally to the philosophy of the Hippies, the youth culture of that era, who had openly promoted mind expansion through the use of drugs and mystical practices. The younger of the two women would have been in her late teens in 1968, so it was possible that, like so many other teenagers of that era, she had become involved in occult practices before going on to join the Sussex-based Friends of Hekate.

Toyne suggested that the older woman, now in her mid 60s, had probably moved into more of an advisory position within the group to allow the younger woman, now in her mid 30s, to take over as High Priestess of Hekate.

As to the London doctor, the third person in the Friends of Hekate's dark controlling triad, Toyne believed that he played a somewhat different role within the group, almost certainly subservient to the two women.

Since the early 1980s, Charles Walker and Toyne Newton had come across very little further evidence of the Friends of

Hekate's presence in and around the Clapham area. Indeed, they felt that the considerable adverse publicity Clapham had attracted over the years, had perhaps driven the group to find a new centre for its occult activities. The final nail in their coffin was, of course, the publication of *The Demonic Connection,* which highlighted the wave of black magic activity currently taking place in West Sussex.

Closing the book, I thought about its implications. There seemed to be little doubt that when Bernard had picked up a connection between the Black Alchemist and the occult goings on taking place inside Clapham Wood, he had been referring to the clandestine activities of the Friends of Hekate.

Therefore, the Black Alchemist and the Friends of Hekate were in some way linked. Perhaps he had now teamed up with certain individuals who either belonged, or had once belonged, to the Clapham-based group. Remember, Bernard had picked up this connection following the Running Well confrontation the previous year, the very first occasion he had clairvoyantly seen the Black Alchemist working with a group.

One person came to mind — the woman with shoulder-length dark hair, described by Bernard as in her 30s, who had turned up in Danbury churchyard on Hallowe'en to carry out the Sword of Dardanus ritual. The same woman who had apparently masterminded the dagger-in-the-heart ritual on Guy Fawkes' Night.

Who then was this woman? She was obviously working alongside the Black Alchemist as he had trusted her to take complete control of the whole Danbury episode which had, of course, strongly featured the power and influence of the Dark Goddess, especially in her guise as Hekate.

It therefore seemed clear that, if any former or current member of the Friends of Hekate could be tracked down by a little investigative journalism in and around the Clapham area, then it could lead me to the identity of the Black Alchemist's female accomplice and, perhaps, even to the identity of the man himself.

Thirty eight
The Ape Dagger

Monday, 7th December, 1987. 'I'll have to read it sometime,' Bernard decided, glancing through the glossy black and white plates in *The Demonic Connection,* after having listened to my brief resumē of its contents. 'Can I borrow it?'

No, the book had to be returned to the library as there was already a fine to pay, so it could not be kept any longer. Anyway, I had ordered a copy from a local bookshop, so he could read that one when I received it.

It was our first get-together at The Griffin since the dagger-in-the-heart sketch over a month beforehand. So, had he received *any* new psychic material since that time?

Still flicking through the pages of the book, he looked up, almost disinterested by the question. 'No, all quiet on the psychic front. Hopefully, we've seen the last of him this time,' he said, a note of optimism in his voice.

I'd heard those words so many times that I just ignored them with a glare.

'What else have you discovered over the past month,' he asked.

Okay, so he wanted to change the subject. I had, at last, found reference to Comarius, the ancient high priest, sage and prophet who had overshadowed Bernard to give him the sickening automatic script on 4th November, following the Maria the Jewess dream. The same character who had taken possession of Bernard's body out in the field behind Danbury churchyard the following night.

I had come across his name, quite by chance, in George Luck's book *Arcana Mundi,* just after the section on Zosimos of Panopolis. Apparently, he had been a Graeco-Egyptian alchemist and high priest of the third century AD. He had also been the author of an alchemical treatise entitled the *Book of Comarius,* dedicated to a lady named Cleopatra the Divine, to whom he had been 'Philosopher and High Priest'.

Referred to as 'the wise woman', Cleopatra was thought to have been an accomplished alchemist herself. However, she was not to be confused with the various queens of that name who had ruled Egypt in the last centuries before Christ.

The *Book of Comarius* begins with an account of how Comarius has conveyed the alchemical sciences to Cleopatra, who had quite obviously been some sort of patron to him. It then turns to more practical matters, such as the properties and uses of certain metals, colours and apparatus. A group of philosophers is then introduced to the text and Cleopatra delivers to them the knowledge she has received from Comarius. It was this last section which had often led scholars to falsely conclude that Cleopatra had been the author of the text, and not Comarius.

George Luck's book, *Arcana Mundi,* then launched into an extract from the *Book of Comarius* where Cleopatra explains how alchemy is the key to the mystery of resurrection. Reading through this, I had discovered a number of statements which quite clearly echoed Comarius' words to Bernard within the automatic script.

As an example, I asked Bernard to read the following extract from the *Book of Comarius:*

> **. . . for they (the plants, the elements and the stones) get nourished in the fire, just as an embryo, nourished in its mother's womb, grows slowly. When the appointed month is near, it is not prevented from coming out . . . but when the tomb (in which they lie) is opened, they will ascend from Hades like the babe from the womb . . . Here you have the sealed mystery.**

And then compare it with the following extract from Comarius' automatic script, scribbled down at high speed in his dining room during November 1987:

> **They (the stones and relics) are nourished in the fire and the embryo grows nourished in its mother's womb.**
>
> **At the appointed time the new child will come. The spirit of the blackness appears and rises up and encircles the child. Clothe yourself. A cry of awaken from Hades will be heard.**
>
> **Arise from your tomb and pit. The voice of resurrection has sounded.**

There were many more such comparisons between the two texts, indicating that they had been penned by the same hand. However, Bernard's automatic text appeared to have a darker, more sinister message, almost as if somebody was distorting the meaning of Comarius' original text.

Yet, having confirmed Comarius' life on earth, and his apparent authorship of the automatic script, a rather nagging question needed answering. Why should a third century Graeco-Egyptian alchemist wish to steal and possess Bernard's soul seventeen hundred years after his life had expired in Ancient Egypt? Hadn't he got anything better to do with his time?

Bernard shrugged his shoulders and looked blank. 'I don't know. Perhaps BA studied the *Book of Comarius* and decided to call upon the man's soul essence to aid him in his own alchemical transmutation.'

And, in doing so, he had created a Comarius thought form which possessed its own individual life essence and intelligence. Yes, it made some sort of sense.

Bernard looked uneasy. 'All this stuff about a new child coming at the appointed time, and things coming out of wombs and pits, does concern me. It brings us back to the idea that BA is attempting to raise something, or bring something into existence. What, or when, I'm not sure.'

Some form of Antichrist?

'Possibly. I really don't know,' he admitted, as he stood up and disappeared off to the bar to buy more drinks.

Opening my briefcase, I brought out the ape dagger. He had

not seen it since its discovery on Guy Fawkes' Night, so I wanted to point out the moon, Saturn and Taurus symbols scratched into its blade. I also hoped that he would agree to psychometrise it to see if he could pick up any information about its previous owner. Enough clues might even lead us to the woman; if, indeed, it *had* belonged to a woman.

Sitting back down at the fireside table, Bernard was handed the ape dagger and shown its astrological symbols. Was there any chance of him psychometrising it?

'No, I'm not attuning to it,' he stated, putting down the artefact as if to emphasise the point. 'I wouldn't get anything anyway.'

Obviously, I disagreed and, after a little friendly persuasion, he gave in and picked up the dagger again.

Slowly rotating it in one hand, and holding a pen close to a clean sheet of notepaper with the other, he began to stare intently into thin air.

At first the psychic saw nothing, but then images of a location began to crystallise in his mind. 'It's night and I see what looks like castle battlements; a wall high up which curves around,' he revealed, as he began to sketch a line of battlements. 'It's a castle perched high up on a hill overlooking a town below.' He sketched in a town.

Assuming that the location was in Sussex, I asked him if he could see the sea.

He slowly shook his head. 'I get no impression of the sea nearby. Only a large river running through the town.'

A long pause followed before he spoke again. 'Behind this wall is a church with a circular path encircling its exterior walls, and a grass churchyard. I see tombstones, but only on one side, its west side, I think. There's a pathway leading from the battlemented wall to an entrance porch on the south side. I also see a corner buttress.' Another break followed to allow him to continue his sketch.

'Outside the wall is a stepped path and an access road, I feel.'

Could he see the castle?

'No. No clear image of the castle. There *is* something behind the church. Although I can't see what; I can only feel its presence, so perhaps it's a ruined castle.' Those final words were thrown away as if only a suggestion.

Completing his drawing, he again concentrated on the battlemented wall. 'There's someone there now, standing below the battlements, facing towards me. It's the same character I saw in Danbury churchyard.'

Who? Paphotia? Maria the Jewess?

'No, the woman with shoulder-length dark hair in the black coat and boots,' he corrected me. 'This time she's wearing a black cowled cloak and is attempting to draw me to her; like a pulling . . . but she's weak . . .'

There was a period of silence before Bernard broke off his vacant gaze and placed the ape dagger down as if to signal an end to the psychometry demonstration. 'She's gone,' he announced, reaching for his cigarette packet. 'I engulfed her image in white light and she disappeared.'

Had the ape dagger belonged to her?

'Yes, I think so,' he confirmed. 'She seems to be connected with this town in some way.'

Did she live there?

'Perhaps. Or connected.'

Where was this town? Sussex?

'No indication. Its just vague stuff really. Isn't it?'

Possibly. However, the imagery itself was not vague. It was clear and precise and, judging by the accuracy of his past material, a town of this appearance existed somewhere; and it was my betting that it was in Sussex. From his description of the location, it would not be that difficult to find.

Tuesday, 8th December. 'It sounds like Arundel, in Sussex,' the bearded antiques dealer suggested from behind his shop counter, after having listened to the description of the town picked up psychically by Bernard in connection with the ebony ape dagger.

As the man had shown some interest in the Black Alchemist affair, following a couple of conversations on the subject, I had promised to keep him up to date on any new developments.

'Arundel's famous castle is perched on a hilltop overlooking the town, just as you describe,' he confirmed, trying to recall his own distant memory of the town. 'On one side of the hill there's a steep drop, whilst on the other side there are some woods, I think. It *is* surrounded by battlements and there *is* a large chapel within the walls of the castle.'

What about an access road to the castle?

'Yes, that's there too. It's all exactly as you say.'

And the castle. Was it a ruin?

'No, not really. It's years since I've been there, so you might be right. Look, I've got a guide to the castle at home. If you're passing this way later on in the week, I'll have it here.'

Thanking him, I left the shop and made my way by car to Grindley's Bookshop, in Leigh Broadway, to take a look at the Ordnance Survey map of the area.

It looked very much as if Bernard had been viewing Arundel, in Sussex. But where was that? I had forgotten to ask the antiques dealer. I also needed to know whether or not the town was near the sea and whether a major river cut through its streets.

Entering the bookshop, I quietly made my way towards the display stand full of Ordnance Survey maps.

A slim female assistant with long blonde hair moved into view by my side. 'Hello. What are you looking for this time?' she asked, in a polite, well-meaning voice.

It was Debbie. She knew something of the Black Alchemist affair, so I told her about Arundel as I attempted to find the correct map.

'I've been to Arundel,' she responded, with reserved enthusiasm. 'The River Arun runs through the town, and it's about five miles inland from the sea; not far along the coast from Worthing.'

Was it a large river?

'Oh yes, huge,' she nodded.

The River Arun. That was what Bernard had seen; and no

wonder he had not felt the close presence of the sea. It was five miles away to the south. And Worthing. Close to Worthing; and therefore close to Clapham?

Unfolding the scarlet-fronted Ordnance Survey map, my eyes scanned the West Sussex coastline until they found first Worthing, and then Arundel. Excitement filled my stomach as I openly proclaimed that Arundel was a mere *five* miles west of Clapham, directly along the A27 road.

The assistant looked at me baffled, yet somewhat bemused, as I shoved the map back into its slot and left the shop in search of any library books on Arundel.

It was beginning to look as if the Black Alchemist's female accomplice came from Arundel; or, at least, she had a strong connection with the town. The fact that it was only five miles from Clapham convinced me even further that she was the link between BA and the Friends of Hekate.

I needed to get down to Arundel as soon as possible. I also needed to make contact with Charles Walker and Toyne Newton to find out if they had any new information on the Friends of Hekate, and to tell them about the Black Alchemist affair. I would write to Toyne that evening and address the envelope to his publishers, Blandford Press. It should eventually reach him via this process.

Friday, 11th December. Having not found much on Arundel in Leigh library, I picked up the castle guide from the antiques dealer and sat down that evening to study its contents.

Seen from the river, or from the east side of the Arun valley, Arundel, it said, was a most imposing Sussex town. Clinging to a shaggy hill, the town was dominated by three architectural structures of significance: its castle, its neo-Gothic Catholic cathedral church, and the parish church of St Nicholas.

Perched high on the crown of the hill, the castle was encircled by a mass of battlemented stone walls, with a keep, a gateway, and a history which stretched back to the time of the Norman Conquest. However, much of it had been restored in the Victorian neo-Gothic style by the same Duke of Arundel who had commissioned the building of the Catholic cathedral church of St Philip Neri, just along the road.

The aerial map in the guide clearly showed the battlemented walls which encircled the castle and incorporated within them the Norman keep and several other embattled buildings. However, it also showed that the only religious edifice in the castle grounds was a private chapel, actually built into the wall itself. However, it did not have a circular path around its exterior walls, it did not possess a grass churchyard with tombstones, and could hardly be described as a church by any stretch of the imagination.

The discrepancy bugged me. Everything else checked out, even Arundel's proximity to Clapham Wood. So what was wrong?

It made me even more determined to get down to the area as soon as time and money would permit.

Thirty nine
The Sword of Dardanus

Thursday, 24th December, 1987. Among the late Christmas cards scattered across the front door mat that morning was a rather more bulky package from Terry DuQuesne.

Opening it, I removed the cover note. He had, at last, discovered details of the Sword of Dardanus and, as I had expected, it was the title of a powerful Graeco-Egyptian ritual. Terry had found it among a collection of similar magical formulas and spells recently translated into English for a new book, entitled *Greek Magical Papyri,* edited by one H.B. Betz and published in Chicago, USA, the previous year.

The pages detailing the ritual — numbers 69 to 71 — had been photocopied and enclosed in the package, and a 'PS' asked me to ring Terry as he had further information on the matter.

Glancing through the photocopies, just the purpose of the Sword of Dardanus rite (or Dardan*o*s as it was spelt in the script) showed its significance to us. For, if successful, it 'immediately bends and attracts the souls of whomever you wish.' Memories of Bernard's psychic material from Hallowe'en came flooding back to me. So I quickly read and digested the rest of the magical formula:

PGM IV. 1716-1870

Sword of Dardanos: Rite which is called "sword", which has no equal because of its power, for it immediately bends and attracts the soul of whomever you wish. As you say the spell, also say: "I am bending to my will the soul of him (or her) NN."

Take a magnetic stone which is breathing and engrave Aphrodite sitting astride Psyche and with her left hand holding on her hair bound in curls. And above her head: "ACHMAGE RARPEPSEI"; and below Aphrodite and Psyche engrave Eros standing on the vault of Heaven, holding a blazing torch and burning Psyche. And below Eros these names: "ACHAPA ADŌNAIE BASMA CHARAKŌ IAKŌB IAŌ Ē PHARPHARĒI." On the other side of the stone engrave Psyche and Eros embracing one another and beneath Eros' feet these letters: "SSSSSSS," and beneath Psyche's feet: "ĒĒĒĒĒĒĒĒ." Use the stone, when it has been engraved and consecrated, like this: put it under your tongue and turn it to what you wish and say this spell:

"I call upon you, author of all creation, who spread your own wings over the whole world . . . (the 'spell' continued on for another couple of hundred words, including some forty goetic barbarous names) . . . Turn the 'soul' of her (or him) NN to me NN, so that she (or he) may love me, so that she (or he) may feel passion for me, so that she (or he) may give me what is in her (or his) power. Let her (or him) say to me what is in her (or his) soul because I have called upon your great name."

The ritual carried on after this, although for my purposes, I'd read enough. In the footnotes it pointed out that the designation 'sword' served as a title for certain types of magical invocations, such as the so-called Sword of Moses, a Hebrew mystical ritual of great antiquity.

Placing down the photocopies, I brought out Bernard's original psychic material, recorded during that fateful October evening, and read them again:

Sword of Dardanus . . . The sword will bend souls as is wished. It will torture. Engrave ACHMAGERARPEPSEI on stone. Burn Psyche. ACHAPA ADŌNAIE BASMA CHARAKŌ IAKŌB IAŌ Ē PHARPHAREI. Tie to tree and burn.

Then, in his summary afterwards, he had posed the question:

> **Is BA using whoever Dardanus is? It relates to fire and the bending of souls in some way.**

It was quite apparent that Bernard had picked up a condensed version of the Sword of Dardanus rite. Before this, I had not really understood what 'bending souls' actually meant. Now it was clear — it was a magical ritual which, if successful, would attract or 'bend' a person's soul using the emotion of false love and passion for the purposes of getting her, or him, to reveal the nature of their power and the contents of their mind. It almost seemed like a corrupt form of love magic of the sort often used in the past, where a witch or wizard would help a person to gain the heart of someone they wanted as their lover.

It was this that the Black Alchemist's female accomplice had been trying to achieve when she had carried out the Sword of Dardanus rite by the upturned tree stump in Danbury churchyard on the night of Hallowe'en. Fortunately for Bernard, it had not worked.

Interestingly enough, the Sword of Dardanus involved the use of an inscribed stone in much the same way that the Black Alchemist appeared to be using them. Indeed, the Mesolithic flint arrowhead, found in the crevice by the upturned tree stump, had been used for the purpose of fixing the intentions of the Sword or Dardanus ritual. In fact, it appeared that, in Gnostic Christian and Graeco-Egyptian magic, the use of inscribed stones and gems were a frequent feature.

A conversation with Terry DuQuesne was clearly in order at the earliest convenience.

Tuesday, 29th December. Finally, after several days of trying, I managed to reach Terry by telephone. I wanted to know more about this new American book which featured the Sword of Dardanus formula; in particular, its availability.

'It's definitely not freely available in this country,' he replied, with some confidence. 'The first I knew of it was when I received an advertising leaflet for the book which came with an issue of *The Hermetic Journal,* earlier this year.'

The Hermetic Journal. Yes, I knew it. It concerned itself with the subjects of alchemy, Hermetica and Rosicrucian literature. However, I was not a subscriber to the publication, and I was pretty sure that Bernard had no knowledge of its existence.

He continued: 'The book had to be ordered direct from the publishers in the States and at £40 to £50 a copy, I doubt whether very many have found their way into this country.'

Who might possess a copy of the book?

'A few students of Graeco-Egyptian magic, perhaps, and one or two classical sections of university libraries up and down the country. That's all. It's an academic book which would be of very little value to anyone other than academics.'

Could there be any possible alternative sources for the Sword of Dardanus formula?

'As far as I am aware, this American book is the first time the ritual has been translated into English,' Terry emphasised. 'And I now realise where it was taken from; and just to show its obscurity, I'll give you its full history as I see it.'

The rite, Terry explained, had originally featured among a collection of magical spells and incantations put together in Graeco-Roman Egypt during the third century AD by an unknown priest magician. Some of the papyri had been set down in Coptic, whilst others were recorded in an awkward form of classical Greek. Each one also contained many goetic barbarous words and used an assortment of Hebrew, Aramaic, Greek and Roman names of gods and goddesses.

During the nineteenth century this book of spells was rediscovered in Egypt by the French and brought back to Paris where the collection became known as *The Great Magical Papyrus in Paris.* Yet despite the interest shown in the collection by classical scholars, it was never translated from its original Coptic and Greek.

The collection laid undisturbed in a Paris library until the

1920s when a German classical scholar, named Karl Preisendanz, had decided to collect together and publish a series of previously untranslated Graeco-Egyptian magical papyri, including the Paris collection, within a three volume work entitled *Papyri Graecae Magicae;* or PGM as it became known among the academic circles. On the left-hand page of each volume was the magical formula in its original form, and on each corresponding right-hand page was Preisendanz' German translation of the text.

The Great Magical Papyrus in Paris, which, of course, included the Sword of Dardanus rite, formed about sixty pages of Section IV of the first volume of PGM, which was published in 1928.

The subsequent volumes of PGM were published in 1932 and 1941 respectively. Virtually all the copies of the third volume were destroyed in Germany during the Second World War, however, several copies of the first two volumes did manage to find their way into the classical sections of certain specialist and university libraries within this country. Yet they were, of course, useless to anyone unless they read either Coptic, classical Greek or German.

Even though I tried to take notes, it was all a little confusing to me. However, the obscurity of the Sword of Dardanus rite was clearly becoming apparent. Anyone who possessed even a basic knowledge of its existence would have required an in depth understanding of Graeco-Egyptian magical papyri.

So, had the Black Alchemist and his female accomplice used the recently published English translation of the Sword of Dardanus, or had they studied the magical formula in its original Greek and German form within a copy of PGM? As early as 1985, Bernard had felt that the Black Alchemist was an academic who worked in a quiet environment, possibly a college or university library. If this was so, then he would have had very little trouble in obtaining a copy of PGM on a library interloan basis.

Terry seemed unconvinced: 'If this man is an academic with such an intricate knowledge of Graeco-Egyptian magic, then what's he doing poisoning holy wells?'

He was, of course, referring to the Black Alchemist's desecration of the Running Well. In answer to this, I suggested that perhaps he was purely a warped and rather unstable psychopath with an obsession for re-working and corrupting ancient magical manuscripts and traditions.

'That may be so. But I almost take this business personally. To know that there is someone in this country with an extensive knowledge of Graeco-Egyptian magic who is corrupting it for their own obscene purposes is a very disconcerting thought.'

I made no comment. Changing the subject again, I mentioned the recent developments concerning the Black Alchemist's female accomplice and her apparent link with Arundel.

'If you want my opinion, I think you'll find that she's going to be the driving force behind the Black Alchemist from now on,' he said, prophetically. 'She is the power. Mark my words.'

I wasn't sure and, after thanking him for his time, I said I would keep in touch.

Terry's closing statement about the Black Alchemist's female accomplice played on my mind throughout the rest of the day. Perhaps he was right. From what little we knew of her, she appeared to be a different sort of character to her male counterpart. Whereas he seemed to be a loner who studied, schemed, brooded and then struck quickly before withdrawing to carefully plan his next move, she was an altogether different animal. She was, I felt, a charismatic person with a lively, outgoing, even sensuous personality; the sort of woman who was likely to take the bull by the horns, so to speak, and attempt to confront us face-to-face. However, there was no way that I was going to upset Bernard by suggesting that he keep a watch out for any strange women unexpectedly turning up on his front doorstep! I wasn't quite sure his wife would understand!

Perhaps it would pay me to forget trying to track down the

Black Alchemist for a while and concentrate my efforts more on the woman.

The new year was to be welcomed in — as in previous years — on the top of Glastonbury Tor, in Somerset. For this reason it seemed like a good idea to drop down into West Sussex on the way home and pay Arundel a visit.

I had still not heard from Toyne Newton, the author of *The Demonic Connection;* which was a pain. So, with the prospect of going to Sussex in the next few days, I felt the best plan of action was to try and contact Toyne's investigative partner — Charles Walker.

Directory Enquiries gave me the address and telephone number of just one C. Walker in Worthing. I rang the number and immediately found myself speaking to the man who, in November 1978, had met the anonymous initiate of the Friends of Hekate and had discovered the demonic mural in the unoccupied manor house, close to Clapham church, the following spring.

We arranged to meet at his home on New Year's Day.

Forty
The Net Closes

Friday, 1st January, 1988. Subdued, and yet without that much of a festive hangover, Ken Smith and I left Glastonbury after breakfast and crossed the dull and wet landscapes of Somerset, Dorset and Hampshire. Low cloud enveloped every ridge of hills and the rain poured down perpetually throughout the journey.

As the car passed from Hampshire into Sussex, during the early afternoon, we were immediately confronted by the mass devastation left by the previous October's hurricane. Fallen trees littered everywhere; whole forests had been left a tangled mess of fallen trunks, uprooted tree stumps and twisted and broken branches. In some areas, the tops of every tree had been violently snapped off like matchsticks around head height, leaving them as an ugly reminder of the enormous brute strength of the terrifying winds that night. I thought that Essex had suffered badly. Yet in comparison with what I was now witnessing in Sussex, it was nothing.

Once in Arundel, we cruised around the town's quaint, almost medieval-style streets looking for the castle. Eventually we found its huge battlemented wall and came to a halt in a small car park at the front of the main entrance gateway.

With the rain still falling, we braved the elements and set out on foot. I needed to clear up the discrepancy concerning Bernard's psychic description of Arundel Castle and its surrounds, just to make sure we *were* in the correct town. He had seen an aerial view of a detached church with a circular path hugging its exterior walls, a graveyard on its west side, and an entrance pathway leading in from an opening in the

The view across the fields to the town of Arundel with its castle clearly visible to the right-hand side of the picture.

embattled wall to an entrance porch on the south side. Yet, as far as I could ascertain, such a place simply did not exist in Arundel, so the matter needed to be sorted out one way or another.

With the battlemented wall to our right, we climbed the hill towards the impressive cathedral church of St Philip Neri. Just past an embattled building incorporated within the towering wall, I noticed a recessed archway behind which I could just make out a Christian edifice which, the signboard announced, was the parish church of St Nicholas.

A gravel path led from the archway *to a porch on its south side,* and strolling along this, I saw that *a circular path* hugged the church's exterior walls.

As Ken and I stood in the pouring rain, quietly studying the assorted gravestones, standing crosses and box tombs — which were only on the western half of the churchyard — I felt a good feeling inside. Bernard had not been wrong. It was *this* church that he had psychically viewed. The discrepancy lay, not in his psychic information, but with the castle guide I had been shown. Its aerial map *had* indicated the position of the church. However, what it had neglected to make clear was that there

Looking through the entrance archway in the embattled wall encircling Arundel castle, the discrepancy in Bernard's psychic material was immediately explained as the parish church of St Nicholas suddenly came into view.

The pyramid-capped tower of St Nicholas' church, just visible behind the embattled wall encircling Arundel castle, as seen clairvoyantly by Bernard.

were *two* battlemented walls encircling the castle; an inner wall and an outer wall.

The outer wall enclosed the parish church of St Nicholas in exactly the way Bernard had clairvoyantly described. The matter had therefore been resolved. So, with this little problem out of the way, we made a quick study of the church's interior before deciding to retire for something to eat.

Taking a seat at the table next to the window in an empty coffee house, I glanced up at the embattled wall on the opposite side of the road, as Ken placed our order with the vivacious young waitress.

As she walked away, Ken removed his soaking wet donkey jacket and placed it on the back of the chair. 'Are you now positive it was Arundel that Bernard saw?'

Yes, I was. There could be little doubt of that any more. The Black Alchemist's female accomplice either lived in the town, or she was strongly connected with it in some way.

'Have you got a name for her yet?' he asked, meaning a Christian name, or a surname.

This amused me. What *could* we call her? We already had the Black Alchemist; or BA for short. So how about the Black Sorceress? Or what about the Black Sorceress of Arundel? BSA for short!

'BSA' Ken repeated, with a incredulous smile, before shaking his head. 'How do you expect anyone to take you seriously with a name like that?'

A sense of humour?

Accepting my word, he found another question. 'So, where do we go from here?'

We were to see Charles Walker at his home in Worthing that evening. I said I would ring him when we arrived in the area. He would undoubtedly introduce us to Toyne Newton.

'What about trying to find BSA?' Ken queried.

Certainly, at some point in the not too distant future, we would have to return to Arundel to see if we could track her down. However, I had the distinct impression that there would be no need to seek her out as she would eventually seek us out herself.

Inside his small lounge, the tall, slim character, with moustache and long hair, listened with his wife as I recounted a condensed version of the entire Black Alchemist affair. My account ended with the details of our visit to Arundel that afternoon and my feelings concerning the Black Alchemist's female accomplice.

Having listened patiently to my story for two and a half hours, Charles could hardly contain his feelings any longer. 'This woman you describe. She sounds *very* similar to the woman in her thirties who apparently controls the Friends of Hekate as high priestess. We have also linked her with Arundel and feel she may live in the town.'

Arundel? My heart sank.

'We have been working with a very talented psychic; an elderly lady, who Toyne knows very well. She's told us that the

Friends of Hekate have used a wooded area just outside Arundel, near the village of Burpham. Toyne has all the details. If you like, I can take you over to meet him tomorrow morning.'

Yes, that would be a very good idea. Yet you say that she may actually live in Arundel?

'Certain psychic clues and other unconfirmed snippets of information have led us to believe that, yes, she may well live in the town.'

Now we were getting somewhere. Was the net finally closing?

Saturday, 2nd January. 'The only thing I can really add to your Black Alchemist story is this psychic material Charles mentioned last night,' the tall, bearded man in a track suit exclaimed, after listening to the entire Black Alchemist story.

Accepting its possible relevance, I sat speaking to Toyne's mother as he left the room for a minute or two.

Returning, Toyne presented me with a sheet of typed notes. It contained the details of three sittings he had made with their elderly female psychic; one in 1982, one in 1984 and the last in 1985.

'The elderly lady who came out with this material is in her eighties and is very ill at the moment,' Toyne revealed, sitting down in an armchair on the opposite side of the room and picking up the ape dagger. 'She knew nothing about the Friends of Hekate, or their activities, so you will see the relevance of what she is saying.'

Nodding in agreement, I began to read the text:

> **29.9.82. The graveyard (at Clapham church) has not been disturbed because necromancy is child's play to these people. This is real devil worship and your life would not be worth a tinker's cuss because they have no human decency left. . .**
>
> **The real brains behind it are by five, with three prime**

movers being two women and one man, a medic. And they move from a distance.

They have also used the wood where no birds sing near Burpham, Arundel.

13.3.84. The younger woman is in her thirties, her main source of money income is blackmail. The medic is the master. They come down once a year, the sacrifice is usually a virgin man or woman, around November 1st, October 31st, or slightly before. The older woman was the original instigator.

They have positioned their activities towards the north. I cannot see the farm, but I feel I am approaching a farm building, but not going in. There must be another building there. I feel that I am underground. Something to do with an underground chasm or cavern. Only for the important meets.

They use the pentagram drawn with white thread. Lady in her thirties very well connected. There is a French connection currently, people come over from France. Lady in her thirties lives in two or more homes, mainly in a London flat. Travels a bit. I get the feeling of a coronet, a crest on the door, a brougham (horse carriage). There are no drugs with the hierachy, neophytes used the mushroom, etc.

10.10.85. The high priestess (the woman in her thirties) is the most dangerous. She looks like a rose but acts like a devil . . . I have gone terribly cold, never felt such evil . . . She is blonde but wears wigs.

Five per cent of the inner circle are involved in show business, public life, etc. When your book is published they will up and go somewhere else. The band will be broken. The nearest you could get to it would be the Hellfire Club, only this (the Friends of Hekate) is more destructive and will create more chaos.

Psychic material must always be treated as pure gobbledegook, unless proved otherwise. However, I was intrigued. The text appeared to confirm many of the claims made in the anonymous letter received by Toyne via *The Unexplained* magazine, in March 1982. Many of its statements concerning the Friend of Hekate's high priestess — the woman in her thirties, who 'looks like a rose, but acts like a devil' — also duplicated our own feelings concerning the Black Sorceress of Arundel. Yet despite the fact that the elderly psychic had indicated that the woman was a blonde, and not dark haired, we too felt that she moved in well-to-do, show business circles where she was fully able to exploit her charismatic charm and elegance.

The psychic's suggestion that the woman lived in two or more homes was also interesting. Perhaps one was in London, and the other was in Arundel. The town was a common location for well-to-do people with holiday homes.

In conclusion, I had to admit that there were marked similarities between our Black Sorceress of Arundel and their High Priestess of Hekate. The Black Alchemist's female accomplice appeared to be an adept occultist who used the powers of the Dark Goddess — Hekate in particular — and possibly even introduced him to the advantages of using this feminine force at the time of the hurricane. We also knew that she was strongly connected with Arundel, where the Friends of Hekate had apparently used a wood near Burpham for their magical operations. But *were* they one and the same?

'I think it possible,' Toyne concluded, with a certain amount of conviction.

Yet in their psychic information there was no mention of the woman in her thirties actually living in Arundel. Where had that idea come from?

Charles looked at Toyne, and Toyne looked back at Charles. It was obvious that they were slightly reluctant to give me an answer to this question, for some reason. Yet then, concluding that it would be okay to tell Ken and I, Toyne shuffled forward in his chair. 'It came from something which the elderly psychic said to us and we followed it on from there.'

Toyne went on to reveal a new lead which he and Charles were currently checking out concerning the woman's association with Arundel.

It was all beginning to make sense. However, it was almost too easy to say that the high priestess of the Friends of Hekate was one and the same as the Black Alchemist's female accomplice.

Having not come to any particular conclusion on the matter, I felt, perhaps, that we should change the subject for a while. So, what else had they discovered about the activities of the Friends of Hekate since the psychic's last message in 1985? Did they feel that the group still existed?

'We're not sure,' Charles answered, taking up the question. 'We've not had any further evidence or information concerning their ritual activities, either in Clapham or anywhere else for that matter.'

'Anyway, if you like I can show you the church and woods this afternoon,' Charles suggested.

That's what I hoped he would say.

'Do you mind if I take a few photos of the ape dagger?' Toyne asked, holding it up.

Of course not. For my own purposes, I wanted a copy of the demonic mural photograph.

'No problem,' Toyne said, leaving the room to find a picture of the mural.

Returning, he handed me a large colour print.

In the light of his conservatory, my camera lense focused upon the demonic mural and, as the image sharpened, I suddenly realised just how powerful it actually was, especially in vivid colour. There was no way that this had been painted by kids, or by idiots dabbling in primary text book magic.

I would have to show a copy of the print to Bernard to see if he would consent to psychometrising it.

We navigated the pitted trackway which snaked its way towards Clapham church as gale-force winds — the worst the country had seen since the previous year's hurricane — gusted wildly across the South Downs.

Bernard's words, spoken as we had sat in the car on the evening of the Running Well confrontation, kept repeating in my mind: 'Now I see more woods, at a place called Clapham, in Sussex. Something's been going on there; ritual, I think. I also see a church nearby, reached down a long, winding road. Not a nice feeling about the place. Best left alone.' Or words to that effect.

Parking the car beneath the tree cover outside the churchyard, Charles and Ken got out and watched as I took a series of photographs of the mostly thirteenth century church. Despite the high winds, there was a clear blue sky and a low winter sun, which made it ideal light for photography.

Carrying on, the three figures stopped to study the various memorials to the famed Shelley family inside the church, before moving back out into the open and tackling the wooden stile on the eastern boundary of the churchyard. From here it was just a short trek across an exceedingly muddy field to the edge of Clapham Wood.

Charles stopped to point out the old manor house where he had discovered the demonic mural in the spring of 1979. It stood to the south of the church amid a cluster of farm buildings, outhouses and barns which made up Clapham Farm. Following its extensive restoration at the beginning of the decade, the manor house was re-christened the Church House. In its driveway were expensive-looking cars, and I wondered whether the current owners were aware of the mural which had once adorned one of its rooms. Probably not.

Inside the woods we were shocked by what we saw. Much of the woodland had been completely razed to the ground by the fierce winds of the hurricane. Miles of dense tree cover had been reduced to a mass of fallen, twisted and tangled mayhem. Some areas had already been cleared, however, other parts were exactly as they had been left following that fateful night in October the previous year.

Never before had I seen anything like it. It was the sort of

As we approached the church of St Mary at Clapham, in West Sussex, Bernard's words kept repeating in my mind: 'Now I see more woods, at a place called Clapham, in Sussex . . . (and) a church nearby, reached down a long, winding road.'

chaotic destruction I would have expected to find after a nuclear holocaust. All parts of the woods were the same. Wherever we went, hundreds of trees littered the ground making it virtually impossible to leave the trackways.

To make matters worse, the gale-force winds were on the increase. As we walked cautiously below what remained of the tall tree cover, we contemplated the possibility of further tree falls as the winds hissed and roared through the woods. It was an eerie sensation which gave the whole situation a very sinister and foreboding ambience.

A little further on we arrived at the Chestnuts, the spot where, in November 1978, Charles had kept his rendezvous with the anonymous initiate of the Friends of Hekate. What he saw shattered him. For instead of a crossways enclosed by dense tree cover and thick undergrowth, all that remained was a wide open space around the old signpost which marked the convergence point of the various footpaths.

Charles Walker stood dumbstruck amid the chaotic destruction within Clapham Wood in the wake of the hurricane.

Charles stared in utter disbelief. 'This wood is totally unrecognisable,' he concluded, shaking his head, as we climbed over yet another fallen tree blocking the path. 'The whole area has been completely devastated. Known sites and specific spots, they simply no longer exist.'

Having seen enough, we decided to head back towards the car.

Pulling out on to the dual carriageway of the busy A27, I thought seriously about the chaotic destruction we had just witnessed in the woods. In some strange way, it almost seemed symbolic of the demise of the Friends of Hekate. It was as if they had covered their own tracks by obliterating their previous meeting places.

In fact, as I drove back into Worthing to drop Charles off at his home, something wanted to tell me that the group no longer existed. It had now fragmented to form new links, new associations and new splinter groups.

In addition to this, I was now pretty sure that its former High Priestess of Hekate was the woman currently working on a magical level with the Black Alchemist — our Black Sorceress of Arundel. The two characters were undoubtedly one and the same.

Forty one
The Summoning

Tuesday, 9th February, 1988. Throughout the day I had the uncanny feeling that something was in the air. The weathermen were predicting another hurricane, and the Black Alchemist seemed to like moving under the cover of high winds.

Ever since the hurricane the previous October, I had been on edge every time gale-force winds had struck, almost as if I could now sense their raw, elemental power.

Yet nothing had happened. Bernard had not picked up any new psychic material on the Black Alchemist situation since the previous December when he had pinpointed Arundel as being in some way connected with the Black Alchemist's female accomplice.

Over the previous weekend, Ken Smith and I had revisited Arundel in the hope of trying to find some trace of BSA. However, our extensive enquiries within bookshops, in antiques shops, and even with the police, had all come to nothing. Despite this, I did feel that we *had* sown a seed. If she did live in Arundel, then she might get wind of the fact that someone was asking awkward questions about her. This would then perhaps tempt her into making further moves in our direction.

By the late afternoon, the predicted hurricane had not materialised in Essex. However, news reports early that evening confirmed that fierce hurricane winds *were* in the process of devastating other parts of the country.

Winds gusting up to speeds of 107 mph had already hit Ireland, North Wales, Northern England and Scotland — all areas which had escaped the previous hurricane six months before.

At least ten people had already been killed as a direct result of the gales. Fallen trees blocked many major roads and railway lines, and nearly 100,000 homes were now without electricity.

And there was more on the way. The hurricane-force winds were moving eastwards and would be in the eastern counties by the early evening. Hurricane K, as they were already referring to the gusting winds, appeared to be on the way.

The high winds were making driving difficult for Bernard as he made his way home from work that evening. The radio said that gusts of up to 65 mph had already been reported in Essex and worse was apparently on the way.

The clock on the dashboard of Bernard's new Montego car showed it was already well past six o' clock. He was to meet Andy at The Griffin just after seven, so there was no time to lose if he was going to be there on time.

The vehicle came to a halt on his driveway and, climbing out, Bernard pulled up the collar of his coat as he made for the front door. Sliding the key into the lock, he turned it until the door pushed open.

On the carpet lay a small, unmarked brown envelope. Picking it up, he stared at it suspiciously. It bore no name or address, and it was sealed. Yet its mere presence sent an instant shiver down his spine. Almost immediately, he felt he knew who it was from, and was glad that both his wife and his daughter had not yet arrived home.

Finding a knife, he slit open its lip and pulled out a tight-fitting sheet of black card, some five inches by three inches in size. On both sides were magical symbols carefully inscribed in pencil which, against the black background, made them difficult to see in the dimly-lit hallway.

Carrying it into the better light of the kitchen, he studied the strange images and tried, in vain, to interpret their meaning. On one side was a large, vertically drawn, updated *Monas Hieroglyphica.* Below this was a more familiar symbol — an oval shape with lines radiating out from its edge, like those which had appeared on some of the early Black Alchemist spearheads.

On the other side were groups of unfamiliar magical characters — two sets on one line and another two below them on a second line. Below these was, what looked like, a long knife with a triangular-shaped blade and a ball-like handle. Inside the blade was a single word — Καλλιστη— which he took to be Greek.

His stomach began to churn wildly and he frowned in annoyance. It was quite obvious that, after nearly three years of searching, the Black Alchemist had finally discovered his full name and address and wanted to make sure that Bernard knew it. But how had he found out? Around the time of the Danbury business the previous autumn, he felt he had been followed home from The Griffin one night. At the time, he had dismissed his feelings as mild paranoia, yet now they seemed to take on a new significance.

Whatever the answer, someone had been to his home that day and left this calling card. So what did it mean? And what would happen next? The hurricane-winds were *his* sort of weather, so what was he up to this time?

A horrible feeling stabbed at his mind. Was someone still around; waiting for him somewhere? In many ways he did not want to know the answer, but for a few brief moments he decided to concentrate his psychic mind on the black card. He allowed just one impression to filter into his conscious thoughts. The card had come, not from the Black Alchemist, but from his female accomplice — the Black Sorceress of Arundel, BSA, as Andy was now referring to her.

Slipping the black calling card back into the small brown envelope, he placed it on the kitchen table and made himself a coffee before leaving for Danbury.

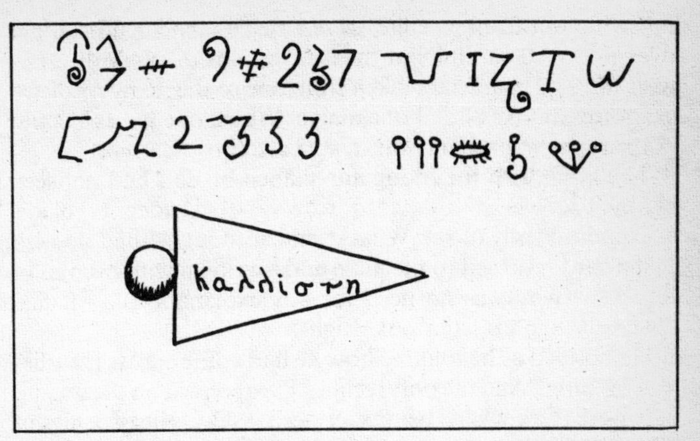

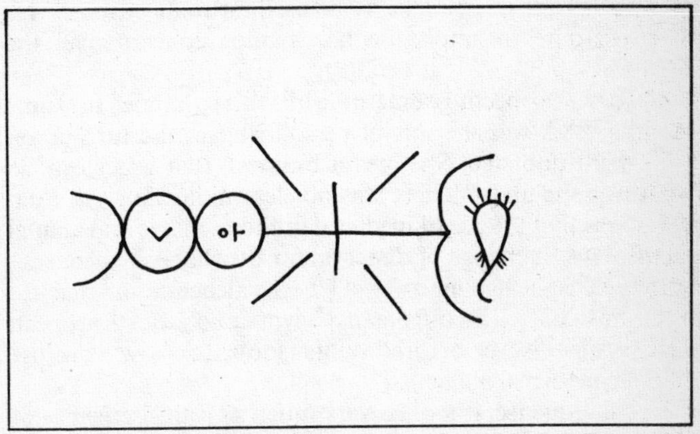

Both sides of the black calling card pushed through Bernard's letterbox, inside a brown envelope, during February 1988.

'Here. This'll give you a shock,' he said, as he threw down a small brown envelope in front of me and wandered over to the bar to order himself a drink.

Sliding out the black sheet of card, I turned it about in the light and tried to make out its pencil-drawn symbols. The updated *Monas* symbol and the small oval shape with the lines radiating out from its edge, gave away its sender. Flicking it over, I looked carefully at the four groups of symbols. They were magical characters taken from one of the many medieval grimoires; books of diabolic magic. Which one though, I was not sure; most probably the *The Clavicle of Solomon.*

The knife with the triangular-shaped blade I had not seen before. However, the word Καλλιστη, inside its blade, was undoubtedly Greek. What it meant though, I had no idea.

Bernard returned to the table and sat down with his pint of Kaliber. There was no need for any explanations — it had fallen through his letter box. Right?

He nodded as he told me how he had come across it earlier that evening. 'And the only feelings I've received on the way up here were of a cockerel being sacrificed. I saw its head being cut off and its feathers being kept and used for some purpose.' He lit a cigarette to emphasise his genuine concern over the situation.

I had been expecting something like this to happen for some months. BSA was the sort of person who would turn up on your front doorstep. She meant business; that was clear. So what was she up to? There was no clear indication. All I did know was that the use of medieval grimoire magic and animal sacrifice was a change of direction for the Black Alchemist.

In the past he had always stuck to the alchemic and magical traditions of Graeco-Roman Egypt and the European Renaissance. Never before had he stooped so low as to use diabolic medieval magic.

In consequence, it looked very much as if this sequence of events was being co-ordinated, not by the Black Alchemist, but by his female accomplice who, it appeared, practised this type of crude ritual magic. If she was the former high priestess for the Friends of Hekate, then it meant that she was already familiar with blood sacrifices.

'Yes, I know,' he stopped me, cutting dead a conversation he did not wish to hear. 'The only feeling I get as we sit here is that each of the groups of symbols were drawn on to the card only after a specific stage had been reached in the ritual. When the whole thing had been completed, it was given to me.'

Intrigued, I wondered whether the calling card had been psychically charged with a message of some sort which might be tapped by the use of psychometry.

He shook his head: 'No, I'm *not* going to psychometrise it. And I'm serious about that.'

Something was obviously going on, so the sooner we knew exactly what was happening, the more of an advantage we would have over the situation. The chances were that she was out there somewhere, waiting and poised to make her next move.

He was still adamant. 'I'm not going to psychometrise that card, and that's final,' he said, stubbing out his cigarette in protest. 'I really don't care what's going on out there. If I ignore them, then they will leave me alone.'

That was a foolhardy attitude which would get us nowhere. Burying your head in the sand was not going to make the problem go away.

Sighing openly, I realised I was fighting a losing battle. He obviously had no intention of psychometrising the calling card, so I decided to drop the matter; for the time being at least. However, just its presence on the table might be enough to spark off something in his mind, so I left it out by the ashtray.

Changing the topic, I turned to other research projects we were working on and updated him on some recent developments.

Several minutes passed before, still speaking, I noticed that Bernard appeared to be miles away; a sure sign that he was viewing a clairvoyant image in his mind's eye. So, what could he see?

The question broke his concentration. 'Oh, er, nothing,' he responded, turning back to me and trying to look interested in my words.

Suspicious, I carried on talking, but still he was not listening. His vacant gaze gave him away. He *was* seeing something. So what was it? A church? A castle? A cave? A holy hill?

He shook his head. 'No, a crossroads; a road junction somewhere.'

A crossroads. A site associated with the worship of Hekate.

'And I don't feel it's far from here,' he added, picking up his half-full pint glass. 'There's someone there. Although I can't make out if it's a real person, or an energy form.'

Now we were getting somewhere. Pretending to be a little disinterested, I continued on our earlier conversation.

Bernard then rapidly finished off his drink, placed down the glass and stood up. 'I can't stay here. Come on, let's go out into the car.'

Assuming that he just wanted to get away from the surrounds of the busy pub, I followed him outside and noted the time. It was 8.50 pm.

The gusting winds roared across the car park as we headed for the car. The hurricane appeared to be with us at last.

Opening the car door, he climbed inside, unlocked the passenger door and started up the engine.

He obviously wanted to go somewhere. So, quickly grabbing a torch from my own car, I pulled open his passenger door, threw in my gear and leapt into the seat, just as the car began to roll away from the spot.

Bernard said nothing. He would not even respond to my words as the vehicle turned right out of the car park and sped off down the hill. He seemed strange; almost somnambulistic. The car clock illuminated the time. It was now 8.57 pm.

Putting his foot on the brake pedal, the car slowed down. Momentarily he hesitated before turning left into a side road and then carrying on.

Several hundred yards down the road a T-junction loomed up ahead and, bringing the car to a halt, he paused for a moment as if getting his bearings, before making a decision to turn right.

Still he said nothing.

Where were we going? To the crossroads he had clairvoyantly seen in the pub? He certainly appeared to be homing in on something. But what? To the left was open farmland stretching away to the south, and to the right were woods.

Bernard then slowed down the car in the middle of the country lane. Apparently realising that we had gone past our destination, he unexpectedly put the vehicle into reverse and back-tracked several yards. Then, finding first gear, he turned the car into a recessed gateway and brought it to a halt.

In front of us was a locked wooden gate which formed the entrance into the car park of Danbury Country Park; a pleasant setting of woods and man-made lakes enjoyed by many visitors to the area.

Turning off the engine, he extinguished the lights. Yet still he said nothing. The time was now nine o'clock precisely.

Gradually he loosened up and turned to me. 'Well, we've been led here for some reason. Something's going on, and I'm not sure what. Come on, let's get out.'

Stepping out into the bitterly cold air, I realised that the gale-force winds were intensifying. Every few seconds a sudden gust would send an unearthly hiss through the woods and a deathly chill through our bodies. Something was building up — on an elemental level at least. But the weather was too much for us, so we got back in the car.

After a few minutes of silence, I asked him what was going on.

He simply shrugged his shoulders in dismay. 'I'm still not sure. It's like a drawing to this spot . . . like a magnet. I can see the same shape . . . the same energy form . . . which is her. She's here somewhere.'

Who? The Black Sorceress of Arundel?

'Yes. But where?' he asked, seemingly searching his own psychic faculty for an answer.

Several more minutes passed as I listened in silence to the heavy winds roaring and whistling through the trees, bending and swaying their branches and trunks until they sounded like creaky rocking chairs.

At 9.14 pm, Bernard switched on the engine. 'I'm going somewhere else,' he announced and, without further word, he reversed out the car and drove off.

'There *was* something here; and possibly still is,' he concluded, 'but I want to go somewhere else now.'

Passing the T-junction where we had turned right on the way to the park entrance, we carried straight on and soon came upon another junction where four roads converged. It was undoubtedly the location he had earlier seen clairvoyantly. However, although he slowed down as we approached this crossroads, he just continued on along the same road without stopping. A large open green then came into view on the left-hand side and Bernard swung the car into its gravel-floored car park. We had apparently reached our new destination.

The location was familiar. On the opposite edge of the green, about 150 yards away, the bright lights of The Cricketer's Inn could just be made out; which meant that we were still in Danbury.

'I don't recognise this spot. Do you?' he asked, glancing about.

Pointing out the pub, he too then realised our new location.

The psychic said very little as we sat patiently waiting for something to happen. The fierce winds whipped venomously across the car park as we stared expectantly towards the headlights of each passing car, wondering whether it would pull in and join us for a shadowy rendezvous of some sort. But none did.

Watching the red and white lights of aircraft criss-crossing through the clear night sky, I contemplated our predicament. The female energy form that Bernard seemed to be experiencing could be likened to the effects of a woman wearing a very heavy perfume. When she enters a room you can smell her aroma, and when she leaves that room her perfume lingers for a time, even though she is no longer there. Should a deaf and blind person enter that room, then they would be unable to tell whether the woman was actually present, or whether they were merely smelling her lingering perfume.

The same thing appeared to be happening to Bernard on a psychic level. He was picking up the close proximity of a female energy form, but seemed uncertain whether she was actually present, or whether he was experiencing her lingering psychic energies, following a visit earlier that day. The intuitive feeling was exactly the same, whether she was present or not.

'I think you're probably right,' he admitted, with a sigh.

'She's out there somewhere; or she was. But there's still some sort of drawing, like a magnet.' He paused to take in his feelings. 'No, I definitely feel that somebody, or something, is still around. I can feel it.'

Stubbing out his cigarette in the ashtray below the dashboard, he turned on the engine once again. 'Come on. I'm going back to the gate. I still get the feeling there's something happening down there.'

The car pulled up in the recessed gateway to Danbury Country Park at 9.35 pm. But something was different; we were not at the same gate. Yet then I understood. The car park inside the woods was, I recalled, linked by a crescent-shaped track with two gates; one an entrance, the other an exit. Earlier on we had drawn up to the entrance gate. Now we sat in front of the exit gate, some eighty yards further back along the road. We talked about the discrepancy, but decided to stay where we were.

'What's in there anyway?' Bernard enquired, nodding towards the darkened treeline.

The lakes.

Without warning, he switched on the car headlights. A trackway and a mass of moving trees was his answer.

Calmly, I suggested that he had probably just given away our presence to anyone who might be lurking in the woods.

He switched them off with an apology.

Another sudden gust of wind tore violently through the treetops. The hurricane had definitely now reached Essex, and it was getting closer. Something had to happen soon. So, was BSA actually out there somewhere?

He frowned in frustration. 'Well, I reckon she's been around here, and I wouldn't be surprised if she, or someone else, is still around,' he said, looking out of the windscreen into the darkness.

It was too cold to go out and investigate. Trees bent and swayed wildly with the sheer force of the terrifying winds. No, there was no way that I was going to go outside, unless I had to.

'Are the woods frequented by black dogs?' he queried. Ghostly ones, with fiery eyes like red-hot coals?

'Yes, that's it.'

No, I knew of no such legend linking phantom black dogs with the woods around Danbury.

Forty two
Contact

The psychic was becoming frustrated at the lack of action. 'Here. Give me that card,' he said, disregarding his earlier refusals to psychometrise it.

Handing him the black calling card, he began to focus his psychic mind on our predicament and waited for a reaction.

With pen and paper poised on my lap, I sat patiently until he started to breathe rapidly, a sure sign that something was happening in his mind.

After a minute or so, I asked him what he felt.

'We walk down to the other gate,' he announced, as he placed the card on the dashboard. 'There's someone down there. Female. However, I don't think she's there herself; not physically at least.'

As we simultaneously opened the doors, a sudden gust of wind sent the black card flying out into the night. My heart sank. Losing that would be disastrous in terms of future research. It had to be found, and fast, before it had a chance to blow away completely. Stepping outside, I searched the grass verge by the side of the car as Bernard stood by. After a few minutes I saw the card sitting in the wet grass. Grabbing hold of it, I slipped it into my document bag and breathed a sigh of relief.

The hurricane-force winds were still on the increase as we approached the other wooden gate in complete silence. Some thirty feet away from our destination, Bernard held out his arm to prevent me advancing any closer and then beckoned that we should stand and face the gate from the opposite side of the road.

The bright headlights of a vehicle approached at speed to reveal a Range Rover which whizzed by without slowing down.

Bernard began to stare intently towards the gate. 'I see the same as before,' he shouted into the wind. 'It's the same woman I saw in Danbury churchyard on Hallowe'en, and in front of the battlements at Arundel. She's just standing there; in front of the gate.'

What was she wearing?

'She's wearing a black, knee-length cloak, with a hood which obscures her face.' With this, he began to slowly advance towards the gate as the wind continued to rush past us with deafening roars which drowned out our speech.

Recalling past situations where Bernard had suffered badly as a result of attuning directly to the warped energies of the Black Alchemist, I emphasised caution. However, I had an idea. We should try approaching her not as a dangerous adversary who wished us harm, but as an equal, with feelings of compassion, not hatred, no matter how inconceivable it might seem. Mentally tell her that we mean her no harm and want only to talk — to make contact. In this way he might be spared any adverse reactions from the energy form.

He nodded his acceptance at my suggestion, as he gradually moved nearer and nearer to the woman, his hair and clothes flapping about in the wind.

Following by his side, I yelled at the energy form directly, confirming our wish to speak with her, provided that she did not try to attack. It was a peculiar situation. However, I actually believed it might work, even though she was an adversary.

As Bernard drew within three feet of the black-cloaked woman, the deafening roar of the wind climbed in pitch and power as she began to reach out towards him with her right hand.

He was tempted, even though he knew it was a terrible risk. Yet he knew that if he wanted to make contact with her mind, then it was the only way. Therefore, with some slight hesitation, he took hold of her hand as an almighty gust of wind tore viciously through the treetops engulfing the entire area and nearly knocking him off his feet.

Contact with his adversary sent electric shock-like jolts through his arm and into his body. He flinched twice at the immediate pain. Yet it was too late to go back. The two minds had now become one. As images and impressions began to flood into his mind, he knew he was now linking directly to her very thoughts. Yet he realised that it had its price, as he felt her searching his mind for similar answers.

His breathing became erratic, and an expression of mental torment formed on his face as the full power of the radiant apparition surged into his body. He had to speak. 'I see pictures and hear names,' he shouted, trying to make himself heard above the constant cacophony of the wind.

'Adonaie . . . a name . . . and Frimost,' he yelled, his hand still linked with hers. 'And Lullington's been done again . . . but nothing left this time.'

With the expression of torment still showing on his face, he paused to compose his thoughts before carrying on. 'I now hear a female talking . . . the drawing on the card *is* of a knife . . . one she possesses . . . and on it are the words: "fairest one". It's steeped in blood . . . I see a ritual going on . . . and a stretched skin on the ground . . . which looks white. It's part of a ritual involving the symbols on the card . . . and the cockerel sacrifice . . . someone is about *here, now.*'

Bernard recoiled backwards, no longer able to withstand the passage of energies flowing into his very soul from the woman. But he was alright. He had not been attacked, and there appeared to be no adverse effects from the ordeal. So, for the moment, he felt satisfied. Yet then a horrific sensation overtook his senses. The car. His mind was trying to tell him something about his car.

'Hell,' he shouted, twisting on the spot as he attempted to crystallise his thoughts. 'The car. We've left the car. We've got to get back to the car. *NOW.*'

He began to walk briskly, before gradually breaking into a

run. The car. Something had happened to the car.

With the gales still racing wildly across the open road, I ran close behind. I heard Bernard mumbling curses under his breath. He had not said so, but the implication was that we had been tricked away from the car for some reason.

It came into sight.

'Give me the torch,' he shouted, in an aggressive tone.

Handing it to him, he frantically began to shine the torchlight into the wheel arches and on to the back bumper as leaves and litter scurried across the grass verge.

What was he looking for?

'I don't like what I feel one little bit,' he seethed, carrying on his search as he moved around to the offside and shone the light into the car's interior. Pulling at the door handle, it came open. 'Damn, I left it open,' he fretted, now shining the light on to the floor below the seat. 'Something's here and we've got to get it out. Go around to your side.'

I tried the door handle. It too came open.

'You didn't lock it.'

Not answering, I just continued to search around the front passenger seat.

Bernard's hand then drew up something from below the corner of the driver's seat, close to the door. 'Here, take this,' he said, a note of resignation in his voice, as he climbed into the seat.

It was another sheet of black card, folded in two and slightly smaller than the first one. Opening it revealed another image in pencil, like those on the card found earlier that evening. It showed a thin-bladed broadsword crossed diagonally over a wand or staff, both of which were covered in magical characters taken from one of the medieval grimoires. I showed it to Bernard.

It annoyed him intensely. 'Right, I'm getting out of here,' he frowned, as he switched on the engine and violently reversed the car out of the gateway. 'I've had enough of this. That's it.'

Facsimile of the symbols drawn on to the black calling card discovered by Bernard shortly after the encounter with the Black Sorceress of Arundel by the gate at Danbury Country Park.

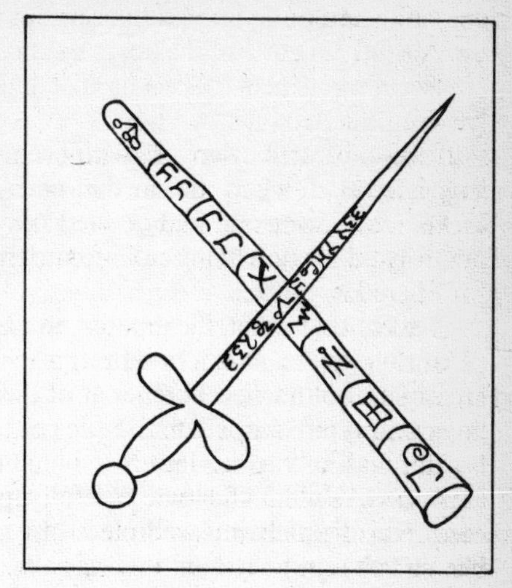

As we drove away, my nose caught a whiff of a peculiar aroma filling the car's interior. It was the smell of perfume; an overpowering, pungent aroma of perfume. It had not been present earlier, so where was it coming from?

Bernard sniffed. 'Yes, I can smell it too. There's certainly nothing in the car it could be. See if you can find the source.'

Pulling up the folded black card, I held it to my nose. No, it was not coming from that. So where then? An air freshener? No, there was not one in the car.

Studying every corner and crevice, as the car continued its journey, I noticed something. In a small cavity within the metal frame that supported the driver's seat was a piece of green paper. Was the stench of perfume coming from that? Probably not. Since Bernard had only owned the Montego for a matter of weeks, it was probably just a piece of rubbish discarded by its previous owner.

As the car came to a halt in the car park at the side of The Griffin, I reached down and pulled out the piece of paper. It stank of perfume. Yet there was more. For across its surface was a clearly recognisable, deep red lipstick smear, as if someone had pulled it across their lips to remove their make-up. Along the centre of the lipstick stain was a small, horizontal grease mark which looked as if it had come from the area between the person's two lips.

It was a bizarre discovery with even deeper implications. It suggested that, when the car had been left unattended by the locked gate, someone had opened the driver's door and left, not only the second black calling card, but also a piece of paper smothered in lipstick and perfume.

In addition to this, the lime-green paper — clearly a female colour — looked as if it had been hurriedly torn away from a larger sheet of narrow notepaper of the sort commonly found in card and gift shops. On the edge of the rough tear were the bottom half of various letters in blue biro which could not be identified. Unlike the two carefully prepared black calling cards, this lipstick-smeared piece of paper looked as if it had been a last minute thought. It was almost a direct response to my conversation comparing psychic energy forms with lingering perfume. It was a chilling thought which Bernard did not like.

It was no ordinary perfume either. It was a pungent, overpowering aroma I had only ever come across once before; and that was under somewhat bizarre circumstances.

During 1983 I had attended seances led by psychic medium Rita Goold, who lived in Leicester. In complete darkness, the apparition of an Edwardian music hall operetta singer, named Laura, would appear to manifest into physical form. It was a remarkable phenomenon and, aside from allowing those present to feel her long dress (Rita would usually wear a simple track suit during seances), the spirit form would cavort around the circle singing songs and emitting an aroma of pungent, almost sickly perfume which would completely vanish when she departed. It was the same perfume as that impregnated on the lime-green piece of paper. Therefore, a call to Rita to find out if anyone had ever been able to identify Laura's perfume, was clearly in order at the earliest possible convenience.

Forty three
Diabolic Magic

Amid the hustle and bustle of the crowded bar, we found a spare table and sat down with our drinks. Pulling out the lipstick-smeared piece of paper, I studied it closely, as Bernard asked if he could use my notepad to scribble down a few impressions and feelings going around in his mind.

The ruby-red smear trailed off to the left-hand side, whilst on the right-hand side the lime-green paper was more creased and crumpled than anywhere else. These points led me to conclude that whoever had wiped it across their lips was right-handed. Looking closely, I could also see that trailing off to the left, an inch or so beyond the red lipstick, was another shiny substance which I quickly identified as a flesh-coloured foundation cream.

Lipstick, foundation, perfume, facial grease and lime-green notepaper all added up to the, perhaps obvious, fact that this item had come from a woman. Not only this, but the rough tear, the unevenness of the lipstick stain, and the grease mark all suggested that the woman had been wearing her make up for some time before she had decided to create this extraordinary calling card. It did not appear planned in any way.

Bernard half listened, as he finished off what he was writing and passed the notepad back to me.

I read his words:

I believe that there were two people in the wood, and most likely male, under orders. Female there in energy form only.

Looking up, I asked him for an explanation. Two people in the wood and they were *both male?* This seemed an unlikely statement considering the fact that we had just found a piece of paper impregnated with lipstick, foundation and perfume. If this calling card had been hurriedly left by two men, then where would they suddenly get hold of make up? It just did not make sense.

'That's what I pick up,' Bernard insisted, sticking to his guns.

No, I had to differ with him on this occasion. It was my feeling that a woman, possibly even BSA herself, had been in that wood whilst we were there. Otherwise the lipstick-smeared piece of paper made a complete mockery of reality.

As Bernard shrugged his shoulders without any further explanations, I read on:

> **The triangle shape (on the black calling card put through his door) is seemingly a knife of sorts and inscribed with Greek, meaning 'the fair one' or 'the fairest one'. Steeped in blood and is new.**

The fairest one. Was this a reference to a man or a woman?

'A woman, I think,' he responded, picking up the lipstick-smeared piece of paper. 'A spirit or goddess. Something like that. Here, I keep smelling that perfume. It keeps wafting up.'

I had noticed. Taking it from his hand, I held it to my nose and sniffed carefully. The aroma was definitely coming from the piece of paper. There was no mistake about that.

'I also pick up something to do with a lamb,' he continued. 'A sacrifice, in connection with the stretched skin and the symbols on the first black card.'

So where had this ritual taken place? Locally, or in Sussex?

'Don't know.'

I felt it might be locally. Could he see anything of the location around the spot where this ritual had taken place?

'Woods, bushes, undergrowth, brambles around a small area, like a clearing. That's all.'

Any more?

'No.'

In conclusion then, it seemed that the Black Sorceress, and at least two of her male accomplices, had carried out a ritual

The piece of lime-green notepaper smeared with lipstick, foundation and perfume, left as a calling card by the Black Alchemist's female accomplice.

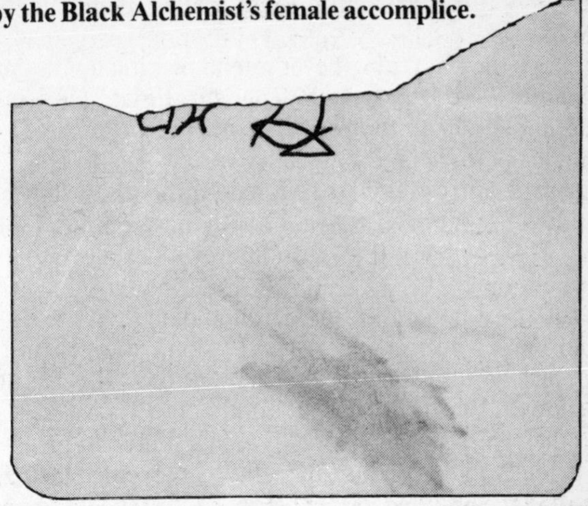

involving the sacrifice of a cockerel and a lamb, during which certain symbols, taken from grimoires, had been drawn at stages on to a black sheet of card. The ritual also appeared to have involved the pinning out of a white animal skin, the use of the cockerel's feathers and the plunging of a dagger into blood – marked with the word Καλλιστη, Greek for 'the fairest one'.

'That's about it,' he concluded. 'And the names Frimost and Adonaie are somehow involved. How would you spell Frimost?'

F-R-E-E-M-O-S-T, I suggested.

He wrote it down. But who was it?

'A person connected with magic, I think. I'm not really sure. And Adonaie — the other name I picked up. How would you spell that? A-R-D-O-N-A-I-E?'

Yes, write it down. I had not come across the name before, but it sounded about right. What about Lullington? What had been going on there?

He yawned as he leant back on his chair and shook his head. 'I don't know. But whatever it was. Nothing was left, so I shouldn't go rushing off down there as you won't find anything.'

His mood then changed. 'Right that's it then.'

What was?

'That's the final thing I ever intend picking up on the Black Alchemist. I've had enough. That's it. Final.' He scrawled a thick line under his notes and wrote the word 'final', before sitting back in defiance.

I sighed with dismay. As I had said earlier on, just by burying your head in the sand was not going to make the problem go away. If he believed that, then he was more naive than I had ever believed.

'You must remember, my wife and daughter know nothing about what's been going on, and I don't want them to find some sick warning on my door mat one day. This has all gone far enough, I'm afraid. If I put out that I will leave them alone, then they will leave me alone. It seems simple to me.'

He really meant it this time, and there seemed little I could do to change his mind. Never before had I seen him so annoyed by any of the supernatural dramas we had been involved in over the past four years.

'Anyway, I'm off now,' he said, as he stubbed out his cigarette, finished off his Kaliber and got up to go. 'What are you doing? Staying here?'

No, I was leaving as well, as I had a lot of things to check out when I got home. But it would not go away. He was a fool to think it would.

He went to answer, but then hesitated. 'Give me a ring.'

Acknowledging his words, and realising that I was fighting a losing battle, I let him disappear out of sight.

Still wearing my coat and fingerless gloves, I scanned the bookshelves for anything on grimoires — the medieval books of diabolical ceremonial magic.

One particular book came to mind, my second-hand copy of *The Book of Black Magic and of Pacts,* by the Victorian occultist, Arthur Edward Waite (de Laurence Company, Inc., Chicago, 1940). It contained lengthy extracts from several well-known grimoires, including the rituals themselves, their methods of preparation, and the ceremonial tools which were to be fashioned and inscribed before the ceremonies could commence.

I had the uncanny feeling that the various symbols inscribed in pencil on to the two black calling cards would be found in this book. So, flicking through its pages, I quickly found what I was looking for. In a chapter devoted to a grimoire entitled the *Book of True Black Magic* — which was, in fact, a bastardised version of the grimoire known as *The Clavicle of Solomon*— I discovered the exact same symbols as those on the wand and short broadsword drawn on to the black card found in the car.

On the same page was a drawing of a knife with a triangular-shaped blade and a ball-like handle, like the one drawn on the black card pushed through Bernard's letter box. It was referred to as a lancet and, although the illustration bore no inscription, its method of preparation called for it to be 'extinguished', or 'steeped', in 'the blood of a mole', among other things.

Studying the drawings of the wand, the sword and the lancet on the two black cards, I realised that they were not only similar, they were *identical* to those in Waite's book.

So far, so good. I then turned my attention to the four groups of curious magical characters drawn on to the first black card. Further on in the same book, I found a chapter on a dark grimoire referred to as *The Sworn Book of Honorius,* a disgusting work of medieval origin, which Waite described as 'perhaps the most frankly diabolical of all rituals connected with Black Magic', the contents of which, he suggested, were to be avoided at all costs.

Studying its pages, which described the preparations and source of the complicated ritual of Honorius, many sentences and symbols began to echo statements Bernard had made earlier that evening. All the elements of the sick ritual he had picked up, along with the symbols on the black card pushed through his letterbox, were featured in the complicated ritual of Honorius.

The lengthy rite was to be carried out in stages at specific times, over a period of several weeks. It culminated in a chosen invocation where one of seven named demons, each associated with a different day of the week, was to be conjured into manifestation for a designated purpose.

As Bernard had suggested, the ritual included the sacrifice of a black cockerel and the use of its feathers, and the sacrifice of a lamb, whose skin was to be removed, pinned out on the ground and then left for a period a time. Various groupings of magical characters were to be inscribed on to the skin of the lamb and on to virgin parchment at certain stages throughout the ritual. These symbols corresponded precisely to those inscribed in pencil on the first black card received by Bernard.

It seemed quite clear that someone, presumably the Black Sorceress and her accomplices, had been following the course of the ritual of Honorius and had actually sacrificed a cockerel and a lamb to comply with its diabolical procedures.

Yet it did not end there. I then discovered two further points of particular significance to the evening. Firstly, the main name of God used to invoke and control the demonic forces within the Honorius ritual, was Adonaie, the name picked up by Bernard as he had made contact with BSA out by the gate. Secondly, in the last section of the ritual of Honorius, where the methods of conjuring the various demons of the week were described, I found the name Frimost — as it was more correctly spelt. It was the demon to be invoked on a Tuesday — which it happened to be that very day. What's more, it was to be invoked *between the hours of nine and ten o'clock at night.*

Our car had initially pulled up at the entrance gate to Danbury Country Park at precisely nine o'clock that evening, and it was at 9.35 pm that Bernard had linked hands with BSA's energy form at the same spot and, among other things, had shouted out the name Frimost.

The implications therefore seemed clear. Someone, perhaps the two men mentioned by Bernard, perhaps even BSA herself, had been bringing the ritual of Honorius to a climax by conjuring into manifestation the demon Frimost between nine and ten that night. What's more, there was a possibility that they had completed this ritual in the woods at Danbury Country Park.

Yet something bugged me. Any knowledgable occultist, whether black or white, knew that grimoire magic was very crude magic which only invoked very low forms of otherworld denizens and supernatural energies. It could certainly not be compared with the powerful Graeco-Egyptian alchemy and magic used in the past by the Black Alchemist.

Only one small link with his own brand of warped Graeco-Egyptian magical activities was present — the Greek word Καλλιστη, drawn within the blade of the knife depicted on the black calling card. So, what did it mean? A call to Terry DuQuesne promptly sorted out a translation.[1] As Bernard had suggested, this word, Kallistee, meant 'the most beautiful lady,' or indeed, 'the fairest lady,' as in the winner of a beauty contest.

Terry suggested that it might be one of the titles of Aphrodite, the Greek goddess of love and beauty.

He was right. A quick check with a dictionary of mythology revealed that Aphrodite had been awarded a golden apple inscribed 'for the fairest', after Paris had judged her to be the most beautiful goddess of all during a beauty contest.

Bernard had also said that this same word had been inscribed by the woman on to her new ritual dagger; the one she had charged with power by steeping it in blood. So why was the Black Sorceress combining a clearly Hebrew/ Christian-based diabolical ritual with the influence of the Greek goddess of love and beauty?

At first, Aphrodite's involvement did not appear to make any sense. However, I then remembered that it was not the first time that the Greek goddess of love had cropped up in connection with the Black Alchemist's female accomplice. On Hallowe'en the previous year, she had used the rite known as the Sword of Dardanus, out in Danbury churchyard, to obtain the power and influence of Aphrodite, among others, in an attempt to 'bend' Bernard's soul. The idea was for him to have fallen into BSA's influence by using the emotional draw of false love and passion, so that he would have revealed, not only his power, but also the contents of his mind. Thankfully for

Bernard, the rite had not worked. However, it looked very much as if she was still attempting to ensnare him by using the same magical current, symbolised by the Greek goddess of love. So what had she been up to this time?

The black calling card pushed through his letterbox had been imbued with a psychic charge, the intention of which had been to draw, or pull, Bernard to Danbury Country Park so that he would leave the car and confront BSA's energy form by the entrance gateway. This had apparently allowed her two male companions to plant the second black calling card and the lipstick-smeared piece of paper inside the vehicle.

Everything about the lipstick-smeared piece of paper seemed to indicate that she was still trying to use love magic to ensnare Bernard. The paper's colour, green, was attributed to the power of both Aphrodite, and Venus, her Roman counterpart. It had been smeared with *her* perfume, *her* grease, *her* foundation and lipstick from *her* own mouth; all factors which would have impregnated it with her own psychic charge.

It had therefore been left in the hope that it would forge a false emotional and mental link between her and Bernard — like a lover being drawn compulsively to his sweetheart. Even the time of year seemed appropriate. The following Sunday was St Valentine's day, a time when men received anonymous cards from admirers and lovers, some of which would be impregnated with perfume.

As to the motives behind all this madness, one could only guess. However, it was clear that, as with the dagger-in-the-heart sketch in Danbury churchyard the previous November, our adversaries had shown how easily they could twist Bernard and I around their little fingers without any problem at all. In a way, it seemed like an exercise in manipulation; an indication of what they could achieve if we stepped out of line or, indeed, if we came too close to the truth.

Forty four
Reprise

Wednesday, 8th June, 1988. For several days now Bernard had been trying to re-read the finished manuscript for Andy's book *The Black Alchemist.*

On first reading it had appeared accurate enough — one or two points here and there which would need changing — but, essentially, nothing major. However, it had felt strange reliving those events again, especially looking at them from somebody else's perspective. In a way, he had not wanted to read the manuscript at all, as it brought back too many disturbing memories which he had been trying to forget.

Still, it *would* have to be proof read again, as he had only scanned through it quickly the first time around.

Retiring into the peace and quiet of the dining room, away from the constant noise of the television and his daughter's hi-fi system, he sat down with a mug of coffee and glanced apprehensively towards the already-opened manuscript. The page in view commenced the chapter concerning BA's Ring of Darkness ritual, and his subsequent desecration of the Running Well, during October 1986.

October 1986, he sighed. It seemed so long ago; and so much had happened since that time. And there still seemed to be no end to the whole affair. He smiled at the amount of times in the book where he had said: 'Right, that's it. This is the final message I ever intend picking up on the Black Alchemist affair.'! Yet then, at some point a little later, he would inevitably receive further psychic material on the subject.

It had happened earlier that year after his encounter with the Black Sorceress of Arundel, out by the gate at Danbury

Country Park. He had categorically stated that he would not pick up any further psychic information on the affair; and then, at the time of the spring equinox, he had received new, unsolicited information about the man's current situation.

He recalled the incident to mind. It had taken place during the early evening of Monday, 21st March, as he had walked into the back garden to close the garage door. Once out in the open, he had been drawn to look up at the new moon. With its two horns pointing upwards, it had contrasted sharply with the planet Venus positioned directly below the convex edge of the slim crescent.

The unique sight had held his gaze for several seconds, at which point he had received the distinct impression that the Black Alchemist was out of the country at that time; in Belgium it seemed, on some sort of 'Grand Tour' of Europe. He was there to track down and purchase a rare magical manuscript being sold as part of a much larger private collection, which had recently come on to the market. The manuscript was essential to the continuation of his alchemical operations, so he would have to have it, whatever the cost.

No further explanatory information had accompanied the impression, and Andy had been unable to establish what exactly he had been after out there in Belgium. However, he had pointed out the interesting fact that the crescent moon, with Venus positioned directly beneath it, looked like the horns of Dee's *Monas* symbol, with the point of its circle directly below the horns. Perhaps it had been for this reason that his mind had, once again, linked with the activities of the Black Alchemist.

Then there had been that odd dream the previous month. But this had been so vague that he had dismissed it as a product of his imagination; despite what Andy had said.

Shaking away these thoughts, he continued to read the pages from the bulky manuscript positioned in front of him, making a few marks here and there with a red felt pen.

An hour passed. He glanced at his watch. It was 10.45 pm.

Reading the chapter entitled *Return to the Well,* he could not help but recall to mind the situation as he had stood in the well hollow, clipboard in hand, waiting for something to happen.

There were the strange symbols he had seen being drawn on a talisman by the Black Alchemist, and then the feeling that their adversary was sitting down in a wood somewhere, meditating on the predicament. Then there had been the eerie feeling of a presence close by, which he just hoped was merely the residue left by the man's earlier visit to the Running Well; not his close proximity. And then, involuntarily, their minds had linked as one, so that he could hear and scribble down his adversary's very thoughts.

His eyes read those very thoughts as he came to them on the page.

Yet then he stopped and looked up. Something was happening. He fretted below his breath. It was the same intruding feeling he had experienced so many times before. He tried to push it away from his mind. But it was no good, the memory of the events in the well hollow that evening in October 1986, was now being replaced by a new, unfamiliar image.

Standing on the top of a low, grassy mound — a tumulus, it seemed — set in a field of long grass and wild summer flowers, close to woods, was the Black Alchemist. As on previous occasions, he was dressed in a black cowled robe. However, in each hand, he held a dagger, their blades crossed high above his head, just like in the dream the previous month, where he had seen the same figure approach him through a long tunnel of swirling grey mist. Yet on that occasion, there had been no indication that the cowled figure had been the Black Alchemist; so he had dismissed the dream; despite Andy saying that, in questing lore, crossed daggers was a sign of provocation; an occult challenge of some sort.

Now the figure stood on a tumulus, silent and motionless, as if patiently waiting for something to happen.

So where was the tumulus? It didn't feel local. Not even in Essex. Possibly down his way somewhere; around Eastbourne perhaps?

Lighting a cigarette to calm his nerves, Bernard thought

hard about the situation. What the hell did he want with him this time? Was he ever going to leave him alone?

Breaking off his concentration, he glanced towards the finished manuscript before getting up to leave the room.

But it was no use, the image remained in his mind, and with it now came the distinct impression that the Black Alchemist was ready and poised for his next move.

Postscript — September 1988

How do you think the Black Alchemist affair will end? That is the question most asked by those who hear the story.

The only answer which can be given is that his next move is patiently awaited, despite the fact that Bernard still refuses to supply any further psychic material on the subject. He wishes only to continue his life, free from the added burden of his acute psychic abilities.

However, there is no way that we *have* seen the last of the Black Alchemist and his female accomplice, the Black Sorceress of Arundel. Even as you read these words, they are building in strength and gathering around them like-minded occultists who have fallen from the true faith. And mark my words. These people are dangerous. If our findings are correct, then they believe they have been chosen to carry through a diabolic plan and will stop at nothing to ensure the fulfilment of that operation.

As any knowledgable occultist will confirm, Sussex is currently a hotbed of black magic activity. Why exactly, no one rightly knows. Yet one point on which they will all agree, is that this activity is growing with intensity. Toyne Newton's book *The Demonic Connection* shows this quite adequately.

Perhaps it is as well to remember the prophetic words of the initiate of the Friends of Hekate, as conveyed to Charles Walker in Clapham Wood during that fateful evening in November 1978: 'We have been using this area for ten years, and plan to continue using it for another ten, after which time we will select other areas in which to spread the word.'

Ten years on from November 1978 brings us to November 1988.

As they say after the first part of a television drama — this story is to be continued.

On a research level, further confirmation of Bernard's psychic material continues all the time. Much of this is outlined within the extensive notes that follow the section entitled ***Questing Slang.***

The single most important discovery has been the location — after nearly three years of searching — of the sequence of magical characters and Greek words which appeared on the Lullington and Rettendon spearheads, and on other Black Alchemist artefacts in either an updated or condensed form.

They were noticed in a book published in 1980, entitled *Alchemy: The Philosopher's Stone,* by Allison Coudert (Wildwood House, London). The entire sequence, as used by the Black Alchemist, is a series of magical symbols — referred to as the Formula of the Crab — originally devised and recorded by Zosimos of Panopolis.

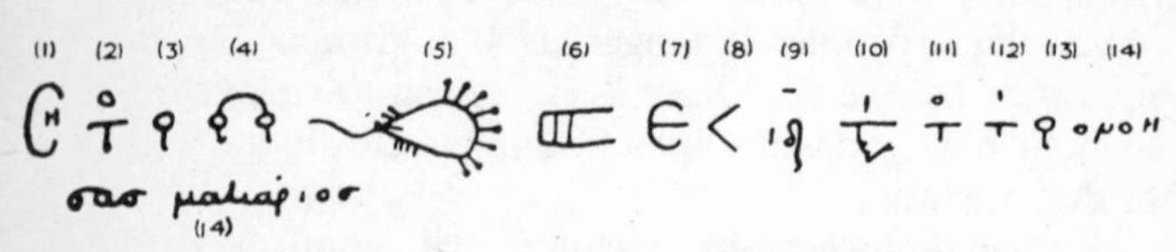

FIG. 4.—The Formula of the Crab (Zosimos).

The so-called Formula of the Crab, as set down by Zosimos of Panopolis, the Graeco-Egyptian alchemist of the fourth century AD.

The crab is symbolised by the fifth character in from the left, which appears to be some form of crayfish. This same symbol has also appeared on its own below the *Monas* symbol on the black calling card pushed through Bernard's letterbox during February this year.

The book said that the sequence of symbols, including the three Greek words, remained undeciphered. However, with the help of Terry DuQuesne, we were, of course, able to identify the three Greek words as Graeco-Egyptian goetic barbarous names.

The heavy perfume impregnated on the lipstick-smeared piece of paper found in Bernard's car has also been identified. One of the sitters at Rita Goold's seances identified Laura's perfume as T-Rose — a rose-based essence which was very popular at the beginning of this century. It is not generally available today, although it is still manufactured, in a synthesised form, by the exclusive Perfumers' Workshop of New York, and is available from top department stores.

According to Caroline Wise, who once worked for a leading perfume manufacturer, T-Rose is an expensive, sickly-smelling perfume which is only usually worn by what she terms as the 'fur brigade.' In other words, expensive-looking women who belong to exclusive upper class and show business social circles—like the Black Sorceress of Arundel perhaps?

Questing Slang

Psychic questing is a new and exciting form of psychical research which takes the psychic out of the seance room and into the landscape. Here are some of the words and terms used by those in the questing community and featured in this book.

Apport: An object which manifests out of thin air by psychic means.

Archetype: The symbolic form of a god, goddess, deity, demon or any other type of supernatural manifestation or image, as previously decided by its accepted history, mythology and designated symbolism.

Artefact: An object, usually of a mystical or religious significance, described, located and discovered by psychic means.

Attune: or **Attuning**. Focusing the mind on a particular object, site or situation, in the hope of picking up psychic information.

Automatic script: or **Automatic writing**. Writing scribbled down by a psychic which is thought to have originated from an external intelligence.

Clairaudience: External voices heard only by a psychic.

Clairvoyance: Images or externalised supernatual forms seen by a psychic. *See also* **Vision.**

Distant viewing: The art of psychically attuning to sites and situations from a distance.

Earthing: The releasing of unwanted, negative energies into the ground using monuments or structures in contact with the earth, such as standing stones, grave slabs and walls of buildings.

Elemental: A supernatural thought form created by magicians, occultists or shamans, either in buildings or out in the landscape. *See also* **Guardians** *and* **Thought forms.**

Energies: or **Earth energies**. Subtle forms of natural energy present in the human body, out in the landscape, and within the universe as a whole, which can be felt, wielded, changed, or channelled by magical processes.

Energy Form: The subtle energy field of the human body that makes up the so-called astral body which can be seen psychically by a psychic either surrounding a person or as a separate externalised form.

Energy matrix: The composite formations of subtle energy patterns present in the landscape.

Familiar: A supernatural entity, usually an animal, said to aid the duties of a witch or shaman. Sometimes it is the energy form they will take to journey in the astral body.

Fixing marker: A psychically or magically-charged object concealed at a site to seal the intentions of a ritual.

Gateway: A spot or location in the landscape where the veil between this world and the next is particularly thin. Such places are much sought after by occultists for the purposes of bringing into manifestation arcane forces and denizens of other worlds.

Kickback: The disastrous result of psychically attuning to a site and picking up negative, harmful energies either left by a ritual trap, by a black magic rite, or inadvertantly by triggering off a site's inherent self-defence mechanism personified as the so-called site guardian. *See also* **Site guardian.**

Meditation: Relaxing the mind, usually with your eyes closed, to use the mental power of visualisation to carry out a ritual.

Negativity: Imbalanced, disharmonious, and often harmful energies present at sites caused either through the collapse of its normally balanced energy matrix, or through the carrying out of warped ritual processes.

Omen: or **Portent.** A meaningful incident interpreted as predicting a favourable or unfavourable future situation.

Overshadow: or **Overshadowing.** This is where both the bodily and mental functions of a psychic are taken over and controlled by an alleged external intelligence. In Spiritualism this is known as trance mediumship.

Picking up: The receiving of new psychic information by a psychic.

Pinning energies: The control, or channelling, of terrestrial energies for magical purposes by means of burying fixing markers, such as daggers, swords or spearheads, around places of power; like stone circles, churchyards or tumuli, for instance.

Place memory: Information impregnated at a location either in a visual, audible or sensory form by past human interaction with the site, either accidentally or on purpose. Such information is only apparent when a good psychic picks up its presence when at the location.

Place psychometry: The ability of a psychic to be able to attune to a site's past history.

Protection ritual: A brief visualisation ritual, with verbal accompaniment, used to set up a psychic barrier around the body in an attempt to give protection against interference from external influences.

Psychometry: The ability of a psychic to be able to pick up data concerning an object's history, simply by touching or holding it.

Quest: Questing or **Psychic questing**. A series of interlinked events and incidents where visions, dreams and supernatural manifestations lead a psychic on towards a specific goal; usually the recovery of a concealed artefact, or the solving of a landscape mystery.

Sacred Site: A specific place or location, usually mystical or religious in origin, which has taken on a spiritual quality.

Site guardian — astral: A thought form, or elemental, created and set up, either on purpose by a priest magician, or accidentally by continued religious or mystical devotion, to guard over the interests of a site or an artefact.

Site guardian — physical: In questing lore, a person chosen by the astral guardian to unknowingly become the living representative of the site concerned. Their role is to prevent harm from coming to the site and to pass on its arcane wisdom and knowledge — often in cryptical form — to genuine visitors. Physical gurdians usually live close to the site and have a lifestyle very much in tune with their own natural environment.

Sketch: A series of interlinked incidents which form only part of an overall quest.

Soul essence: or **Spirit**. The part of the human mind left after death which either reincarnates through successive incarnations or operates as an independent intelligence accessible to psychics.

Super-psychic: or **Direct information psychic**. A highly gifted psychic who can consistently produce accurate and factual psychic material, which includes names, dates and places. The term is presently only applied to those psychics, or modern-day shamans, who work within the questing field.

Synchronicity: A meaningful coincidence which occurs to either confirm a prior decision or give some clue as to an up-and-coming decision or situation.

Thought form: A supernatural entity or manifestation, with its own basic intelligence and personality, created either accidentally by religious devotion at a location, or on purpose by a mystic, occultist or shaman to carry out a specific magical function.

Trance state: A form of deep relaxation or meditation used to obtain psychic information. Very often overshadowing will take place during trance states.

Vision: A meaningful externalised clairvoyant image, or apparition, seen by a psychic.

Visualisation ritual: The use of mental images and pictures to manipulate subtle energies through the power of psychokinesis, or mind over matter.

Notes

Portent

1. This entire account is accurately constructed from Bernard's recall of the ritual when he made contact with the stone spearhead in Lullington churchyard on Thursday, 30th May, 1985. The spoken words were devised from our subsequent knowledge of the ritual, gleaned from further psychic information and later research. *See* Chapters Four and Five.

Chapter Two — Wilmington

1. Details of Wilmington Priory's ecclesiastical immunity, along with its alleged unorthodox religious activities, were only realised on Tuesday, 4th June, 1985, when Nigel Pennick showed me his copy of *The Wilmington Giant* by Rodney Castleden.
2. See above.

Chapter Three — The Guardian

1. The information concerning Peter of Savoy, Pevensey Castle and the repair of its defences was not discovered until after our visit to the Sussex Downs.

Chapter Five — The First Matter

1. I later found that the name Peredur is thought to derive from the title 'steel spear.' See Rachel Bromwich, *Trioedd Ynys Prydein — The Welsh Triads, etc.,* (University of Wales Press, Cardiff, 1978). Obviously, this would have some bearing on the planting of the inscribed spearhead at Lullington by the Black Alchemist.
2. I am pretty sure that the Black Alchemist chose Lullington because of its association with the episode in the Peredur story concerning the beheading of the white stag, as proposed by S.F Annett in 1932.

   In Zosimos' vision — and within alchemy in general — the removal of the head of the alchemist is seen as the symbolic extraction and rebirth of his divine soul.

In alchemy, the stag represents the soul of the alchemist. Therefore, a sacred site with a tradition connected with the severing of a stag's head would be the ideal choice as a place of rebirth for an alchemical transmutation.

By substituting the severed head of the Zosimos ritual with a spearhead — and thus utilising the Peredur link with the site — the Black Alchemist used this ritually-charged object to confirm and fix the intentions of his alchemical transmutation.

He knew that once the spearhead had been removed — as in the stealing of the stag's head in the Peredur story — it would signal his achievement of the First Matter stage, known also as the Black Man, the Negrido, or the Crow's Head. This would be reflected in the next part of the Peredur account where the black man then rises out of the mound. The Black Alchemist would then be able to continue on to the next stage in his ritual.

Chapter Seven — The Dome of Kent

1. *Remien Vigilia* and *Ratio Experimentia,* as well as the image of the cave picked up psychically by Bernard in The Griffin, derive from illustrations in Henricus Khunrath's *Amphitheatrum Sapientiae Aeternae,* Hanau, 1609.

   On the base of one of the two front columns of the portico inside the alchemical laboratory in one illustration, are the words *Ratio* and *Experimentia* — 'reason' and 'experiment' — the two words the alchemist must never tire of uttering.

   Above the door at the end of the same laboratory are the words *Dormiens Vigilia* — 'while sleeping watch' — a reference to the constant vigil the alchemist must keep over his transmutation, lest it get out of control and be ruined.
2. *The True Glass of Alchemy* is an alchemical treatise written in 1683 under the pseudonym 'Roger Bacon'.
3. Subsequent research showed that the Priest of the Sanctuary in Zosimos' vision *was* named Ion. See C.G. Jung's *Alchemical Writings,* for instance.

Chapter Eleven — St Anne's Castle

1. The statement concerning the virtues of the *Monas* echo Dee's own words on the symbol.

   According to Allison Coudert in her *Alchemy: The Philosopher's Stone,* Dee considered his *Monas* a talisman which embodied all the powers of the universe and that by contemplating it men would absorb these powers and experience transformation. He praises God for allowing the *Monas* to give men 'such great wisdom, power over creatures and large dominion.' Among many other statements, he also explains how the point at the centre of the *Monas'* circle represents 'the centre of all things'.

All this implies that the sender of the message was familiar with Dee's own interpretation of the *Monas Hieroglyphica.*

Chapter Sixteen — Nine Nights to Live

1. Subsequent study of the symbols on the reverse of the Rettendon spearhead have thrown a new light on the movements of the Black Alchemist that evening.

   I now believe that the Black Alchemist started his ritual at the Running Well *and then* moved out to create the Ring of Darkness, starting with Rettendon churchyard and then visiting the other three sites in a *clockwise* perambulation, not in an anti-clockwise motion as we had assumed at the time.

   This would make sense of many things. It would explain why BA was able to find the Running Well across the fields, since it would still have been light when he commenced his journey through the Runwell countryside. It would make sense of the number 1 on the Rettendon spearhead and explain why it contained the same series of symbols found on the Lullington stone, and why its reverse contained symbols confirming the Ring of Darkness ritual. It would also make sense of the number 2 on the Runwell stone, and explain why Bernard felt that he was in the vicinity when we passed through South Hanningfield. The Black Alchemist had probably just completed his ritual as we had entered the area from the other direction.

Chapter Seventeen — Back to School

1. John Dee is well known for his 'spiritual' diaries which contained transactions of his many psychic communications. I feel that Bernard's impression concerning someone who 'keeps a diary' was a reference to Dee; especially as his next impressions turned out to be references to Dee's *Monas* symbol.
2. Robert Turner's book was not discovered until some weeks after the Running Well confrontation.

Chapter Eighteen — Return to the Well

1. The scribbled foreign characters were later identified as Greek by Terry DuQuesne. However, only the first two words — 'This is . . .' could be made out before the characters became illegible.
2. Inside St Mary's church, Runwell, is a medieval purbeck coffin known locally as the Prioress' Tomb. Its lid depicts a diamond-shaped design referred to as the Runwell Cross. It is thought to have belonged to one of the prioresses of the convent allegedly attached to the Running Well. When the coffin was opened during restorations in 1907, it was found to be empty. *See The Running Well Mystery* pages 15-17.

3. Their incessant use of bellows earned alchemists the derogatory title *'puffer,'* or *'soulfleur.'*
4. The section from 'It is found . . .' to '. . . rejected by all.' has been taken, almost word-for-word, from an essay entitled *Gloria Mundi,* featured in a collection of alchemic texts published in 1678 under the title *Musaeum Hermeticum.*

   Obviously, Bernard's Elizabethan alchemist spirit guide, who died long before 1678, can call upon source material from later alchemic traditions, a common feature with direct information psychics.
5. Kether is a Hebrew Cabalistic term describing the highest ethereal plane of existence, or the first manifestation of God within this universe.
6. The '10 rooms' is a reference to the ten spheres, or planes, of existence within the teachings of the Cabala.
7. The '32 steps' refer to the ten spheres of existence and the 22 paths connecting each of the ten spheres, as shown on the Cabalistic glyph, or visual aid, known as the Tree of Life. They also refer to the 22 picture cards, or Major Arcana, of the Tarot pack.
8. Neshama, Yecidah and Chia are three of the ten aspects of the divine soul, as set down in Cabalistic tradition. Ain Soph, the so-called Limitless One, is, according to Cabalistic tradition, one of the three primary manifestations of God beyond this universe.
9. *Caput Corvi* is Latin for Crow's Head. It is one of the names of the First Matter stage in the alchemical transmutation. *Corpus Invisible* is Latin for the invisible body, the soul of the alchemist, one must assume.
10. Since october 1986, each of the titles given to Bernard by the Elizabethan alchemist have been located. In order, they are:

    Abu'l Qasim al-Iraqui, *The Book of Knowledge, Concerning the Cultivation of Gold,* edited and translated by E.J. Holmyard, Paris, 1923.
    Artis Auriferae, Quam Chemian Vocant . . ., Basilaea, 1610.
    Bonus, Petrus, *Pretiosa Margarita Novella de Thesauro ac Pretiosissimo Philosophorum Lapide . . .* edited by Janus Lacinis, Venice, 1546.
    Musaeum Hermeticum, 1678. Translated by A.E. Waite, London, 1893.
    Ko Hung, *The Nei P'ien of Ko Hung: Alchemy, Medicine, Religion in the China of AD 320.* Translated by J.R. Ware, Cambridge, Mass., USA, 1966.
    Khunrath, Henricus, *Amphiteatrum Sapientiae Aeternae, Hanau, 1609.*
    Stolcios, Daniel, *Viridarium Chymicum . . .* Frankfurt, 1624.
    Dee, John, *Monas Hieroglyphica,* Antwerp, 1564.

    Interestingly enough, as least half of these books were not published until after the death of Bernard's Elizabethan alchemist spirit guide. However, this in no way detracts from the authenticity of the communication as it has been shown how direct information psychics appear to be able to tap information from what has been referred to as the occult pool of knowledge. See *Strange Phenomena,* No. 2, October 1979.

Chapter Twenty Seven — The Foul Virgin

1. To suggest that the hurricane was selective in its targets may not be as absurd as it might at first seem. Aside from the horse chestnut tree in Danbury churchyard, other prominent sites featured in this book were also destroyed that night.

At Lullington, for instance, around half of the wooded grove surrounding the churchyard was destroyed; as were a great number of the beech trees surrounding Ide Hill churchyard, symbolically stripping the village of its title — the Dome of Kent. The North Downs area around Ide Hill was one of the worst hit areas of the hurricane. On several occasions Ide Hill was featured on national television because its electricity supply had still not been switched back on some days after the hurricane.

Inside Shenfield Common only a few trees were taken down by the hurricane. However, no less than four of the trees which made up the clearing used by the Black Alchemist were destroyed, including the one beneath which the stone spearhead had been located. Today, the clearing is a mass of fallen tree trunks amid a wide open space next to the railway line; nothing more.

In Rettendon, the lightning-struck tree which stood at the very centre of the Runwell Cross landscape geometry — and adorned the front cover of *The Running Well Mystery* — was also taken down.

The extraordinary destruction of Clapham Wood is described in chapter forty.

From what I have heard from a number of mysteries researchers in the south of England, it would appear that a great number of sacred trees — or trees which formed copses around sacred sites — were destroyed that night, disharmonising local energy fields on a wide scale.

Chapter Thirty One — The Arrowhead

1. For references to the name Hekate being derived from the Egyptian root Hekau, see *Cults of the Shadow,* Kenneth Grant, Frederick Muller Ltd., London, 1975. Also *Goddesses of the British Museum,* p.20.

Chapter Thirty Five — The Perfect Master

1. I later discovered that the two statements inscribed on the ape dagger were taken, virtually word-for-word, from sayings in the *Theatrum Chemicum Britannicum,* a collection of alchemical essays published in 1652 by Elias Ashmole.

The first of these, 'All haile to the noble companie' may be found on page 278 within the statement:

All haile to the noble Companie

Of true students in holy alchemie
Whose noble practice doth men teach,
To vaile their secrets with mistie speach.

The 'noble Companie' would therefore imply students of alchemy.

The second statement, 'A parfet master made them call' may be found on page 103 of the same volume:

A parfet Master ye maie him call trowe,
Which knoweth his Heates high and lowe.
Nothing maie let more your desires
Than ignorance of Heates and your Fiers.

This implies that a 'parfet Master' is an accomplished alchemist.

2. The so-called Alchemical Tree symbolises the growth of the transmutation and the Philosopher's Stone. In association with the dagger-in-the-heart ritual in Danbury churchyard, the Alchemical Tree is best explained in a sixteenth century alchemical treatise entitled *De Alchimia.* It describes how it grows from a corpse lying in its coffin, which symbolises the alchemical vessel, or womb. The corpse is the seed, the divine spark or soul, which must die before it can germinate, or be reborn. Sitting serenely within its fully-grown branches is the Royal Child, the fully-developed fruit of the alchemical opus.

   It would appear as if the Black Alchemist was attempting to utilise this concept in Danbury churchyard.
3. Bolos, I later discovered, was a reference to Bolos of Mendes, who lived in Egypt around 200AD, or 200 BC in some accounts, and wrote what is considered to be the oldest extant alchemical text, the *Physica Kai Mystika.*

Chapter Thirty Seven — The Friends of Hekate

1. The speech used in Charles Walker's meeting with the anonymous initiate has been taken, with kind permission, from Toyne Newton's book *The Deomonic Connection.* According to both Charles and Toyne, it represents an accurate acount of the conversation between the two men.

Chapter Forty Three — Diabolic Magic

1. The call to Terry DuQuesne was not made until the following day.

Selected Bibliography

Questing

Collins, Andrew, *The Sword and the Stone,* Earthquest Books, London, 1983.

Phillips, Graham, and Keatman, Martin, *The Green Stone,* Granada Publishing Ltd., London, 1984.

Phillips, Graham, and Keatman, Martin, *The Eye of Fire,* Grafton Books, London, 1988.

Alchemy

Burland, C.A., *The Arts of the Alchemists,* Wiedenfeld & Nicholson, London, 1967.

Coudert, Allison, *Alchemy: The Philosopher's Stone,* Wildwood House, London, 1980.

Redgrove, H. Stanley, *Alchemy: Ancient & Modern,* EP Publishing Limited, Wakefield, 1973 (1st 1911).

Dr John Dee

Dee, Dr John, *The Hieroglyphic Monad,* Samuel Weiser, Inc., New York, 1975 (1st 1564).

Morgan, Chris, ed., *Strange Oxford,* Oxford Golden Dawn Publishing, Oxford, 1986.

Suster, Gerald, ed., John Dee, *Essential Readings,* Crucible, Wellingborough, 1986.

Turner, Robert, ed., *The Heptarchia Mystica of John Dee,* Arkana, London, 1986.

Graeco-Egyptian Alchemy and Magic

Betz, H.D., ed., *Greek Magical Papyri,* Chicago, 1986.

Hopfner, Th., ed., *Griechisch — Aegyptischer, Offenbarungs-zauber. Vol.1,* Amsterdam, 1974 (1st 1922).

Luck, George, *Arcana Mundi,* Crucible, Wellingborough, 1987.

Preisendanz, Karl, *Papyri Gracae Magicae, Vol.1,* Teubner, Leipzig, 1928.

Scott, Walker, ed., *Hermetica, etc., Vol.IV,* Shambhala Publications, Inc., 1985 (1st 1936).

The Hurricane

Ogley, Bob, *In the Wake of the Hurricane,* Froglets Publicatons Ltd., 1988.

Landscape Mysteries

Castleden, Rodney, *The Wilmington Giant,* Turnstone Press Ltd., Wellingborough, 1983.

Collins, Andrew, *The Running Well Mystery,* Earthquest Books, London, 1983.

Collins, Andrew, *The Knights of Danbury,* Earthquest Books, London, 1985.

Graves, Tom, *Needles of Stone,* Granada Publishing Ltd., London, 1980 (1st 1978).

Medieval Apocalyptism

Emmerson, Richard Kenneth, *Antichrist in the Middle Ages,* Manchester University Press, Manchester, 1981.

The Occult

Cavendish, Richard, *The Black Arts,* Routledge and Kegan Paul, London, 1974 (1st 1967).

Newton, Toyne, *The Demonic Connection,* Blandford Press Ltd., Poole, 1987.

Seligmann, Kurt, *The History of Magic,* Pantheon Books, New York, 1948.

Waite, Arthur Edward, *The Book of Black Magic and of Pacts,* L.W. de Laurence, Chicago, 1940 (1st 1910).

Yates, Frances A., *The Rosicrucian Enlightenment,* Paladin, St Albans, 1975.

Index

INDEX

INDEX